Cross-platform UI Development with Xamarin.Forms

Create fully operational applications and deploy them to major mobile platforms using Xamarin.Forms

Paul F. Johnson

[PACKT]
PUBLISHING

open source*
community experience distilled

BIRMINGHAM - MUMBAI

Cross-platform UI Development with Xamarin.Forms

First published: August 2015

Production reference: 1210815

Published by Packt Publishing Ltd.
Livery Place
35 Livery Street
Birmingham B3 2PB, UK.

ISBN 978-1-78439-119-5

www.packtpub.com

Credits

Author
Paul F. Johnson

Reviewers
Yaroslav Bigus
William Harrington
Christopher Martin
Frédéric Mauroy

Commissioning Editor
Akram Hussain

Acquisition Editor
Subho Gupta

Content Development Editor
Ritika Singh

Technical Editor
Parag Topre

Copy Editors
Relin Hedly
Sonia Mathur

Project Coordinator
Judie Jose

Proofreader
Safis Editing

Indexer
Monica Ajmera Mehta

Graphics
Disha Haria

Production Coordinator
Nilesh R. Mohite

Cover Work
Nilesh R. Mohite

About the Author

Many years ago, from the fountains of Mount Olympus came forth upon the planet a man, a mystery, and an enigma. Over many years, he grew; he developed amazing biceps, an intellect to rival the greatest minds in the universe, a personality larger than a fair-sized moon, and a smile that would melt the hearts of the iciest of witches. He fought in wars, raged battles against injustice, and was generally an all-round amazing type of guy.

This is not his story.

You see, while he could do all of this really cool stuff, he couldn't work his mobile, and worse, he was clueless about how to make his own apps. Then stepped forth a nice chap from Liverpool, and with a bit of patience, he showed him how to do it.

This is his story.

What made this Scouser worthy of helping the man from Olympus? The simple answer is experience. You see, he was there at the outset of the home computer boom of the early 1980s. He developed code in BASIC, Z80, the 6502 and ARM assembler, C, C++, C#, Pascal, and FORTRAN. He has won awards for programming and is a published author with Packt Publishing.

Add these together and you can see why he was a worthy teacher. That, and he makes a killer cup of coffee!

Paul (for that is his name) is 44, lives with his wife, dog, cats, and son and drinks way too much coffee! You can normally find Paul on the Facebook Xamarin Developers group, where he is an admin. He is currently in the planning stage for a follow up of this book, but this time, he is concentrating on using XAML instead of pure C# to develop Xamarin.Forms applications. This will combine his lifetime love of Dr. Who with his other love that is to create fun code.

He is currently in the middle of buying enough coffee to fuel him through it - Brazil is on high alert!

Acknowledgments

This book could not have been written without my wife, Becki. She took up the slack when I needed to work and did not complain when, instead of sunning myself in Turkey on holiday, I was tapping away on the laptop to ensure that the deadlines were met. Her patience, love, companionship, and poking are the reasons why this is done. Thanks, baby.

I also owe a fair amount of thanks to my son, Richard. He knows just when to make me a drink and when to leave me to get on with things. He also enjoyed testing code for me on his phone.

William Harrington helped a fair bit with the creation of the Azure code. It's really not my strong area, and he stepped in to help me out at the very last moment. I should also mention that originally, Andrei was supposed to do this, a part of which he did do. Unfortunately, before I could get to the Azure part, my subscription expired.

The folks over at Stack Overflow and the Xamarin Developers' Facebook group also get an honorable mention. They say in space no, one can hear you scream. Thank goodness for cyberspace where they most certainly can!

I must also thank Ritika, Subho, and Parag at Packt Publishing. They have made writing this book an absolute pleasure with their good humor, sage-like advice, and for generally being there when I had the writer's block. It is my hope that I will work with them on future books for Packt Publishing.

Other mentions:

Unlike the last book, there have been fewer people involved, so there should be fewer to thank. I must thank the chaps over at Xamarin (including Bryan Cistanich and Charles Petzold) for giving me a chance to work with them. I would also like to thank Roger Darlington, Roy Heslop, Scott Sullivan-Reinhart, Jax, Lynn, Anne, Terry, the Xamarin Developers' group, Scott Bradley and the Postmodern Jukebox, who played pretty much nonstop during the second half of writing this book, Jock Graham, Hollie and Jack Harrington, and John King. Last but not least, I would like to thank my graphic artist, Ella Monea, Bonnie Shown, Charlene Bibby, and John Cartmell.

Here's to the next book, folks!

About the Reviewers

Yaroslav Bigus is an expert in building cross-platform web and mobile applications. He has 7 years of experience in development and has worked for companies everywhere, from Leeds to New York. In development, Yaroslav uses the .NET Framework, Python, JavaScript, AngularJS, jQuery, Underscore, and Xamarin.

He is currently working at an Israeli start-up called Tangiblee as a full-stack developer. Previously, Yaroslav reviewed *Xamarin Mobile Application Development for iOS, Paul F. Johnson, Packt Publishing; iOS Development with Xamarin CookBook Dimitris Tavlikos, Packt Publishing; Learning JavaScript Data Structures and Algorithms Loiane Groner, Packt Publishing;* and *Mastering JavaScript High Performance Chad R. Adams, Packt Publishing.*

William Harrington lives and works at his family's cattle station, Olga Downs, in Northwest Queensland, Australia. He attended James Cook University, Townsville. At the age of 20, he established his own company, Harrington Systems Electronics, which sells the NLIS RFID tag reader—The Pipe Reader—that he designed and manufactures. He also received the AgForce President's Innovation Award in 2005. In 2006, he graduated with honors as a computer systems engineer and received the Queensland Primary Industries Young Achiever Award. Since then, he has gone on to design the uSee remote monitoring system, a revolutionary and low-cost remote monitoring solution.

Having a home-based company has become part of a unique diversification strategy for the family and has provided them with the opportunity to stay on the land. Due to a never-ending passion for technology, William speaks regularly on many topics, so he can bring a futuristic version of the technology that will possibly exist in the next decade.

Since 2011, he has also been a director and programmer for Farm Apps Pty Ltd, developing smartphone and tablet apps that increase farming efficiency.

He enjoys traveling and brewing beer at home.

William works alongside his wife, Hollie, having recently welcomed their young son, Jack, into the world.

Christopher Martin has been a software developer for over 20 years. He started his career working for Advanced Development Methods for Ken Schwaber, who codeveloped the Scrum process with Jeff Sutherland in the early days of the Agile development movement. He went on to write the user interface for the award-winning and top-selling e-commerce software, Online Merchant and Online Merchant Gold.

For the past 5 years, Christopher has concentrated mainly on mobile development and has published several native developed applications for iOS, Android, and Windows Phone. For the past year, he has worked on several projects, using Xamarin and utilizing his native development experience along with C# and the .NET development stack.

Today, Christopher consults through his company, Desert Gadgets, for Alpha Software as a solutions engineer. He creates demo mobile applications and instruction videos using Alpha Anywhere—a low code, rapid application development environment to build HTML5 and hybrid business apps that look and feel like native apps. You can find more information about Christopher and Desert Gadgets at `www.desertgadgets.com`.

Frédéric Mauroy discovered computers in the mid-eighties along with the joy of programming with BASIC. This new-found passion naturally led him to pursue an education in IT, where he learned C and C++. His first job let him hone his skills in C, and he later slid toward C# with the amazing .NET Framework. Having worked mainly in ASP.NET, he also developed Windows applications and, more recently, mobile applications for Android and iOS, using PhoneGap and Xamarin.

He has made mobile applications for Viashopia and Alert112, which can be found at `http://mauroy.eu`, `http://fredericmauroy.com`, `http://viashopia.com`, and `http://alert112.com`.

www.PacktPub.com

Support files, eBooks, discount offers, and more

For support files and downloads related to your book, please visit www.PacktPub.com.

Did you know that Packt offers eBook versions of every book published, with PDF and ePub files available? You can upgrade to the eBook version at www.PacktPub.com and as a print book customer, you are entitled to a discount on the eBook copy. Get in touch with us at service@packtpub.com for more details.

At www.PacktPub.com, you can also read a collection of free technical articles, sign up for a range of free newsletters and receive exclusive discounts and offers on Packt books and eBooks.

https://www2.packtpub.com/books/subscription/packtlib

Do you need instant solutions to your IT questions? PacktLib is Packt's online digital book library. Here, you can search, access, and read Packt's entire library of books.

Why subscribe?

- Fully searchable across every book published by Packt
- Copy and paste, print, and bookmark content
- On demand and accessible via a web browser

Free access for Packt account holders

If you have an account with Packt at www.PacktPub.com, you can use this to access PacktLib today and view 9 entirely free books. Simply use your login credentials for immediate access.

This book is dedicated to anyone who wants to learn and wants to progress.

Enjoy!

Paul

Table of Contents

Preface

One of the pleasures of working in the mobile arena is the speed of development and the improvement in the toolchains. Being at the forefront of allowing the "write once, deploy many times" paradigm, Xamarin never sits still in making life easier for the developer.

Although having C# as the basis of writing code made the business logic (consider anything not to do with the user interface as the business logic) of an app much easier to cater to, it did leave a terrible chunk missing: to employ specialized developers for the UI. Then, the game changed.

There was a new technology out there, an uncharted territory, and that territory was Xamarin Forms. Instead of just one platform, with Xamarin Forms, we have three platforms. The dream of one language for all mobile devices comes another step closer. With Xamarin Forms, the mythical 100 percent code-sharing nirvana for the user interface and program is within reach.

What this book covers

Chapter 1, *In the Beginning…*, talks about planning your app from the backend to the frontend.

Chapter 2, *Let's Get the Party Started*, discusses views and gadgets. It teaches you how to add a Forms project to your current project in addition to the application life cycle, inversion of control, web views, and maps.

Chapter 3, *Making It Look Pretty and Logging In*, focusses on the UI abstraction. It shows you how to style your UI, custom renderers, triggers, and positioning.

Chapter 4, *Making Your Application Portable*, discusses the considerations for a PCL. It provides information on how to move code from a nonPCL to a PCL.

Chapter 5, Data, Generics, and Making Sense of Information, talks about everything you ever wanted to know about generics, but were too afraid to ask. This involves reflection and how to use LINQ to make the manipulation of data much simpler.

Chapter 6, A View to a Kill, takes the UI to the next level. This chapter demonstrates how to bring the Android application to Xamarin Forms in order to produce a universal app.

Chapter 7, Connect Me to Your Other Services, focusses on Azure, REST, and WCF.

Chapter 8, What a Bind! talks about the power behind a data-driven application.

Chapter 9, Addressing the Issue, discusses how to use the device address book.

Chapter 10, This is the World Calling…, focuses on how to use the device hardware with your Xamarin forms application using GPS and maps.

Chapter 11, A Portable Settings Class, talks about the different strategies to implement a settings system that will work on all platforms.

Chapter 12, Xamarin Forms Labs, takes a quick glimpse at how to extend the UI through the Xamarin Forms Labs community project.

Chapter 13, Social Media into the Mix, teaches you how to add Twitter and Facebook to your app.

Chapter 14, Bringing It All Together, brings all the parts of the app together, enabling you to create your own app.

What you need for this book

- To make the best use of this book, you will need at least the indie version of Xamarin.

- To compile for iOS, you will need a Mac or Mac in the cloud service.

- The instructions for this can be found in the book for Windows users. You can also find the information on how to include the Xamarin.Forms libraries and how to add Xamarin.Forms for the Windows Phone project to your existing Xamarin.Forms project created under Xamarin Studio for Mac.

- You can get a copy of the Xamarin installer at www.xamarin.com; follow the download links and download it for your preferred environment.

- For Visual Studio users, you will need to install either VS 2013 or VS 2015 community editions. Both contain the required components that can be used with Xamarin.

Who this book is for

This book is for developers who no longer wish to be restricted to a single platform, but would rather be able to create once and deploy thrice. It is intended for those who don't wish to waste their time having to reinvent the wheel every time they wish to create an app for another platform.

Most of all, it's meant for those who just wish to write good apps.

Conventions

In this book, you will find a number of styles of text that distinguish between different kinds of information. Here are some examples of these styles, and an explanation of their meaning.

Code words in text, database table names, folder names, filenames, file extensions, pathnames, dummy URLs, user input, and Twitter handles are shown as follows: " Click on upload, and upload the .p12 file you have just exported from the keychain tool."

A block of code is set as follows:

```
[<key>NSLocationAlwaysUsageDescription</key>
  <string>Can we use your location</string>
<key>NSLocationWhenInUseUsageDescription</key>
  <string>We are using your location</string>
```

New terms and **important words** are shown in bold. Words that you see on the screen, in menus or dialog boxes for example, appear in the text like this: "Select **File | Export** and give the file a name."

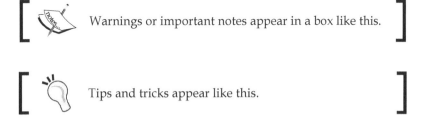

Warnings or important notes appear in a box like this.

Tips and tricks appear like this.

Reader feedback

Feedback from our readers is always welcome. Let us know what you think about this book—what you liked or may have disliked. Reader feedback is important for us to develop titles that you really get the most out of.

To send us general feedback, simply send an e-mail to feedback@packtpub.com, and mention the book title via the subject of your message.

If there is a topic that you have expertise in and you are interested in either writing or contributing to a book, see our author guide on www.packtpub.com/authors.

Customer support

Now that you are the proud owner of a Packt book, we have a number of things to help you to get the most from your purchase.

Downloading the example code

You can download the example code files for all Packt books you have purchased from your account at http://www.packtpub.com. If you purchased this book elsewhere, you can visit http://www.packtpub.com/support and register to have the files e-mailed directly to you.

Errata

Although we have taken every care to ensure the accuracy of our content, mistakes do happen. If you find a mistake in one of our books—maybe a mistake in the text or the code—we would be grateful if you would report this to us. By doing so, you can save other readers from frustration and help us improve subsequent versions of this book. If you find any errata, please report them by visiting http://www.packtpub.com/submit-errata, selecting your book, clicking on the **errata submission form** link, and entering the details of your errata. Once your errata are verified, your submission will be accepted and the errata will be uploaded on our website, or added to any list of existing errata, under the Errata section of that title. Any existing errata can be viewed by selecting your title from http://www.packtpub.com/support.

Piracy

Piracy of copyright material on the Internet is an ongoing problem across all media. At Packt, we take the protection of our copyright and licenses very seriously. If you come across any illegal copies of our works, in any form, on the Internet, please provide us with the location address or website name immediately so that we can pursue a remedy.

Please contact us at copyright@packtpub.com with a link to the suspected pirated material.

We appreciate your help in protecting our authors, and our ability to bring you valuable content.

Questions

You can contact us at questions@packtpub.com if you are having a problem with any aspect of the book, and we will do our best to address it.

1
In the Beginning...

By virtue of using a mobile device, you will have used a messenger app of some description or the other (as well as any number of other apps). As time has moved on, so have the apps. For the humble messenger software, you can now add sound, video, and audio, and have it extend over many messages (a message was traditionally 160 characters, as it was only used by telecom operatives to send small messages informing others of their progress or a fault in the system). How did the apps metamorphose to the apps we have today? The answer is simple—planned changes.

In this chapter, we will cover the following topics:

- Application planning
- Application setup
- Creating the correct provisioning profile for iOS
- The database model

Application planning

In the 1990s, there was a piece of software for the Acorn RISC OS range of machines called **SBase**. The software was one of the most stable, intuitive, and above all simple-to-use applications. I was surprised many years later to find out that this was not down to unit testing, A-B testing, or anything like that. The reason was that before a single line of code had been written, absolutely everything was written by hand first. Not code (this would not be a good plan), but a detailed storyboard and flow.

After a month or so of planning, the work of coding began. However, as the author knew what would go where, the final development time was much less than the time it would have taken, had he just sat down and started coding.

The design templates

There are quite a number of different design templates freely available for download (a quick search on `https://images.google.com/` will show them). The following template will be used in this book:

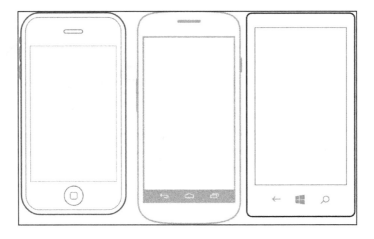

For each new view, a new design will be drawn. While the app will never be a one-to-one representation of the design, it should be close and give an idea of how all sections would work together.

It is also a good idea to use piece of flowcharting software when creating a flow. Again, there are plenty of pieces available, but through trial and error, one of the best that I have found is called the yEd Graph Editor (`http://www.yworks.com/en/products/yfiles/yed/`).

When creating any piece of software, it's also a good plan to have a *shopping list* of the features that you would like to see in the final application.

A messenger – a shopping list of features

The shopping list should feature everything that you want in the app rather than everything that you think should be in the app. If you have a large budget, then the shopping list can be longer. Remember, the longer the list, the larger (and more complex) the application.

The basics of any messenger application UI comprises of the following lists:

- Contacts
- Add and remove contacts
- Message composition, add sound, and pictures

- Message summary
- Message display or text to speech
- Message delete
- Login/register/forgotten password
- Forced synchronization

The following are a few details about the basics:

- Contacts can be from Facebook or your contacts, and should also provide a summary of the contact
- Messages need to be entered via a keyboard or **speech to text** (**STT**)
- Messages need to be able to include pictures (not video) and sound
- Message notifications (new messages) are required
- Forced synchronization causes the app to download all messages and contacts from the server

Speech to text and text to speech

Speech to text is a vital addition to most applications to facilitate those who are visually impaired. These facilities are available on all mobile platforms, and the inclusion will greatly improve the scope and range of users who can take advantage of your new app.

Speech to text is not the same as adding sound to a message; adding sound is different.

Other considerations

While Android is a very open platform that allows users to create their own apps for messaging, iOS is very prescriptive over what you can and cannot do. For example, to create a text message, you must use their text message service and software. This is fine, except that it ties you in strongly to what Apple provides, and doesn't give the end user any different an experience; so why should they bother using what you have over what Apple supplies?

To remove this requirement, a web service can be used. The use of the web service gives a number of advantages:

- No requirement to use the built-in messaging software
- Offline storage
- Notifications

- Large amount of storage
- Routing facilities
- Ability to download messages to any device

This final point is of great importance for this application.

Cross-platform considerations

As the name of this book includes Xamarin, and you are reading this, you will be aware that we are using C# for the core language. This will already be giving a massive advantage in terms of code sharing (for example, all the data services, SQL, and core code will be the same, irrespective of the platform), and also by using one of the more recent additions to Xamarin. It also means that the user interface can be shared by using `Xamarin.Forms`.

We can also swap between devices. On my desk, I have to handle a range of Android devices (tablets and phones), a couple of Windows Phones, a couple of iPhones, and an iPad. At any given time, I may have two of the phones on me, and want to use the app on either of the devices. Not only will the data structure need to be the same but ideally, a similar user interface is needed. This is not to say that each platform version cannot make use of some specific tweak on each platform, but the overall experience needs to be the same.

A secondary aspect to having a cross-platform application is to have a common settings file. All three platforms store user data in a different (and largely incompatible) way meaning that for personal data and app settings, a common profile needs to be established. This can be achieved either online, offline, or both, each having their own advantages and disadvantages:

Method	Advantage	Disadvantage
Offline	Locally stored App can be used out of network coverage	File can be corrupted Not portable between devices
Online	Permanently available Unlikely to become corrupted by app failure Can be used by any device	Requires connection (updates may therefore not always be in sync)
Both	Portable App can be used when not in network range Unlikely to be corrupted Can be used on any device	Synchronization

Obviously, from a portability and usability point of view, having both as options is the best way forward; however, synchronizing changes may be an issue: which is the newer settings file?

Language considerations

It is no longer acceptable to have apps run in a single language. While it was the norm to say, "Hey! I'm English, so everyone can understand English" a number of years ago, there is no valid reason why that now needs to be the case, as all devices are able to localize given the correct language file.

The issue though is that to have every language covered would cost a fortune—many (human) language translators charge between £50 and £100 per hour (at the time of writing), so unless you're part of a larger organization with deep pockets, this can be ruled out.

Online translation services

The next consideration would be to use the likes of Google Translate for the language files used within one version of the app. This is not a bad idea but has a simple problem: though the likes of Google Translate are getting much better, it fails to recognize the context of a sentence so the translation may be incorrect. That said, if the translation is for a *message 3 of 10* (stored as `message %0 of %1` in the localization file), the returned translation to German would be correct.

This allows translations to any language covered by Google (or the translation service you choose to use).

The only remaining issues are storage of the translated messages, and having them as usable across all platforms.

Consider how Android and iOS store localized strings:

- **iOS**: The text for translation is stored within the language file like the following code:

  ```
  "Common.Save"="Save";
  ```

- **Android**: This is more in line with a standard XML format, as shown in the following code:

  ```
  <string name="Common.Save">Save</string>
  ```

Android is closer to a standard XML format while iOS as a `Dictionary<string,string>`. The two are not easily translatable and really, there isn't a simple, cross-platform way to translate text.

However, there is a way around this issue, which also means that should Google add further languages to their system, further language files need no longer be created. The only caveat is that it requires at least one language file to store the translation data in a database on the device and on the server (for others to use).

While this may be initially slow for grabbing the translation file from the server, it won't be slow later on.

The internal data structure

Windows Phone, iOS, and Android all come with an implementation of SQLite (though Windows Phone does require the package to be installed via nuget). This means that we can have the same data structure for all platforms apart from being able to match up to the server with minimal issues. The code for accessing the databases will be covered in *Chapter 5, Data, Generics and Making Sense of Information*; here we will discuss the data table classes.

Any database can be considered as a series of disparate objects that may or may not be linked. Each of these objects is an entry in a data table.

Consider the following example of a book, author, and publisher:

The Newton-le-Willows Community Library has a hundred books on Android development. For argument's sake, they have only one edition and a single author for each book. Each book has the following information stored on it: the ISBN, price, author, publication date, and publisher.

The ISBN number is unique to each book, so it is never replicated making it perfect as what is known as a **Primary Key**. The author may have written any number of books (not only on Android, but possibly in Chemistry and the UK Armed Forces between 1960 and 1965, for example). A name is also not unique—I went to school with three people who had the same name as me.

The publisher too, will have a table containing information such as their address.

In terms of a database structure, the publisher and the author will have what is known as a *one-to-many relationship* with the book (the meaning is literally that—one publisher or author to many books) going **FROM** the publisher or author table **TO** the book. Going **FROM** the book **TO** the author or publisher shows a many-to-one relationship.

To complete this triangle, there will be a relationship between the publisher and the author. As the publisher is a single entity using multiple authors, it will have a one-to-many relationship with the authors.

The ISBN number will have a *one-to-one relationship* with the publisher and the author.

The messenger data structure

For each table, the key data stored needs to be defined. We have, in our application, a simple set up:

- The message
- Contacts
- Backend storage
- The language

Each of these will need defining.

The message

A message contains a number of pieces of information

- A unique identifier
- Who it is from (a contact)
- Date and time sent
- Attachments (though this will be from a separate table, linked by ID)
- The previous message Id

The previous message Id is important for message threading. The first message in any thread will have a value of -1. It is then just a case of moving through the message identifiers to correctly thread a message.

Attachments can be either an audio file or an image. It is never a good idea to store these on a device within the database, as it leads to massive slowdown of the application (SQLite was never designed to store **BLOB** (**Binary Large OBject**) data types).

Contacts

Contacts are anyone (including you). A contact can be anyone invited to share in the app with you; it can be read from your mobile device directory or obtained via the likes of Facebook. Each contact will have the following information:

- Contact ID
- Name

- E-mail
- Phone number
- Last-used date
- Username

Each message is linked to another message as well as to a contact.

Backend storage

While it is fine to have storage on the device, there needs to be an external server somewhere. Currently, there are two main players when it comes to external servers if you are unable to host things yourself. They are Microsoft Azure and Amazon. Both offer the same sort of facilities, but given that Xamarin uses the .NET framework, it makes slightly more sense to use Azure.

The configuration and setting up of an Azure service is covered extensively in *Chapter 14, Bringing It All Together*.

Making sure the messages get through

Part of ensuring that messages get through as soon as they are sent is to use a push notification. Essentially, this is sent out from the server to the application. Unfortunately, the procedure for getting this to work is not the same for Android and iOS.

Setting up for Android

For Android, push notifications are a simple affair, as shown in the following steps:

1. Register the application with Google and obtain an API key.
2. Once you have this, go into the Azure portal, click on **Mobile Services**, select the service name, and then select **Push**.
3. To obtain the key, go to `https://console.developers.google.com/start`, and click on **Create Project**. Enter a new project name. After sometime, the project will appear on the console.
4. Next, select **Add an API** and switch on the **Google Cloud Messaging for Android** option.

5. Now select the credentials and create a new Public API access key. You will see the following displayed. Over here, select **Server Key**:

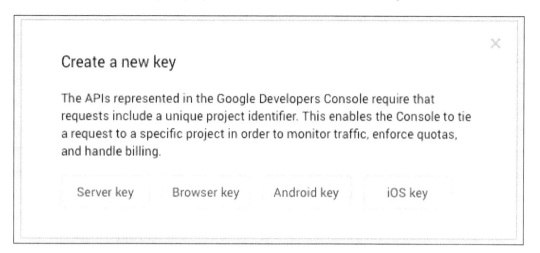

6. After this point, you will need to just create a new key by selecting **Create**:

7. Once the API key has been created, copy and paste it onto the Azure push services page (shown in the following screenshot):

8. Once complete, select **Save** and Android is set up, server side, to send a push notification.

Setting up for iOS

For push notifications to work on iOS, you will need a valid iOS developer account with Apple (currently this costs $99 per year). Assuming you have such an account, log in.

If you already have a developer profile set up, skip to the *Creating and configuring for push notifications* section.

Creating your iOS profile

The certificate is your digital signature that can be used for any application, for any given team. The use of certificates enables developers to work on different teams and still have a valid signing certificate. Creating a certificate is simple enough:

1. Click on your Applications folder and navigate to **Utilities | KeyChain Access**.

2. From the Menu bar, select **Certificate Assistant | Request a Certificate From a Certificate Authority…** (as shown in the following screenshot):

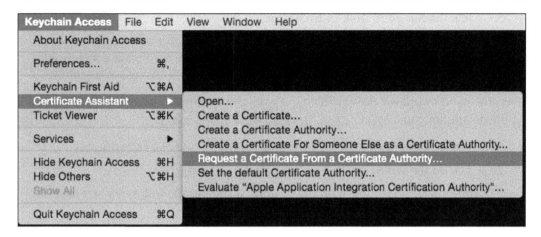

3. Once this has been clicked, you will be presented with the following window:

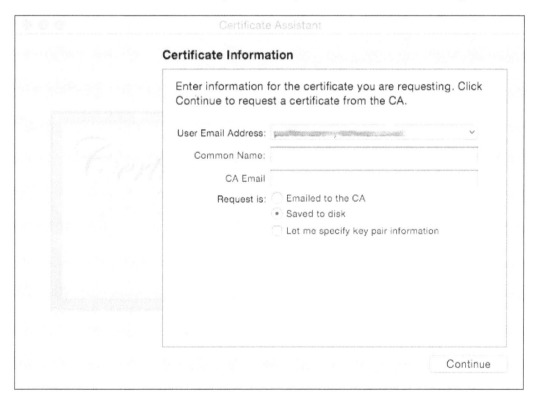

4. Fill in the **User Email Address** using the address that the Apple developer account is registered with.

5. Click the **Saved to disk** radio button.

6. When these have been filled in, select `Continue`. After a few moments, you will be asked where to save the certificate. Give the certificate a meaningful name and save. You can now minimize the Keychain Access application.

You now need to upload the certificate. Again, this is simple enough. Log into your Apple developer console (`https://developer.apple.com/`):

1. Click on **Certificates, Identifiers and Profiles**, and select **Certificates**.

2. Click on the **Add** icon.

3. You will be presented with the options shown in the following screenshot:

4. You will need to create at least an **iOS App Development** and an **App Store** and **Ad Hoc** certificate.

5. The process for creating either of these certificates is the same. Select the certificate type, and click on **Continue**.

6. You will be presented with an information page that covers how to create your certificate (performed in the preceding steps). Click on **Continue**.

7. The next page allows you to upload the certificate you previously created to the Apple Developer portal. **Click Choose File**, navigate to where you saved the certificate, and click on **OK** to upload.

8. Once the file has been selected, click on the **Generate** button. After a while, the certificate can be downloaded. Download and double click on the certificate to install.

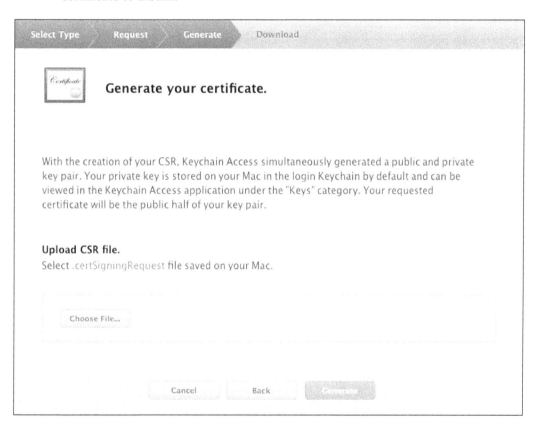

9. You can check whether the certificate has been installed by checking the Keychain Access application.

Creating and configuring for push notifications

We now have to create a profile for our application. On the developer portal, select Identifiers.

1. Select the **+** button to create a new app.

2. Fill in the **App ID** description (this is just a name for the app).

3. Add an explicit app ID. This is recommended to be a reverse, domain-style string (for example, com.packt-pub.messenger).

4. Towards the bottom of the page, you will need to select **Push Notifications**.

5. Once complete, you will be presented with something similar to the following screenshot:

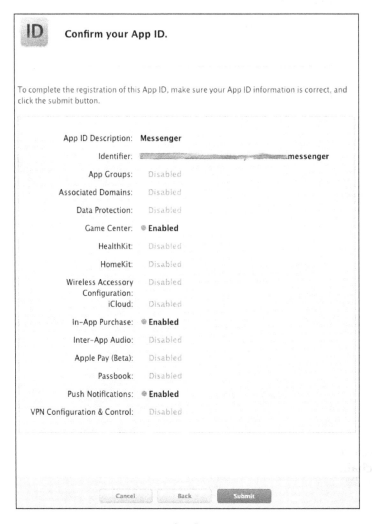

ID   **Confirm your App ID.**

To complete the registration of this App ID, make sure your App ID information is correct, and click the submit button.

App ID Description:	**Messenger**
Identifier:	▓▓▓▓▓▓▓▓▓▓▓▓▓▓▓▓▓▓.messenger
App Groups:	Disabled
Associated Domains:	Disabled
Data Protection:	Disabled
Game Center:	● **Enabled**
HealthKit:	Disabled
HomeKit:	Disabled
Wireless Accessory Configuration:	Disabled
iCloud:	Disabled
In-App Purchase:	● **Enabled**
Inter-App Audio:	Disabled
Apple Pay (Beta):	Disabled
Passbook:	Disabled
Push Notifications:	● **Enabled**
VPN Configuration & Control:	Disabled

Cancel   Back   **Submit**

6. Once you are happy with all the selections, click on **Submit**.

7. Next, a certificate has to be generated for the notifications. If you're used to creating a certificate, generate two—one for development and one for distribution. If you're not, follow the instructions used for generating your initial certificate.

8. Select the app created from the App IDs page on the developer site (as seen in the following screenshot):

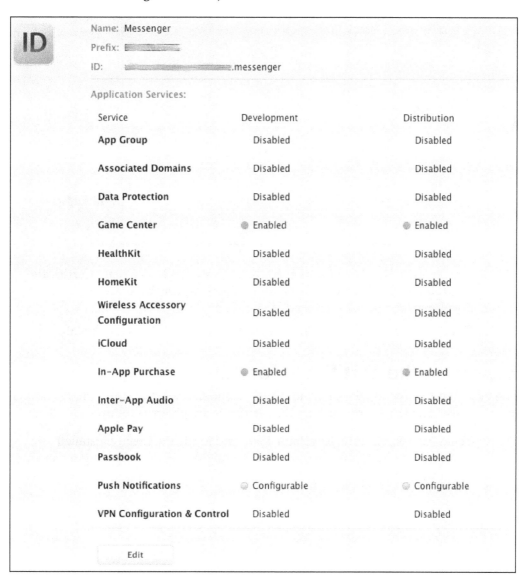

9. Select **Edit**.

10. Go to the section marked **Push Notifications**.

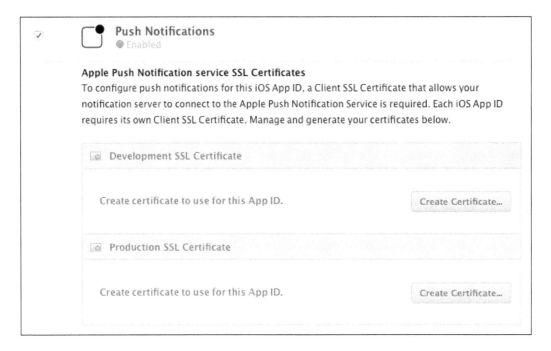

11. Starting with the **Development SSL certificate**, click on **Create Certificate** and follow the on-screen instructions. When requested, select the development certificate created in step 7.

12. Once generated, download the certificates and double-click to install.

Exporting the certificate for Azure

The final step for creating the push notifications for Azure is to export what is known as a `.p12` file. The steps for exporting the certificate are given as follows:

1. To access this, start the **Keychain Tool**, and locate the freshly installed development push notification entry (highlighted in the following screenshot):

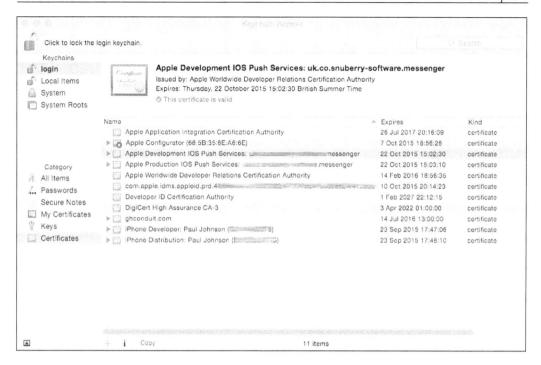

2. Select **File | Export** and give the file a name. Then click **Save**, as shown in the following screenshot:

3. This needs to be imported into Azure. As with Android, go to **Mobile services | Push**, and move to the **Apple** section:

4. Click on upload, and upload the .p12 file you have just exported from the keychain tool. Ensure that **Sandbox** is selected when requested. When complete, you will see the following screen:

Azure, iOS and Android push notifications are now set correctly on the server side.

Adding packages to your application

For the application to be able to access the Azure services, it requires an additional package. You can manually create it, but it is easier to use the NuGet package. I will cover this in detail in *Chapter 3*, *Making It Pretty and Logging In*.

Summary

We've covered quite a lot of information in this chapter, from enabling push notifications to registering your app with Google and Apple, and by now you should have at least an appreciation for what is involved in even the simplest of applications.

In the next chapter, we will start looking at the user interface and at using Xamarin forms for the application UI.

2
Let's Get the Party Started

This chapter is primarily involved with the introduction of the Xamarin Forms library, and its incorporation within your applications. In particular, we will cover the following topics:

- Setting up for Xamarin Forms
- How Xamarin Forms work
- Adding a Windows Phone project to your app

What is Xamarin Forms?

Xamarin Forms is known as a user interface abstraction library. It operates as a **Portable Class Library** (**PCL**), sitting on the target platforms and feeding in the UI elements that the application needs. It is as good as it sounds! Application user interfaces can be quickly constructed as a large amount of any other code can be shared.

 The Xamarin Forms library also allows you to access the platform hardware through injection with UI customization, through custom renderers. Both of these topics are covered later in the book.

Being an abstraction layer, only those elements with an analogous element on all of the target platforms are covered. For example, at the time of writing, there is not a single checkbox in forms and graphics on tab pages, for Android gives nothing.

This library is also part of a PCL. The PCL itself only supports a subset of the standard .NET library classes, namely those that are supported on all platforms. This leads to quite a few issues, such as the likes of the `File` class within `System` is simply not there as there is no guarantee that the targets will have the same class. This seems daft when you consider that everything supports files. This is both true and false. Mobiles and desktops have a file system, but embedded devices or devices with a sole project that needs no form of storage may have a custom build of the .NET libraries to exclude the classes not required (though they can be implemented using Wrapper classes).

 A Forms-based application also has a distinct life cycle which will be covered later in this chapter.

Xamarin Forms are split into four main areas:

* Pages
* Layouts
* Views
* Cells

Pages

A page occupies the full screen in most cases. A page acts the same as `Page` on a Windows Phone and `UIViewController` on iOS. It is important to note that on Android they are more like a `Resource.Layout` and are certainly not an `Activity`.

 Code examples for each type of page are given in `Chapter 2/Pages` directory within the code, supplied with this book.

There are five types of pages, given as follows:

Type	Description
ContentPage	It contains a single view.
MasterDetailPage	A page that has two panes for the page. Typically, the master will contain the likes of a menu with the detail the content.
NavigationPage	A page that contains a navigation bar. Pages are kept on a stack and can be jumped between. The Navigation bar can handle buttons on either side of the bar as well as a title.
TabbedPage	A container page. The TabbedPage acts as a container holding the content pages associated with each tab.
CarouselPage	A page that allows for sweeping across to show other views.

Layouts

A layout is a container that can hold other layouts or views. There are seven different layouts, given as follows:

Layout	Description
ContentLayout	Used as a base class for user-defined views. Holds a single element.
Frame	A parent containing a single child that can be framed.
ScrollView	A view capable of being much larger than the screen on the phone. If the content doesn't exceed the screen size, the scrolling has no effect and acts as a standard view.
AbsoluteLayout	A view that positions child layouts at specified positions using anchors to define the placing and size.
Grid	A layout containing multiple views arranged in rows and columns (such as would be found on a camera picture viewer).
RelativeLayout	A layout that positions elements relative to each other using constraints.
StackLayout	One of the most commonly used layouts. It positions the child elements in a line. The layout handles the child bounds, so any user defined bounds are overwritten.

 Code examples for each layout are given in Chapter2/Layout directory.

Views

A view is the likes of a Button, ActivityIndicator, or Label. The 19 different types of views are given as follows:

View	Description
ActivityIndicator	Typically used to show the progress of time (such as when something is being downloaded, or a calculation is taking place).
BoxView	Allows a solid colored box to be drawn.
Button	A standard UI button.
DatePicker	Produces a Date-picker control specific to the platform.
Editor	A multi-line text editor control
Entry	A single-line text entry control.

View	Description
Image	This view holds an image from the host platform. These should be placed where graphics normally go (Resources/Drawable on Android, Resource on iOS, and Assets on a Windows Phone).
Label	A non-editable text view. Can span across multiple lines.
ListView	Displays a collection of data in a vertical list.
OpenGLView	OpenGL is typically used for games or other graphically intensive code.
Picker	A spinner control that allows for picking from a list of items.
ProgressBar	Similar to an activity indicator.
SearchBar	An entry control used for searching.
Slider	A sliding method for entering a value controlled linearly.
Stepper	A view that allows for movement between user defined values using a + and – button.
Switch	A toggle view.
TableView	This is not the same as an iOS UITableView; it is closer to the Android TableView which holds rows of cells.
TimePicker	Similar to a DatePicker, but for time.
WebView	A view that allows HTML to be shown either generated from the app or using as an online resource.

 Examples for this section are discussed in Chapter2/Views.

Cells

A cell can be considered as a specialized view that describes how each item within a TableView or ListView is drawn. There are four cell types, given as follows:

Cell	Description
EntryCell	A cell containing a label and single-line entry element.
SwitchCell	The same as a switch, but with a label before it.
TextCell	A cell containing both a primary and a secondary text field.
ImageCell	A text cell that also contains an image.

 Examples for this section are in Chapter2/Cells.

So, how does this all work?

What follows gives you an idea on how Forms works. It is not the full story; that would take a great deal of time. What follows should suffice.

Before you consider how Xamarin Forms works, you need to consider how any application works, or its life cycle. The following screenshot shows the life cycles of Android, iOS, and Windows Phones applications.

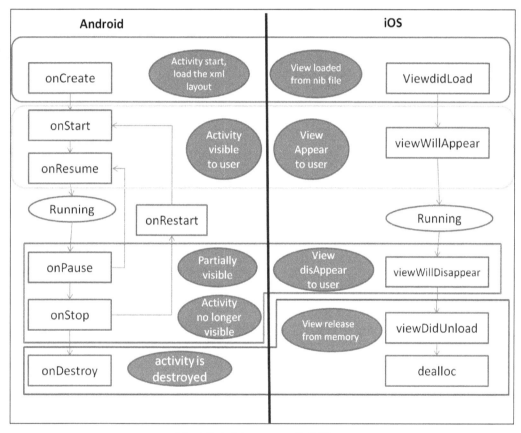

http://i.stack.imgur.com/Jn6MZ.png

The life cycle for a Windows Phone is not quite the same, as is shown in the following diagram:

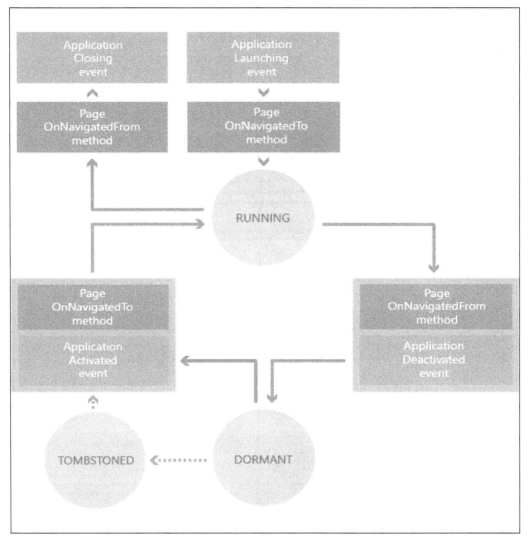

http://edglogowski.azurewebsites.net/wp-content/uploads/2013/10/WinPhoAppLifecycle_thumb.png

In effect, they follow the process:

1. Start
2. Make the UI visible
3. Handle events
4. End

As all three follow the same routes and are using the same language, it should be possible to create a library that handles all these facilities. The problem is linking it in. Do you create three libraries with the same method names, but map down to different UI element names and call those from within the PCL?

Essentially, that is what is done (there is a lot more to it than that in reality). The library is instantiated on the platform with the UI being constructed from the code in the PCL. The PCL tells the platform, "I want a button in the middle of the view". Android uses a vertical layout, adds a button with the linear layout gravity set as center. The PCL then says, "the click event calls a method inside of the PCL, so redirect to that when it's called", and so on.

The life cycle is also used (though in a simpler way) as follows:

- `OnStart()`: This method is called when the app starts
- `OnSleep()`: This method is called when the app goes into the background or when the app terminates naturally (not a crash)
- `OnResume()`: This method is called when the app comes back from the background

Storing information

A static `Dictionary<string, object>` called `Properties is also available` for storing information within the application(accessed through `Application.Current.Properties`).

It follows all the usual rules for dictionaries. The `Properties` dictionary is a persistent type (in other words, the dictionary stays even in the `OnSleep()` state or when restarted. This is very useful to prevent the loss of information even when recovering from a crash.

Instantiating Xamarin Forms within an app

We instantiate Xamarin Forms within each supported platform of the app. Xamarin Forms support the following platforms:

- Android
- iOS
- Windows Phone

Android

Typically, an activity to start an activity class looks like this:

```
public class MyActivity : Activity
{
    protected override void OnCreate(Bundle bundle)
    {
        base.OnCreate(bundle);
        // then whatever you need to do
```

To start a Xamarin Forms app, this changes as we are not inheriting the Activity but a FormsApplicationActivity, or more precisely:

```
public class MyActivity : global::Xamarin.Forms.Platform.Android.
FormsApplicationActivity
{
    protected override void OnCreate(Bundle bundle)
    {
        base.OnCreate(bundle);
        global::Xamarin.Forms.Forms.Init(this, bundle);
        LoadApplication(new App());
    }
}
```

iOS

As with Android, we inherit FormsApplicationDelegate in AppDelegate instead of the usual UIApplicationDelegate:

```
[Register("AppDelegate")]
public partial class AppDelegate : global::Xamarin.Forms.Platform.iOS.
FormsApplicationDelegate
{
    public override bool FinishedLaunching(UIApplication app,
NSDictionary opts)
    {
        global::Xamarin.Forms.Forms.Init();
        LoadApplication(new App());
        return base.FinishedLaunching(app, options); // must have this
line in!
    }
}
```

Windows Phone

Windows Phone instantiation is a two-part process. The next section shows how to add a Windows Phone project to your application (if the project was started on a Mac). At the end, you will find what needs to be altered in the `xaml` and `xaml.cs` files.

Adding Windows Phone to your project

If you're using Windows Phone, you'll be using Visual Studio. The instructions that follow are for Mac users wanting to add a Windows Phone package. However, from adding the libraries, the instructions are for both VS and for those adding a Windows Phone package.

Import from Mac into Visual Studio

This can be performed via Git or any other means you want. Simply follow these steps:

1. Open the project using **File | Open**. Once loaded, you will see something like the following screenshot:

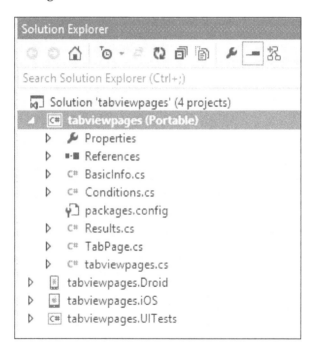

2. Select the portable package. From the menu, select **Add | New Project**:

📥	Build Solution	F6		'Portable)	
	Rebuild Solution				
	Clean Solution				
	Run Code Analysis on Solution	Alt+F11		:s	
	Batch Build...			nfig	
	Configuration Manager...				
🎁	Manage NuGet Packages for Solution...				
📑	Enable NuGet Package Restore			:s.cs	
				roid	
	Web Essentials	▶		)S	
📰	New Solution Explorer View			lTests	
🖧	Show on Code Map				
	Calculate Code Metrics				
	Project Dependencies...				
	Project Build Order...				
	Add	▶		New Project...	
⚙	Set StartUp Projects...			Existing Project...	
📲	Add Solution to Subversion...			New Web Site...	
📲	Add Selected Projects to Subversion...			Existing Web Site...	
	Subversion	▶	🗔	New Item...	Ctrl+Shift+A
	Paste	Ctrl+V	⁺🗔	Existing Item...	Shift+Alt+A
🔤	Rename		📠	New Solution Folder	
↪	Open Folder in File Explorer				
🔧	Properties	Alt+Enter		New	

3. After you select **New Project**, you will be met with the new project window:

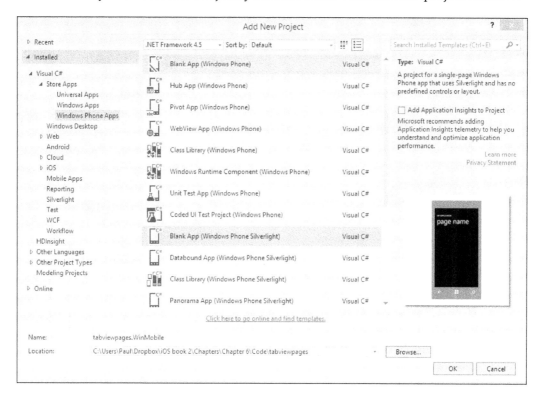

4. Select **Blank App (Windows Phone Silverlight)**. Give the application a name, and click on the **OK** button. Visual Studio will add a blank Silverlight application.

5. Once the **OK** button has been clicked, you will be presented with the target OS. Select either Windows Phone 8 or 8.1.

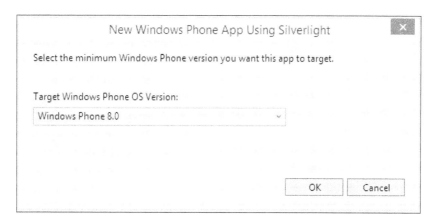

And there you have it! Your two-platform app created on a Mac now supports three platforms through your PC.

Adding the libraries

The application created is a standard Windows Phone application—it is not yet a Xamarin Forms application. You will need to install the library from NuGet.

1. To do this, highlight the **References** menu. Then from the pop up menu, click on the **Manage NuGet Packages...** option:

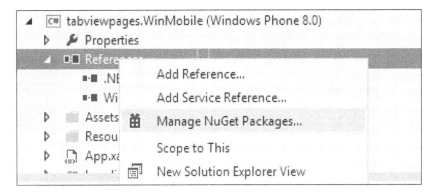

2. The NuGet library window will open. In the search box, type xamarin forms:

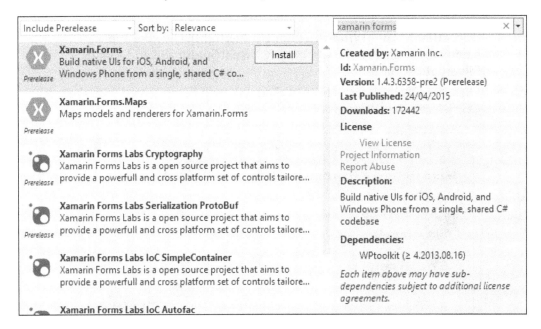

3. Click on **Install** to install the library. NuGet will install the library and any dependencies it relies on.

4. Next, we need to reference the PCL library. This can be found through the reference manager. Select **Solution | Projects**, followed by the PCL name (in the following example, it is `tabviewpages`; if you accept the defaults when you create a Xamarin Forms app, the PCL will always just be the name of the project).

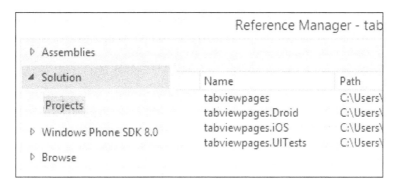

5. When the PCL is clicked, a tick box will appear to the left of the name. Click on the box, and a tick will appear. Select **OK**.

The app is now nearly ready!

Modifying the XAML code

The final part is modifying the XAML code to tell the app that it is a Xamarin Forms application, not a Windows Phone application.

1. Select the `mainpage.xaml` file (this is the file that creates the base UI). Modify the code as given in the following screenshot:

```
1  <phone:FormsApplicationPage
2      x:Class="tabviewpages.WinMobile.MainPage"
3      xmlns="http://schemas.microsoft.com/winfx/2006/xaml/presentation"
4      xmlns:x="http://schemas.microsoft.com/winfx/2006/xaml"
5      xmlns:phone="clr-namespace:Xamarin.Forms.Platform.WinPhone;assembly=Xamarin.Forms.Platform.WP8"
6      xmlns:shell="clr-namespace:Microsoft.Phone.Shell;assembly=Microsoft.Phone"
7      xmlns:d="http://schemas.microsoft.com/expression/blend/2008"
8      xmlns:mc="http://schemas.openxmlformats.org/markup-compatibility/2006"
9      mc:Ignorable="d"
10     FontFamily="{StaticResource PhoneFontFamilyNormal}"
11     FontSize="{StaticResource PhoneFontSizeNormal}"
12     Foreground="{StaticResource PhoneForegroundBrush}"
13     SupportedOrientations="Portrait" Orientation="Portrait"
14     shell:SystemTray.IsVisible="True">
15
16  </phone:FormsApplicationPage>
```

The important lines here are lines **1** and **5**. The first says that it is using a `FormsApplicationPage` (rather than an `ApplicationPage`). Line **5** specifies the namespace and the assembly to be used.

2. Next `mainpage.xaml.cs` needs to be modified, as shown in the following screenshot:

```csharp
using Microsoft.Phone.Controls;
using Xamarin.Forms;
using Xamarin.Forms.Platform.WinPhone;

namespace tabviewpages.WinMobile
{
    2 references
    public partial class MainPage : global::Xamarin.Forms.Platform.WinPhone.FormsApplicationPage
    {
        // Constructor
        0 references
        public MainPage()
        {
            InitializeComponent();
            Forms.Init();

            LoadApplication(new tabviewpages.App());
        }
    }
}
```

3. The application has been set as a Xamarin Forms application. All that needs to be done is to set the Windows Phone app as the start application. Select the project name, and on the context menu, select **Set as Start Up Project**.

4. You will notice that unlike Android and iOS, the PCL has to be launched by preceding the `App()` with the PCL namespace. This is due to Windows Phone already having its own `App` class.

5. Test the code by compiling. When it works, you will see the UI:

Dependency injection

Another important aspect of Xamarin Forms is based on something called **Inversion of Control (IoC)**.

Inversion of Control?

Once the app has started, the PCL runs the show; it is in control. However, certain things have to use the device or facilities on the device, and so control is passed to the application (control has been inverted). This can be considered using the following diagram:

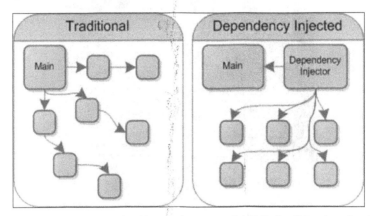

https://jonlennartaasenden.files.wordpress.com/2015/01/traditional-vs-di.gif

IoC and Dependency Injection go hand-in-hand. DI (as the name implies) injects information directly into the PCL. There is a rule, though, to do this: the class being called must have a default constructor for the class (normally, the default constructor for any class is not required).

Implementing DI

Let's take the following example for DI. A PCL only contains a subset of the standard libraries; one important omission is anything to do with the filer. When you create a SQLite database though, a file has to be written, which cannot be done within the PCL.

To access the code on the platform, an interface class is constructed within the PCL (you will see this a lot within the book as you progress):

```
using SQLite.Net;

namespace MyApplication
{
  public interface IDatabaseConnection
  {
    SQLiteConnection Connection { get; }

    string ConnectionString { get; }
  }
}
```

On the platform, `IDatabaseConnection` is inherited and implemented:

```
[assembly: Xamarin.Forms.Dependency(typeof(DBManager))]
namespace MyApplication.Droid
{
  public class DBManager :IDatabaseConnection
  {
    private readonly string documentsPath = Environment.
GetFolderPath(Environment.SpecialFolder.Personal);
    const string sqliteFilename = "myapplication.db3";

    public SQLiteConnection Connection
    {
      get
      {
        string libraryPath = Path.Combine(documentsPath, "..",
"Library");
        var path = Path.Combine(libraryPath, sqliteFilename);
        var plat = new SQLite.Net.Platform.XamarinAndroid.
SQLitePlatformAndroid();
        var conn = new SQLiteConnection(plat, path);
        return conn;
      }
    }

    public string ConnectionString
    {
      get
      {
        var pDocs = Path.Combine(documentsPath, "myapplication.db3");
        return string.Format("{0}; New=true; Version=3;PRAGMA locking_
mode=EXCLUSIVE; PRAGMA journal_mode=WAL; PRAGMA cache_size=20000;
PRAGMA page_size=32768; PRAGMA synchronous=off", pDocs);
      }
    }
  }
```

We can then access the `Connection` within the PCL using the following code:

```
using (var sqlCon = DependencyService.Get<IDatabaseConnection>().
Connection)
{
  // do whatever you need here
}
```

Customizing the UI

While the basic UI elements are available, to do anything interesting (such as customizing buttons), a custom renderer has to be created. These are covered fully in *Chapter 6, A View to a Kill*, which deals with the user experience, as well as other places within the book.

Gestures, maps, and WebViews

Gestures, maps, and WebViews are very commonly used user-interface facilities. While they are all in Xamarin Forms, we will see that they are not as extensive as if they were native versions.

Gestures

All mobile devices have some form of a sweep system. The iOS is especially rich when it comes to having a multi-touch user interface. As with everything to do with Xamarin.Forms, it only covers the basic type of touch, essentially the only one supported on all platforms.

> Code for the following is given in Chapter2/Gestures.

Gestures are not enabled on all types of gadgets (for example, gestures are not enabled for dragging pins on a map). This is because only tap detection is currently supported.

Adding a gesture recognizer

In this example, we'll add a gesture recognizer to a label. Labels usually don't have a click event.

1. Let's create the label:

```
var count = 0;

var label = new Label()
{
  Text = string.Format("You have clicked me {0} times", count),
  TextColor = Color.Red,
  BackgroundColor = Color.White
};
```

2. Next is the creation of the gesture recognizer. One of the nice things about the gesture recognizer is that the number of taps required to activate the tap can be defined. If it is set to more than one, there is a finite time between clicks. If the tap is too slow, then the event is ignored:

```
var tapGesture = new TapGestureRecognizer
{
  NumberOfTapsRequired = 2
};
```

3. The gesture recognizer reacts to the `Tapped` event:

```
tapGesture.Tapped += (s, e) =>
{
  count++;
  if (count % 2 == 0)
  {
    label.BackgroundColor = Color.Red;
    label.TextColor = Color.White;
  }
  else
  {
    label.TextColor = Color.Red;
    label.BackgroundColor = Color.White;
  }
  label.Text = string.Format("You have clicked me {0} times",
count);
};
```

4. Finally, the `tapGesture` has to be added to the label itself:

```
label.GestureRecognizers.Add(tapGesture);
```

That is all there is to adding a gesture recognizer to a gadget.

WebViews

The WebView UI is handled by the platform's native browser. This is simple enough for Windows Phone, and iOS, but Android is currently moving over to using Chrome. Whichever you have selected will be used. If you are using this on Android, ensure that the `INTERNET` permission is set.

 A WebView example is in `Chapter2/Webviews`.

The view is able to display a standard webpage or a page generated in code.

Displaying a web page

The browser is called into life using the following line of code:

```
var myBrowser = new WebView();
```

To point the browser to a website, set the Source property to point to the website:

```
var myBrowser = new Webview
{
  Source = "http://www.farmtrack.co.uk"
};
```

Displaying a generated web page

To have a WebView show a page generated in code, an HtmlWebViewSource object has to be created. Essentially, this is a string with HTML in it. Once created, the browser Source property is set to point at the HtmlWebViewSource object:

```
var htmlSource = new HtmlWebViewSource
{
    Html = @"<html><body><h1><center>Hello World!<center></h1></
body></html>"
};
myBrowser.Source = htmlSource;
```

Displaying a web page from a file

There are occasions when you would want to display a webpage stored as a file within the app. The file is normally read into a string and the string is displayed. The issue is that within the PCL, a great deal of the file library is missing.

There are a couple of solutions to this. The first is to use reflection with an EmbeddedResource, as follows:

```
var assembly = typeof(LoadResourceText).GetTypeInfo().Assembly;
var stream = assembly.GetManifestResourceStream("myNamespace.
myFileToLoad.ext");
var data = "";
using (var reader = new StreamReader(stream))
    text = reader.ReadToEnd();
myBrowser.Source = text;
```

The next solution is to use DependencyService. This has to be implemented on each platform before it will work on any of them. The dependency service is used in conjunction with the BaseUrl property of WebView. The BaseUrl property lets WebView know the path to use when resolving a URL. However, these will be stored on the device.

As we saw earlier, to access the platform from within the PCL, an interface is used:

```
public interface IBaseUrl { string GetBaseURL(); }
```

We then create `HtmlWebViewSource`. Here, an image and a stylesheet are included. These are stored on the device itself. They are resolved by `BaseUrl` being followed down to the device:

```
var htmlCode = new HtmlWebViewSource
{
    BaseUrl = DependencyService.Get<IBaseUrl>().GetBaseURL(),
    Html = @"<html><head>
<title>Test webview</title>
<link rel=""stylesheet"" href=""myCSS.css"">
</head>
<body>
<h1>Testing 123</h1>
<p>This is a test</p>
<img src='Images/logo.png' />
</body>
</html>"
};
myBrowser.Source = htmlCode;
```

As we are using a dependency service, the dependency interface has to be implemented on the platforms.

Displaying a web page from a file – iOS

Store the files in `Resources`, and set the build action to `BundleResource`. The dependency looks like the following piece of code:

```
[assembly: Dependency(typeof(BaseUrl_iOS))]
namespace WebViewExample.iOS
{
  public class BaseUrl_iOS : IBaseUrl
  {
    public string GetBaseURL
    {
      return NSBundle.MainBundle.BundlePath;
    }
  }
}
```

Displaying a web page from a file – Android

The code to be included should be stored in the `Assets` directory and the build action set to `AndroidAsset`. The dependency looks similar to the iOS version but the base URL becomes `file:///android_asset/`:

```
[assembly: Dependency(typeof(BaseUrl_Android))]
namespace WebViewExample.Android
{
  public class BaseUrl_Android : IBaseUrl
  {
    public string GetBaseURL
    {
      return "file:///android_asset";
    }
  }
}
```

Displaying a web page from a file – Windows Phone

Windows Phone is fairly similar to Android. Any images should be placed in the `Assets` directory:

```
[assembly: Dependency(typeof(BaseUrl_WinMobile))]
namespace WebViewExample.WinMobile
{
  public class BaseUrl_WinMobile : IBaseUrl
  {
    public string Get()
    {
      return "";
    }
  }
}
```

Maps

As with `WebView`, the map system uses the native system. While it means that the users have an interface they are familiar with, from a developer's point of view, a number of hoops have to be jumped through in order to get the maps to work.

 The map example is in `Chapter 2/Maps`.

The map requires an additional library installation from NuGet: `Xamarin.Forms.Maps`. Once installed, the library has to be instantiated on each platform after the main `Forms.Init()` call. The library is called into being using `Xamarin.FormsMaps.Init();`.

The `Init()` method should be placed in `FinishedLaunching` (iOS), `MainActivity.cs` (Android), and `MainPage.xaml.cs` (Windows Phone).

Setting up on iOS

The following needs to be added to the `info.plist` file if you're developing for iOS 8. iOS 7 doesn't need this, though it does no harm adding it:

```
<key>NSLocationAlwaysUsageDescription</key>
   <string>Can we use your location</string>
<key>NSLocationWhenInUseUsageDescription</key>
   <string>We are using your location</string>
```

Setting up on Android

A valid Google maps v2 API key is required. This is the same as if you were developing for Android and required a map. Once you have the key, paste the key into `Properties/AndroidManifest.xml`:

```
<meta-data android:name="com.google.android.maps.v2.API_KEY"
   android:value="Key_Value_Goes_Here" />
```

You will also need the following permissions setting: `AccessCourseLocation`, `AccessFineLocation`, `AccessLocationExtraCommands`, `AccessMockLocation`, `AccessNetworkState`, `AccessWifiState`, and `Internet`.

Setting up on Windows Phone

To have maps working on Windows Phone, the `ID_CAP_MAP` and `ID_CAP_LOCATION` capabilities flags set. These are found by clicking on the `WMAppManifest.xml` file within the `Properties` folder. Once you have double clicked on the XML file, select the **Capabilities** tab and select the two capabilities required.

Adding a map

The map control is simple to create and add onto a `ContentPage`:

```
var theMap = new Map(MapSpan.FromCenterAndRadius(new Position(-2.962,
53.430), new Distance(0.3)))
{
  IsShowingUser = true,
  HeightRequest = 100,
  WidthRequest = 960,
  VerticalOptions = LayoutOptions.FillAndExpand,
  MapType = MapType.Hybrid // can also be Street and Satellite
};

Content = new StackLayout{ Spacing = 0, Children = { theMap } };
```

Adding a zoom facility to a map

A simple method of adding a zoom to the map is to add in a `slider`, and change the map zoom by reacting to the `ValueChanged` event:

```
var mySlider = new Slider(1, 10, 1); // goes from 1 to 10 in steps of
1
mySlider.ValueChanged += (s,e) =>
{
    var newZoomLevel = e.NewValue;
    var latlongdegs = 360 / (Math.Pow(2, newZoomLevel));
    theMap.MoveToRegion(new MapSpan(theMap.VisibleRegion.Center,
latlongdegrees, latlongdegrees));
};
```

Sticking a pin in it

There are four types of pins: `Generic`, `Place`, `SavedPin`, and `SearchResult`. Their names describe what they are typically used for. Pins are not pullable and only have limited capabilities (though they can be extended through custom renderers).

```
var mapPin = new Pin
{
    Type = PinType.Place,
    Position = new Position(-2.962, 53.430),
    Label = "Liverpool FC",
    Address = "Anfield, Liverpool"
};
theMap.Pins.Add(mapPin);
```

Summary

From the get-go, Xamarin Forms gives you the ability to create an app on the three main mobile platforms without many problems. Most of the standard UI elements are present, and enable the production of feature-rich applications. As we will see in later chapters, using custom renderers as well as being able to access the hardware-specific facilities can extend applications.

In the next chapter, we'll be looking at how we can improve upon the user experience by modifying the user interface to make it more friendly and intuitive.

3
Making It Look Pretty and Logging In

While `Xamarin.Forms` provides the basics of a user interface experience, it provides just that—a very basic user interface, functional but plain. With a bit of effort though, it is possible to produce custom UI components across the various mobile platforms.

In this chapter we shall:

- Understand how Xamarin Forms performs the UI tasks
- Look at the customization of the user interface using a custom renderer
- Apply these changes to allow for an improved user login experience

Introducing the standard UI login experience

Held within the source code examples in this chapter, you will find a simple Xamarin.Forms application called **BasicUI**. All the code for this section is taken from there. It is very minimal. When executed, you will see the following:

The iOS and Android UIs

While these are purely functional, they don't exactly look nice. The problem is that we can't change the look and feel very easily. This is due to the technology behind Xamarin Forms.

Abstract this, abstract that

If you think of any user interface, you will find a lot of commonality, as given in the following table:

UI element	Android name	iOS name
Label	TextView	UILabel
Editable text	EditView	UITextView
Image	ImageView	UITextField
Table	Table Layout	UIImageView
View	View	UITableView
		UIView
Dropdown	Spinner	UIPickerView
Lists	ListView	UITableView

Each of these will have their own properties (such as size and color), and each will have their own events. The point is that there is a commonality between all the mobile platforms. If you remove these commonalities and create a layer to deal with these elements, it is known as an **abstraction layer**. This layer sits between the device and the application to provide the functionality.

However, the problem lies in what you can do with these elements. For example, each button will only have a basic click event, as that is the only event guaranteed to be implemented on the target platforms. Altering the size of an element is also difficult. If you consider the massive range of Android devices available for both phones and tablets and the variation in pixel depths, you can rapidly appreciate the difficulty in implementing sizing. This is why the height/width properties are a finite size.

When size really does matter

If you consider just the Android implementation (shown in the following screenshot) and a native implementation rather than a Forms implementation, we could ensure that the entry section will have a uniform size in one of two ways, given as follows:

1. Create a vertical linear layout with a weight of 1, and into that place two horizontal linear layouts, each with a weight of 3. Add a TextView into each (layout weight = 1) and an EditText element (weight 2). It will now look like the following screenshot:

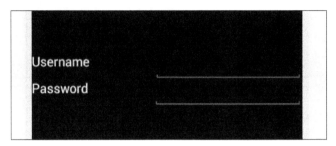

Figure 1

2. Create a TableLayout. Make the stretch column be column 1. Place TextViews into column 0 of each row and EditText into column 1. Finally, change the layout_span property of EditText elements to 2. You will end up with something similar to the following screenshot:

Figure 2

Both have their merits and both have their detractors. The weighted view (*Figure 1*) will always ensure that irrespective of the device, the text on the left will always fill one-third of the view, but with that there will always be some dead space.

The table version (*Figure 2*) will always fill the screen (the position of the elements can be moved from the edges by putting a left and right margin on the table layout itself). The problem is that tables aren't graceful. By that I mean that as you move down to smaller size screens, the columns tend to break and in other cases, the rendering of tables can also be slower. An android table layout is very similar to an HTML table in concept.

As far as Xamarin Forms are concerned, they have no understanding of weights. While a Table is possible, it is closer to an Android `ListView` (or iOS `UITableView`) than a table layout.

The question is how to tell Xamarin Forms to make the label one-fourth of the screen size with the text box filling the other three-fourths, given that we've established that this is an abstraction layer and so has no understanding of the hardware running it.

We could guess, but that would end up invariably with a complete mess that may render correctly on an iPhone 4S, Galaxy S3 Mini, or a Nokia 525 but look terrible on a Z3, iPhone 6+, or the top-of-the range Windows Phone device.

Let the device help you

While the abstraction will have zero idea on the hardware sitting underneath it, we can let the device tell the library the screen dimensions quite simply.

In the PCL, add the following to the main project launcher `cs` file (for the `SizeUI` example, it is `SizeUI.cs`):

```
public static Size DeviceWindowSize { get; set;}
```

 A Xamarin Forms `Size` is not the same as a `System.Drawing.Size`.

To set `DeviceWindowSize` within the platform code, you will need to add the following code, all of which needs to come before the `LoadApplication(new App());` line.

- For Android (in the launcher source file):

```
App.DeviceWindowSize = new Size(Resources.DisplayMetrics.
WidthPixels / Resources.DisplayMetrics.Density, Resources.
DisplayMetrics.HeightPixels / Resources.DisplayMetrics.Density);
```

- For iOS (in `AppDelegate.cs`):

```
App.DeviceWindowSize = new Size(Resources.DisplayMetrics.
WidthPixels / ResourcesApp. DeviceWindowSize = new Size(UIScreen.
MainScreen.Bounds.Width, UIScreen.MainScreen.Bounds.Height);.
DisplayMetrics.Density, Resources.DisplayMetrics.HeightPixels /
Resources.DisplayMetrics.Density);
```

- For Windows Phone (in `MainPage.xaml.cs`):

```
App.DeviceWindowSize = new Size(Application.Current.Host.Content,
ActualWidth, Application.Current.Host.Content.ActualHeight);
```

Once we have this code, we can then start to modify the UI to ensure that the label and edit text boxes have the correct size.

Within `Login.cs`, you will see the following code:

```
var quarter = App.DeviceWindowSize.Width / 4;
```

We can see a `WidthRequest` in each `Entry` of `3 * quarter` and `Label` of `quarter`. This will request (but not necessarily give) a width of three-fourths of the screen width.

With the `Padding` property within `StackLayout` set to `10`, this will give a uniform padding around the stack itself. We can add further padding within each of the children if we wish in the same way, should it be required.

The new layout looks more uniform now (and if you test on a range of devices, you'll see that the UI remains the same, irrespective of the screen size). There is a difference between iOS and Android, but there is already an improvement, as shown in the following screenshot:

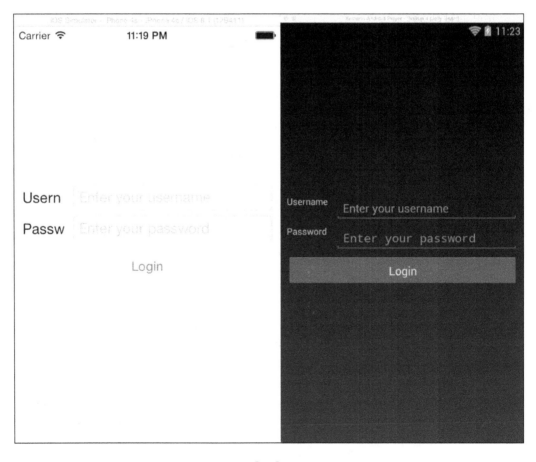

That button, though…

As it stands, the login button occupies the full screen and is the standard native button. We can change the physical size of it in the same way as we changed the physical size of Label and Entry, but it is still ugly. The mobile platforms allow for a great deal of customization of the user interface. We've seen that we're fairly limited to what we can do within the abstraction layer. To do anything else, we need resort to something called a **custom renderer**.

The custom renderer

When the abstraction layer comes to doing something, the interface needs to call a rendering routine. The renderer is different on each platform, but still delivers the same experience by taking the code generated and reworking it on the platform.

The custom renderer allows for the device to render something that is not a direct part of forms. It provides complete flexibility in how the controls look and behave, and can include platform-specific code to implement the native SDK features. Typically, this is performed by inheriting the base class (such as a Button) and applying something to it in the PCL, which then needs the platform to render the new UI elements.

Creating a custom renderer

The first step in creating the custom renderer is to create the custom class. In the CustomRenderer source code, you will see that it really is just a case of inheriting the base class:

```
public class NewButton : Button
{
  public NewButton()
  {
  }
}
```

Nothing is being added to the button, so this is fine as it stands. The Button instance within the Login source code needs to be changed to use NewButton:

```
var btnLogin = new NewButton()
{
  Text = "Login",
};
```

Next up is the implementation of the custom button. This has to be performed at the platform level rather than the PCL.

All the renderers have some commonality:

```
[assembly: ExportRenderer(typeof(NewButton),
typeof(NewButtonRenderer))]
```

and:

```
protected override void OnElementChanged(ElementChangedEventArgs<T>e)
```

The content of the override is what changes between the implementations. For our purposes, we shall change the color of the text and the background as well as customize the shape.

Customizing for Android

Android is capable of many things. Altering the color is simple, but we need to use some XML for the shape. In the `Resources/Drawable` directory is a file called `RoundedButton.xml`:

```xml
<?xml version="1.0" encoding="utf-8"?>
<selector xmlns:android="http://schemas.android.com/apk/res/android" >
 <item android:state_pressed="true" >
    <shape android:shape="rectangle"   >
        <corners android:radius="3dip" />
        <stroke android:width="1dip" android:color="#5e7974" />
        <gradient android:angle="-90" android:startColor="#345953"
android:endColor="#689a92"   />
    </shape>
 </item>
<item android:state_focused="true">
    <shape android:shape="rectangle"   >
        <corners android:radius="3dip" />
        <stroke android:width="1dip" android:color="#5e7974" />
        <solid android:color="#58857e"/>
    </shape>
 </item>
<item >
    <shape android:shape="rectangle"   >
        <corners android:radius="3dip" />
        <stroke android:width="1dip" android:color="#5e7974" />
        <gradient android:angle="-90" android:startColor="#8dbab3"
android:endColor="#58857e" />
    </shape>
 </item>
</selector>
```

We will set the color of the text to be white. All this can be performed within the renderer:

```
[assembly: ExportRenderer (typeof(NewButton),
typeof(NewButtonRenderer))]
namespace CustomRenderer.Droid
{
  public class NewButtonRenderer : ButtonRenderer
  {
    protected override void OnElementChanged(ElementChangedEventArgs<
Button> e)
    {
      base.OnElementChanged(e);
      if (Control != null)
      {
        Control.SetBackgroundResource(Resource.Drawable.
RoundedButton);
        Control.SetTextColor(global::Android.Graphics.Color.White);
      }
    }
  }
}
```

Implementing on iOS

iOS is a UI-feature rich system, so we can perform tasks like adding borders, colors, and so on very simply:

```
[assembly: ExportRenderer(typeof(NewButton),
typeof(NewButtonRenderer))]
namespace CustomRenderer.iOS
{
  public class NewButtonRenderer : ButtonRenderer
  {
    protected override void OnElementChanged(ElementChangedEventArgs<
Button> e)
    {
      base.OnElementChanged(e);
      if (Control != null)
      {
        Control.BackgroundColor = UIColor.FromRGB(130, 186, 132);
        Control.SetTitleColor(UIColor.White, UIControlState.Normal);
        Control.Layer.BorderWidth = 0.8f;
        Control.Layer.BorderColor = UIColor.FromRGB(45, 176, 51).
CGColor;
```

```
            Control.Layer.CornerRadius = 10f;
        }
      }
    }
}
```

When the code is compiled and run, you should see something like the following screenshot on the device:

Whenever a new button is required, simply calling NewButton instead of Button will produce the new button on the screen.

A complex UI example

The custom renderer is not restricted to simple user interface elements; it also covers gestures and other platform specific operations as well as more complex user interface elements (including the likes of composite buttons). The source code for CompositeUI shows how this can be performed. At this point, knowledge of how the UIs of specific platforms work is essential.

As with the simple UI button example, we start by inheriting the button:

```
public class NewCompositeButton : Button
{
  public NewCompositeButton(string text, string filename, bool
imageOnLeft = true)
  {
  }
}
```

Notice that this time we are passing in three values:

- The text to render
- The image filename
- The position of the image

The implementation for each platform is greatly different. Android, for example, uses `int` for the drawable rather than the filename, but the images are always in `Resources/Drawable`. For iOS, the image can be anywhere in the app. Android has `ImageButton`, but the image is always above the text.

There are two caveats to the creation of a custom renderer:

- The first is that if you create a non-parameterless constructor, you must also provide a parameterless constructor for the renderer.
- The second is that the first method hit in the renderer is not the default constructor but the override `OnElementChanged`. This second caveat causes an issue when creating a non-standard UI element. To avoid that problem, Xamarin Forms allows you to pass data from the PCL to the native renderer in much the same way as it gets data from the native platform: the use of `get;set;`.

As with the `CustomUI` example, we create the new button in the same way as before, creating a class that inherits `Button`:

```
public class NewCompositeButton : Button
{
  public NewCompositeButton()
  {
  }
}
```

This is then called from within the PCL, but we also have to set the text and filename to load and where it is to be placed on the button:

```
App.text = "This is a cow";
App.filename = "cow.png";
App.onTheLeft = true;

var btnComposite = new NewCompositeButton(){ };
```

The hard work then comes within the platform-specific code.

An Android custom renderer

As with any custom renderer, we first need to state that it is a custom renderer and the type of renderer to inherit:

```
[assembly: ExportRenderer(typeof(NewCompositeButton), typeof(NewCompos
iteButtonRenderer))]
namespace CompositeUI.Droid
{
  public class NewCompositeButtonRenderer : ButtonRenderer
  {
```

We have a small issue with passing a filename: Android doesn't use filenames for the image; it uses `Resource.Drawable.Id` (an `int`), so first we need to translate the filename to a resource ID:

```
public int GetResourceIdFromFilename(string filename)
{
  var fn2 = filename.Replace('-', '_');
  fn2 = fn2.Split('.').ToArray()[0];
  var res = Resources.GetIdentifier(fn2, "drawable", Android.App.
Application.Context.ApplicationInfo.PackageName);
  return res;
}
```

We can then use `SetCompoundDrawable` to position the image and set the `TextAlignment` property to put the text on the left or right:

```
var draw = Resources.GetDrawable(GetResourceIdFromFilename(App.
filename));
var other = Resources.GetDrawable(Android.Resource.Drawable.
ButtonStar);
Control.SetBackgroundResource(Resource.Drawable.RoundedButton);
Control.SetCompoundDrawables(App.onTheLeft ? draw : other, other,
!App.onTheLeft ? draw : other, other);
Control.SetTextColor(Android.Graphics.Color.Black);
Control.Text = App.text;
Control.TextAlignment = App.onTheLeft ? TextAlignment.ViewEnd :
TextAlignment.ViewStart;
```

An iOS custom renderer

iOS is a much simpler affair. Again, we need to tell the application that we are using a custom renderer and the render type to use:

```
[assembly: ExportRenderer(typeof(NewCompositeButton), typeof(NewCompos
iteButtonRenderer))]
namespace CompositeUI.iOS
{
    public class NewCompositeButtonRenderer : ButtonRenderer
```

After this, it is really just a case of creating `UIImageView` and `UILabel` and placing that onto the button as well as setting the background on the button:

```
if (Control != null)
{
    // Set the background
    Control.BackgroundColor = UIColor.FromRGB(130, 186, 132);
    Control.SetTitleColor(UIColor.White, UIControlState.Normal);
    Control.Layer.BorderWidth = 0.8f;
    Control.Layer.BorderColor = UIColor.FromRGB(45, 176, 51).CGColor;
    Control.Layer.CornerRadius = 10f;
    // do the rest of it
    var image = new UIImageView(new CGRect(App.onTheLeft ? 4 : (nfloat)
App.DeviceWindowSize.Width - 36, 8, 24, 24))
    {
        Image = UIImage.FromFile(Path.Combine("Graphics", App.filename)).
Scale(new CGSize(24, 24))
    };
    var label = new UILabel(new CGRect(App.onTheLeft ? 32 : 4, 8,
(nfloat)App.DeviceWindowSize.Width - 36, 21))
    {
        Text = App.text
    };
    if (App.onTheLeft)
    {
        Control.AddSubviews(new UIView[]{ image, label });
    }
    else
    {
        Control.AddSubviews(new UIView[]{ label, image });
    }
}
```

Implementing a login screen

There are a couple of things to consider with a login screen, as follows:

1. The login backend (are we using our own system or one of the social network systems).
2. Position of the UI elements within the screen.
3. Making it look good other than by custom rendering.

The login backend is dealt with in *Chapter 7, Connect Me to Your Other Services*.

UI positioning

Xamarin.Forms allows for a large degree of positioning options, all of which look different. The following are examples of how iOS renders four buttons using the different styles, as shown in the following screenshot:

As you can see, there are a lot of options for the position. We can also set the position by altering the `Padding` property either within the UI element, or within the holder element.

Making it look good

One of the more interesting new features that have come out with Xamarin Forms 1.4 are **triggers**. You can think of a trigger as an event that alters the UI rather than causing an action to occur.

For the likes of login UI, we can use a trigger to show the user which `Entry` has focus.

 The following code can be found in the section on `Triggers` in the source examples.

The following code example shows how we can do some interesting things with a trigger, but it will require some explaining:

```
public App()
{
  var userEntry = new Entry()
  {
    Placeholder = "Username",
  };
  var passEntry = new Entry()
  {
    Placeholder = "Password"
  };

  var trigger = new Trigger(typeof(Entry))
  {
    Property = Entry.IsFocusedProperty,
    Value = true,
  };
  trigger.Setters.Add(new Setter{ Property = Entry.
BackgroundColorProperty, Value = Color.Green });
  trigger.Setters.Add(new Setter{ Property = Entry.TextColorProperty,
Value = Color.White });
  trigger.Setters.Add(new Setter{ Property = Entry.ScaleProperty,
Value = 1.2 });

  var style = new Style(typeof(Entry));
```

```
        style.Triggers.Add(trigger);

        Resources = new ResourceDictionary();
        Resources.Add(style);


        MainPage = new ContentPage
        {
          Content = new StackLayout
          {
            Padding = new Thickness(20, 50, 120, 0),
            VerticalOptions = LayoutOptions.Center,
            Children =
            {
              userEntry, passEntry
            }
          }
        };
    }
```

The snippet starts off by creating two `Entry` elements and sets the placeholder text to show what is needed. Nothing new in this!

Next is defining the trigger. The trigger has a property value pair that acts as an `if` condition.

In simple terms, let's look at the following lines:

```
var trigger = new Trigger(typeof(Entry))
{
  Property = Entry.IsFocusedProperty,
  Value = true,
};
```

They can be considered as being equivalent to the following code:

```
if (UIElement is Entry)
{
  if (Entry.IsFocused == true)
    {
        // add what to do via Setters
    }
}
```

The setters have then to be inserted. These tell the UI what to do and are all `BindableProperty` types (in other words, you can't have a property that cannot be bound to, so `TextColor` is not allowed, but `TextColorProperty` is fine), as shown in the following code:

```
trigger.Setters.Add(new Setter{ Property = Entry.
BackgroundColorProperty, Value = Color.Green });
trigger.Setters.Add(new Setter{ Property = Entry.TextColorProperty,
Value = Color.White });
trigger.Setters.Add(new Setter{ Property = Entry.ScaleProperty, Value
= 1.2 });
```

The following code will be in terms of what the code actually means within the `if` condition:

```
if (UIElement is Entry)
{
  if (Entry.IsFocused == true)
    {
      var entry = UIElement;
      entry.BackgroundColor = Color.Green;
      entry.TextColor = Color.White;
      entry.Scale = 1.2;
    }
}
```

This is just a part of the story though. Each trigger is part of a style that in turn has to be stored within a `ResourceDictionary`. Why is it done like this? If you consider how Xamarin Forms interacts with the underpinning platform and what we're actually writing, then the platform will need a resource to grab the metadata from.

What we have done is set a whole pile of properties that are reliant on a condition being met. We can't actually write it as an `if` statement as metadata doesn't work that way. It has to be more about how the XAML version would be written whereby we have a `Resource` which has a `Style` having a `Trigger`. In essence, we have `Dictionary<string, object>`, where `object` is a style that has a trigger in it.

Using EventTrigger

Triggers are essentially, if you recall, events. As such, we can use the `EventTrigger` class to bind an element to an event. For our login, we should not allow the **Login** button to be enabled unless the `Entry` element has some text in it and the password is longer than six characters.

There are two important aspects to the `EventTrigger` source example:

1. The `Entry` and `Button` elements are defined at the `App` level rather than in the login UI code.

2. `TriggerEvent` itself is a class that inherits `TriggerAction` for the element.

Typically, we would only be acting on the element itself rather than testing the contents of the two elements and then changing the state of a third element.

The `EventTrigger` class is set up like the following code:

```
// define the trigger event - this will be for both Entry elements

var trigEvent = new EventTrigger()
{
  Event = "TextChanged"
};
trigEvent.Actions.Add(new ValidateEntryTriggerAction());

// add the trigger event to the Entry element

App.Self.userEntry.Triggers.Add(trigEvent);
App.Self.passEntry.Triggers.Add(trigEvent);
```

It is different from the first example in that we're not setting a style and resource, as what we're doing (again this is in effect, not necessarily what it is) is to create an event handler:

```
public class ValidateEntryTriggerAction : TriggerAction<Entry>
{
  protected override void Invoke(Entry sender)
  {
    if (sender.StyleId == "username")
    {
      if (!string.IsNullOrEmpty(sender.Text) && !string.
IsNullOrEmpty(App.Self.passEntry.Text))
        App.Self.loginBtn.IsEnabled = true;
      else
        App.Self.loginBtn.IsEnabled = false;
    }
    else
    {
      if (!string.IsNullOrEmpty(sender.Text) && sender.Text.Length > 5
&& !string.IsNullOrEmpty(App.Self.userEntry.Text))
        App.Self.loginBtn.IsEnabled = true;
      else
```

```
        App.Self.loginBtn.IsEnabled = false;
    }
  }
}
```

If you consider `TriggerAction<Entry>` to be `EventArgs`,
`ValidateEntryTriggerAction` as the handler, and `Entry` sender to be `object`
sender, then we have the basis for a standard .NET event. The difference is that
while we create this, we have to invoke the event itself (this invocation is performed
under the hood of .NET events but has to be exposed here).

Further trigger enhancements

There are two further actions that we can apply to our `Entry` elements;
`EnterActions` and `ExitActions`. These perform a specified action when the element
has been entered or exited.

 The source for this can be found in the book code's
`EntryExitActions` folder.

As with `EventTrigger`, the `Entry` and `ExitActions` are treated in much the same
way, as given in the following code:

```
var userEntry = new Entry()
{
  Placeholder = "Username"
};
var passEntry = new Entry()
{
  Placeholder = "Password",
  IsPassword = true
};

var triggers = new Trigger(typeof(Entry))
{
  Property = Entry.IsFocusedProperty,
  Value = true
};
triggers.Setters.Add(new Setter{ Property = Entry.
BackgroundColorProperty, Value = Color.Green });
triggers.Setters.Add(new Setter{ Property = Entry.TextColorProperty,
Value = Color.White });
triggers.EnterActions.Add(new FadeTriggerAction());
```

```
triggers.ExitActions.Add(new FadeTriggerAction());

var style = new Style(typeof(Entry));
style.Triggers.Add(triggers);

var resource = new ResourceDictionary();
resource.Add(style);

userEntry.Triggers.Add(triggers);
passEntry.Triggers.Add(triggers);
```

This time though, we have included a setter (which will also need the creation of a
`Style` and `ResourceDictionary` for the platform to refer to).

The `FadeTriggerAction` class sets the opacity to 1 when the `Entry` element is
focused, or `0.5` when not focused:

```
public class FadeTriggerAction : TriggerAction<Entry>
{
  protected override void Invoke(Entry sender)
  {
    if (sender.IsFocused)
      sender.FadeTo(1);
    else
      sender.FadeTo(0.5);
  }
}
```

Summary

We have covered a lot in this chapter. If you've followed the chapter and looked at
the code examples, then you should have an understanding now on how Xamarin
Forms goes about both simple and more complex tasks and some of the ways you
can use the native platform to provide facilities not available in the PCL.

In the next chapter, we shall be looking at how we can make the best use of the
Portable Class Library, the power behind a Forms application.

4

Making Your Application Portable

Part of the advantage of using the .NET Framework to create an application is that it is possible to write the core of the application, and this core will work on anything supported by the .NET Framework. This is great until you hit a simple issue—what happens if the platform itself does not support a feature? This is when a portable common library comes in handy.

In this chapter, we will cover the following topics:

- The advantages and disadvantages of using a PCL
- Writing your PCL

PCLs – the pros and cons

One of the biggest advantages of using a **PCL** (**Portable Class Library**) is that as the name suggests, the library contains only code that is guaranteed to run on all .NET platforms. You write it once, you deploy it once, and everything can use it. This differs greatly with a shared library that has no guarantee of running on all .NET platforms.

> For more on PCLs, refer to http://developer.xamarin.com/
> guides/cross-platform/application_fundamentals/
> pcl/introduction_to_portable_class_libraries/.

This may not make a great deal of sense—surely, everything should be able to run the .NET code, irrespective of whether it is running Mono, Microsoft .NET, or GNU .NET. This is not an unreasonable assumption to make, but let's think about this logically.

If you consider a piece of hardware capable of running some flavor of .NET, you cannot unreasonably think that it will have some form of storage, some form of output, and anything else you would expect to find on a computer, mobile phone, or laptop. Here, though is the biter—when dealing with a portable library, you have to assume that everything is working only on a base level of hardware. There is no guarantee that the hardware will have storage, a keyboard, a video output, or anything of this nature.

To this extent, the libraries that can be used or shipped with a PCL is only a subset of the full .NET base. This does leave a number of problems or questions:

1. If you don't have access to parts of libraries (such as hardware access), how can they be implemented?

2. If you don't have full range to all of .NET, what is the point of having a PCL?

The answer to the first question is quite complex, so I'll answer it after the the second question.

If you don't have the full .NET base, what is the point of having a PCL?

The point of having a PCL is to avoid code replication where replication isn't required. Think of it as you get it right once, you test it, and deploy it. As with a library book, it gives you the core, but not the specifics.

Take the example of a database and its access to data. To enter a code in the database, one can use this:

```
public void AddOrUpdateGroup(GroupsSQL gr)
{
  lock (dbLock)
  {
    using (var sqlcon = DBConnection)
    {
      sqlcon.Execute(DBConstants.DBClauseSyncOff);
      sqlcon.BeginTransaction();
      try
      {
        if (sqlcon.Execute("UPDATE GroupsSQL SET id=?, " +
          "__updatedAt=?, group_name=?, joined=?, left=?, ismember=?, event_id=?, group_type=? WHERE id=?",
          gr.id, gr.__updatedAt, gr.group_name, gr.joined, gr.left,
gr.ismember, gr.event_id, gr.group_type, gr.id) == 0)
          sqlcon.Insert(gr, typeof(GroupsSQL));
```

```
        sqlcon.Commit();
      }
      catch (Exception ex)
      {
        #if DEBUG
        Console.WriteLine("Error in AddOrUpdateGroup - {0}--{1}",
  ex.Message, ex.StackTrace);
        #endif
        sqlcon.Rollback();
      }
    }
  }
}
```

To get the data back, use the following code:

```
public T GetSingleObject<T>() where T:IDatabase, new()
{
  lock (dbLock)
  {
    using (var sqlCon = DBConnection)
    {
      sqlCon.Execute(DBConstants.DBClauseSyncOff);
      sqlCon.BeginTransaction();
      string sql = string.Format("SELECT * FROM {0}",
  GetName(typeof(T).ToString()));
      var data = sqlCon.Query<T>(sql).FirstOrDefault();
      return data;
    }
  }
}
```

There is nothing difficult with this code, but consider that this will be exactly the same on every application. If you were to write something similar to WhatsApp or Viber, the Android version, the iOS version, Windows Phone, and desktop will in all probability store data internally using the same technique.

As this storage forms part of the business end of the application (here, business can be taken to mean that it is the part that does all the hard work), it would make sense to write the code once and deploy it multiple times.

It is here that we hit an issue with using a PCL, which is where the first question comes in.

If you don't have access to parts of libraries, such as hardware access, how can they be implemented?

A simple answer is that anything platform-specific has to be dealt with in the platform code. This is fine, but it leads to an obvious question. If the platform code deals with the likes of the filer, how can a library have access to the filer? Should the library not provide a common code as the name implies?

The answer is that under normal circumstances, as with a textbook, the main control application (the platform) dips into the library and pulls out the information required.

In a PCL, this is in part the case. In another part of the case, there is a process that takes place called **Inversion of Control** (**IoC**). The library takes control to get something from the control application in order for the library to return the data back to the control application.

It is here that something known as **Dependency Injection** takes place. Here, the library injects something from the control application. Typically, this injection is obtained using an interface.

Is there a processor speed hit?

Typically, there isn't a massive hit.

The following table summarizes the pros and cons of using a PCL. There are other advantages and disadvantages, but these are the main ones:

Pros	Cons
This separates out business and nonbusiness logic and allows greater number of available platforms	This uses a subset of the standard .NET libraries, so the likes of the filer and console are not available
This allows rapid application development	There is a requirement to add additional code to access platform-specific features
This can be run on anything that supports .NET	
This writes once, uses many	
This is easier to debug and unit test	
There is no significant speed degradation	

Writing your PCL library

For this, I'll use my DBManager class. It is simple to understand and see how things change. The source for this is included in the code examples.

Examining the code

The class itself starts by creating the database. This is performed by creating a database file on the device's storage. As this requires access to the filesystem, it will need to be handled in the platform code.

The majority of the code from thereon can be handled by the PCL.

Wait. The class works by using a connection string that is created when the database is created. The connection string can be accessed by an interface and then uses the dependency injection to place the connection string in the query.

The following is an old version of the code:

```
using SQLite;
public class DBManager
{
  public DBManager()
  {
    SQLite3.Config(SQLite3.ConfigOption.Serialized);
    dbLock = new object();

    pConnectionString = Path.Combine(AppDelegate.Self.
ContentDirectory, "mydatabase.db");
    connectionString = string.Format("{0}; New=true; Version=3;PRAGMA
locking_mode=EXCLUSIVE; PRAGMA journal_mode=WAL; PRAGMA cache_
size=20000; PRAGMA page_size=32768; PRAGMA synchronous=off",
pConnectionString);
  }

  string pConnectionString, connectionString;
  object dbLock;

  public string DBPath
  {
    get { return pConnectionString; }
  }

  public string ConnectionString
  {
    get { return connectionString; }
  }
```

The following is the new version of the code. It is used to make this PCL compliant with a couple of changes. The first version is used to create an interface to be able to access the platform code:

```
using SQLite.Net;

namespace MessengerApp
{
  public interface IDatabaseConnection
  {
    SQLiteConnection Connection { get; }

    string ConnectionString { get; }
  }
}
```

The database creation method in the platform part now becomes this:

```
public class DBManager :IDatabaseConnection
{
  private readonly string documentsPath = Environment.
GetFolderPath(Environment.SpecialFolder.Personal);
  const string sqliteFilename = "mydatabase.db";

  public SQLiteConnection Connection
  {
    get
    {
      string libraryPath = Path.Combine(documentsPath, "..",
"Library");
      var path = Path.Combine(libraryPath, sqliteFilename);
      var plat = new SQLite.Net.Platform.XamarinAndroid.
SQLitePlatformAndroid();
      var conn = new SQLiteConnection(plat, path);
      return conn;
    }
  }

  public string ConnectionString
  {
    get
    {
      var pDocs = Path.Combine(documentsPath, " mydatabase.db ");
      return string.Format("{0}; New=true; Version=3;PRAGMA locking_
mode=EXCLUSIVE; PRAGMA journal_mode=WAL; PRAGMA cache_size=20000;
PRAGMA page_size=32768; PRAGMA synchronous=off", pDocs);
    }
  }
}
```

An important change (other than the interface) is that the PCL version uses SQLite. NET, rather than SQLite. The main difference is that the .NET version is designed for use with PCL libraries and will require a platform-specific plugin to also be installed along with the SQLite.NET library.

 The platform in the preceding code example is the `var plat = new SQLite.Net.Platform.XamarinAndroid. SQLPlatformAndroid();` line. This changes for any platform that is targeted.

While we have the interface to access the data, we still need to tell the code that is in use with the dependency injection with the following code:

```
[assembly: Xamarin.Forms.Dependency(typeof(DBManager))]
```

This needs to be placed before the `namespace` line. The code is now available for the PCL. Let's go back to the code comparison!

The old code

The following code adds the data to the database:

```
public void AddOrUpdateLanguages(Languages l)
{
  lock (dbLock)
  {
    using (var sqlcon = new SQLiteConnection(ConnectionString))
    {
      sqlcon.Execute(Constants.DBClauseSyncOff);
      sqlcon.BeginTransaction();
      try
      {
        if (sqlcon.Execute("UPDATE Languages SET id=?, " +
          "is_deleted=?, key=?, locale=?, value=?, __
updatedAt=?,device_id=?" +
        "WHERE id=?",
        l.id, l.is_deleted, l.key, l.locale, l.value, l.__updatedAt,
l.device_id, l.id) == 0)
          sqlcon.Insert(l, typeof(Languages));
        sqlcon.Commit();
      }
      catch (Exception ex)
      {
        #if DEBUG
```

```
          Console.WriteLine("Error in AddOrUpdateLanguages - {0}--{1}",
    ex.Message, ex.StackTrace);
        #endif
        sqlcon.Rollback();
      }
    }
  }
}
```

> While the standard .NET 4.5 format is that you don't need a
> default constructor in a class, with a Xamarin.Forms class
> using **Dependency Injection (DI)**, the default constructor
> must be included. The DBManager class, while it does use DI,
> is not using anything from Xamarin.Forms, so the default
> constructor isn't required. However, it never harms to include
> the default constructor.

There are two issues with this code:

1. SQLConnection(ConnectionString): This is a platform-specific code
2. Console: This is not guaranteed to be available on the target, so it cannot be used

The first issue requires an injection to be used. The second issue can be resolved by replacing Console with Debug.

The new code

The following is the new code. I am making the assumption that the injection has succeeded:

```
public void AddOrUpdateLanguages(Languages l)
{
  lock (dbLock)
  {
    using (var sqlcon = DependencyService.Get<IDatabaseConnection>().
Connection)
    {
      sqlcon.Execute(Constants.DBClauseSyncOff);
      sqlcon.BeginTransaction();
      try
      {
        if (sqlcon.Execute("UPDATE Languages SET id=?, " +
          "is_deleted=?, key=?, locale=?, value=?, __
updatedAt=?,device_id=?" +
```

```
        "WHERE id=?",
        l.id, l.is_deleted, l.key, l.locale, l.value, l.__updatedAt,
l.device_id, l.id) == 0)
        sqlcon.Insert(l, typeof(Languages));
        sqlcon.Commit();
    }
    catch (Exception ex)
    {
        #if DEBUG
        Debug.WriteLine("Error in AddOrUpdateLanguages - {0}--{1}",
ex.Message, ex.StackTrace);
        #endif
        sqlcon.Rollback();
    }
    }
   }
 }
```

With these small changes, the same database code can be used on any .NET platform capable of using a PCL.

A secondary example of a universal settings file and how it is moved to PCL is available in the accompanying source code repository.

Other options for PCL

If you are able to guarantee that the target platforms will have the facilities you need and they are handled in the same way with the same directories that are able to be accessed in the same way (for example, Android being a Linux-based system, certain directories cannot be accessed, but the application itself has access to all the directories that it owns, as well as any public directories).

On iOS, Apple has locked down a large number of directories that look like they should be available (they are listed with IntelliSense when you look at the environment path), but on compile time, the app crashes because you have no access to certain directories. As a result, a **Shared Code Library** (**SCL**) can be used.

[PCL libraries cannot be used on versions of .NET before 4.0.   ]

Summary

PCL libraries are a great step forward in code reuse. They can be used for a large number of situations and aid in rapid application development. They are simpler to debug than having the same code in every version of the application. Overall, it helps in application construction.

When it comes to `Xamarin.Forms` applications, the core is a PCL. This is then fed to the platform-specific code.

In the next chapter, we will take a closer look at the database helper class and how to get the best from it.

5
Data, Generics, and Making Sense of Information

.NET provides the developer with a rich library of code which enables us to process and manipulate data with or without a database. We also have generic types and database style manipulators using LINQ. In short, .NET gives the developer all the tools required for complex and speedy data manipulation.

In this chapter, we shall be covering the following topics:

- Using generics to speed up development
- Using LINQ to make queries simpler to use and extract the correct information
- Writing the database helper class
- Using reflection within the SQL helper class and elsewhere

A history lesson

In the beginning, if a developer needed to store data then the way to do this was array based. There was nothing inherently wrong with arrays, except that you had to initialize them so they could only have a finite size, and trying to add past that size would result in something known as *undefined behavior* (meaning that just about anything could happen, though usually it would result in a crash). Eventually, it was possible to resize arrays, but this was difficult.

For anything more complex than a straight array, it was not a simple task. A linked list was possible (this can be considered as being a structure linked to another instance of the structure). The useful aspect of a linked list was that it was forever expandable and could be traversed up and down the list to find data. The downside was that the developer had to remember to clear the unused structures or risk running out of memory.

.NET generics

With the advent of .NET 2.0, this problem was solved; Microsoft introduced generics to the mix. The generic classes are instantiated once and then you can add to them as many times as you like. The framework itself does the memory management for the list, so they can be considered as an ever-extendable array.

In which case, why are they called generics as arrays have a definite type (`string`, `int`, `byte` and so on)? The answer to that is the `type` argument. A .NET generic takes a generic type (typically referred to as `T`). This `T` can be anything — even another generic (for example, there is nothing to stop you from having `List<Dictionary<T, List<U>>>`, the caveat being that `T` and `U` will need to be defined somewhere).

This obviously will mean that you can create not only a list of strings, but a list of classes, structs, UI objects, and pretty much anything you want. Unless the generic has a global scope or `static` type, when the class that the generic is defined in goes out of scope, the **Garbage Collector** (**GC**) destroys that instance, thereby freeing up the memory.

The difference between a generic and collection, therefore, is that collections are for dynamic arrays of a type.

Restrictions on using a generic class

Generic classes and types are nothing new; C++ had them way before .NET was a twinkle in the eyes of Microsoft. Code such as the following would be used:

```
public T myMethod(T var1, T var2)
{
   return var1 + var2;
}
```

This led to a problem: what exactly was T? The way early C++ compilers would solve this would be considered very primitive now. The compiler would take every compatible type where the + operator could be applied and create a compiled virtual method for that type. There could also be a serious speed hit with using generic methods, as the runtime would need to determine which of these virtual methods would need to be called at any one point.

Modern compilers trace back to the source that calls a method and only creates the methods based on the addressing types. They also rename the methods internally to avoid hitting the performance.

T can only ever be of one real type at any one time; you cannot have T foo and T bar where the second T is not the same type as the first.

.NET handles generic types in one of two ways: either as a modern C++ compiler would, or for data structures, by having something to hang on to.

The following code is a perfectly good C# method definition:

```
private List<T> getMyData<T>(string id)
{
  // method code
}
```

In this instance, the method takes a string and returns a List of type T. The real flexibility comes, though, when dealing with classes.

Say we have a number of classes for the database. The following code will not be allowed:

```
private List<T> getMyData<T>(T myClass)
{
   return sql_query_get_list("id", myClass.id);
}
```

The question is why would this not be permitted? The T objects are all of the same type. The problem is that the compiler doesn't have a clue what T is. This causes a problem. What if we want to use generic types as part of an SQL call (such as the preceding example)?

The solution boils down to the class structure. Database classes invariably have some form of commonality between them (such as `id` values). Say our classes all have `string id` and `DateTime __updatedAt` defined within them. If we create an `interface` class to these properties, we can then use generics within methods, shown as follows:

```
public interface IIdentity
{
   string id { get; }

   DateTime __updatedAt { get; set; }
}
private List<T> getMyData<T>(T myClass) where T:IIdentity
{
   return sql_query_get_list("id", myClass.id);
}
```

Essentially, here we have told the compiler that you don't know what `T` is, but there is a guarantee that there will be a `string` and `DateTime` object called `id` and `__updatedAt`.

The generic methods

For our purposes here, the majority of the classes in use are held within the `System. Collections.Generic` and `System.Collections.Specialized` namespaces. The following table is a subset of the ones that will be used within our app:

Name	Namespace	What it does	Example
List<T>	Generic	This creates a list of objects.	var myList = new List<string> {"a","b","C"};
Dictionary<T, U>	Generic	This creates a dictionary based on a key/value system. There can be multiple keys to a value, but not multiple keys to a value.	var myDict = new Dictionary<string,int> {{"a", 1}, {"b", 2}, {"C", 12}, {"d", 2}};
NameValue Collection	Specialized	This creates a form of lookup that allows multiple values to a single key.	var myNVC = new NameValueCollection {"fred",1}, {"harry", 2},{"harry", 3}, {"joe", 4}};

Lists can be accessed in the same way as a standard array. For example, refer to the following code:

```
var myList = new List<string>{"a","b","C"};
Console.WriteLine("Element 1  = {0}", myList[1]);
```

This code would result in b being placed on the console output. In a similar way, the contents of the List array can be altered:

```
Console.WriteLine("Element 2 contains {0}", myList[2]);
myList[2] = "hello";
Console.WriteLine("Element 2 now = {0}", myList[2]);
```

The console output would be as follows:

Element 2 contains C

Element 2 now = hello

This same addressing-by-element method applies if the List array contains a class:

```
class myHolderClass
{
   public string name {get;set;}
   public int number {get;set;}
   public double value {get;set;}
}
var classList = new List<myHolderClass>();
// add some data into the List - make sure there are 5 elements in
there
classList.Add(new myHolderClass {name="James", number = 1, value =
22.714});
classList.Add(new myHolderClass {name="Ash", number = 8, value =
2.714});
classList.Add(new myHolderClass {name="Hollie", number = 30, value =
122.714});
classList.Add(new myHolderClass {name="Becki", number = 34, value =
22.1714});
classList.Add(new myHolderClass {name="Will", number = 30, value =
22.7124});

Console.WriteLine("Ash's number = {0}", classList[1].number);
classList[1].number++;
Console.WriteLine("Ash's new number = {0}", classList[1].number);
```

The output is as follows:

Ash's number = 8

Ash's new number = 9

This makes the list a very handy collection to have. Dictionaries can be handled using an array reference in the same way as `List`:

```
var nameData = new Dictionary<string, string>
{
    {"Ashleigh", "Daughter"},{"Richard", "Son"},
    {"Becki", "Wife"}, {"Beer","Drunk"}
};
Console.WriteLine("nameData[2] = {0}:{1}", nameData[2].Key,
nameData[2].Value);
```

The output is as follows:

Becki:Wife

The benefit of using the reference-based system is that it is possible to alter the value of a particular dictionary entry due to `Value` having both a `get` and `set` accessor.

Typically, the `Value` from a `Dictionary` object is found using `TryGetValue`:

```
var nameData = new Dictionary<string, string>
{
    {"Ashleigh", "Daughter"},{"Richard", "Son"},
    {"Becki", "Wife"}, {"Beer","Drunk"}
};
string answer = "";
bool test = nameData.TryGetValue("Wife", out answer);
Console.WriteLine("Answer = {0}", test ? answer : "Not found");
test = nameData.TryGetValue("Elephant", out answer);
Console.WriteLine("Answer = {0}", test ? answer : "Not found");
```

The output is shown as follows:

Becki

Not found

Completely opposite to `Dictionary`, we have the `NameValueCollection`. Whereas a `Dictionary` will let you have multiple `Keys` with a single `Value`, the `NameValueCollection` allows you to have multiple values for a key:

```
var myCollection = new NameValueCollection
{
    {"Paul", "Author"}
    {"Becki", "Wife"},
    {"Becki", "Solicitor"}
};

foreach(var ket in myCollection.AllKeys)
    Console.WriteLine(key);
```

The output is shown as follows:

```
Paul
Becki
```

With these three generic types, the question that really needs to be asked is why do we need them?

Consider the standard messenger app. The app is capable of sending to a single person, multiple people, or from a single person (if you consider receiving a group message, that group message will not have originated from everyone, but from one source; even if each person on the message list replies, it is still only from a single person).

The names for these generics are a collection; they can be used as a storage medium. If we have a data object, it is possible to store an entire message thread, like the following line of code:

```
var threadMessages = new Dictionary<Guid, List<Messages>>();
```

This gives any message thread a single dictionary object that can then be sorted or manipulated to produce the UI in any style we want. It is possible again to create a List array of these Dictionary objects:

```
var threadedMessageList = new List<threadMessages>();
```

Perfect! A List containing a Dictionary object that contains all the messages, which can be accessed by a Key value. What could be the problem?

Simply put, the amount of data (and therefore memory) required for each message thread is the answer. Say we have a thread containing 100 messages. This is not 100 strings for the message thread, but 100 full copies of the message object. Each of these objects will require memory, not only for storage but also for manipulation. This slows down the software, and potentially, may also cause the app to crash.

This may also seem to be a good way to organize data. The problem lies in how the data is stored and accessed. Data comes into the app independent of any message thread; it's data and has no idea as to which thread it belongs to. That data is stored in an internal SQLite database and used whenever it's needed.

With this in mind, can we create a way to still use one of these storage collections for the messages? As it stands, no. There is no way to link one data set to another. The way to get around the issue is to create something known as a **linked list**, and there is nothing new about linked lists; they have formed the basis of many a beginner's C and C++ course. As the name suggests, this is a data structure that links one object to another. This list could be extended indefinitely by creating a new object and placing it at the top of the stack. The n+1 position of the stack is always null, so testing for null will show the number of objects in the list. Searching through the list was a case of starting at 0 (the first object) and searching through until whatever was being looked for was found or the next object was null.

Modern linked lists

Essentially, linked lists have not changed. Every time a new instance of the object is required, it is instantiated and added to the top of the list. The big differences are the way in which the list can be searched, and how the list is constructed.

Each list has its own ID and a parent ID. The top of each message thread starts with -1 for the parent and the own ID. The next instance on the list will have the parent as the previous ID for the parent of itself. This means that by comparison of the two ID fields, it is possible to grab all the objects for a particular list. If we store these two fields as Dictionary, we have a small memory footprint containing the absolute minimum amount of information for the thread. This will also be fast as we're only storing two pieces of information in the Dictionary object.

At this point, you may be thinking (quite rightly) that a thread may have a few hundred messages, and that the order the data is read in is not always going to be the correct chronological order, so the actual threading, while it contains all the messages, will not always be correct. After all, all that Dictionary contains are two IDs.

There are options available that allow for the correct order to be used. It is possible that rather than using a Dictionary collection, we use a List collection that contains the whole thread, and we then manually create a duplicate temporary List which contains the original List in the correct chronological order.

This is fine but slow, as the List has to be iterated through for the number of items in the List - 1, with the DateTime stamps compared. If the List is small, the time taken will not really matter. However, if the List is large, the time taken will be considerable. Remember also that each member of the List will be a complete object of the message and so may contain a fairly large chunk of data. It may thus end up being a memory hog.

It is also possible to use some form of complex tracking system on DateTime based on the ID, timestamp, and some other parameter. This approach is error-prone and needlessly difficult to use.

Thankfully, all of this boredom is dispelled with the use of LINQ.

LINQ me up baby – yeah!

LINQ gives the developer the power of SQL but for collections. It is not uncommon to order data coming from an SQL database for given parameters (such as searching on a property and outputting the data based on surname and the output ordered DateTime, then the first letter of the first name property), but in terms of collections prior to LINQ manipulation, it literally meant iterating through each piece of data.

In terms of our message collection, we can construct our lists like the following:

1. From the SQLite database, grab all messages with a parent id of -1.
2. Using the initial list, perform the following steps:
    1. Iterate through the list.
    2. From the SQLite database, grab messages where parentid == id and store it in a List collection.
3. On the List, use LINQ to order by DateTime.
4. Store the ids in a Dictionary collection.

Simple! At the end, there will be a Dictionary with the initial ID followed by the List of IDs.

The code would look like the following. In this example, DBManager is a helper class that is used for data insertion, updating, and retrieval:

```
var messageDict = new Dictionary<string, List<string>();
var initialMessages = DBManager.GetListOfObjects<Messages>().
Where(t=>t.parentid == "-1");
foreach(var init in initialMessages)
{
  var newMessages = DBManager.GetListOfObjects<Messages>.Where(t=>t.id
== t.parentid).Orderby(t=>t.__createdAt).Select(t=>t.id).ToList();
  if (newMessages.Count != 0)
    messageDict.Add(init.id, new List<string>{newMessages});
  else
    messageDict.Add(init.id, new List<string>{init.id});
}
```

Jumping into the code

The preceding example may look a bit hairy, but let's have a look at what it actually does. The first thing to understand is what `DBManager.GetListOfObjects<T>()` actually does.

As the name suggests, this method will return a `List<T>` of all the objects of type T. Before you jump and scream that I have actually done exactly what I said was a bad idea, you need to consider the part after the method call. This is the LINQ part. While it is true that all the objects of type T are returned, only those where the selection parameter holds are stored, which is exactly what happens when you have an SQL call along the lines of the following:

```
var data = select (*) from T where parentid=="-1";
return data;
```

In terms of memory efficiency, the data being drawn from the database can be considered almost as if it is part of using a construct, in that once whatever has been selected has been used, the rest is disposed of, and the garbage collector does what it is supposed to do.

At this point, we only have a list of messages where the `parentid == "-1"`.

The next line after the iteration is slightly more complex in that we have a chained LINQ statement. Again, the same database call is made, but this time, we only store the message list where the `id == parentid`. This list is then sorted based on the `DateTime` that the message object was created and finally we store only the ID part of the message object. The result is a `List<string>` collection.

Finally, there is a check on the number of messages (remember, if the message is the first message on the thread and there has yet to be a reply, then the message itself is both the ID for the `Dictionary` as well as the first member of the `List<string>` collection) and the list stored.

Wait, hold on, that's wrong!

Those who have been alert may have spotted what may seem like an error and quite a schoolboy error at that; sure we have a `Dictionary` with the initial id and a `List` of message id's, but will that `Dictionary` also be correct in terms of the `DateTime` stamps? After all, up to this point we've simply done a quick data grab, sorted the messages on the `__createdAt` property, and stored them. How do we know that the `Dictionary` order is correct for the `DateTime` stamp?

If you spotted that error, well done!

Fortunately, this error is quite simple to fix. Remember, we have a `Dictionary` with the `Key` (the first parameter) being the message ID where the `parentid == "-1"`. To sort the issue, the initial grab of the `parentid` messages can have the additional LINQ query `OrderBy(t=>t.__createdAt).ToList()` added as follows:

```
var initialMessages = DBManager.GetListOfObjects<Messages>().
Where(t=>t.parentid == "-1").OrderBy(t=>t.__createdAt).ToList();
```

The `Dictionary` is now correct for the `DateTime` stamp when the message parent was created and the messages themselves.

The database helper class

All smart phones come with a version of SQLite installed (including the likes of the Blackberry range), and while SQLite provides a number of inbuilt methods of storing data, they are often cumbersome and in terms of what they do (or how they do it), aren't exactly clear.

The second problem is that the connection has to be made every time a query is to be made.

Thankfully, it is more than possible to write a helper class that deals with the creation, insertion, amendment, and retrieval of data.

There are a number of advantages to having a helper class in this situation:

- All the data methods are in one place (reducing the number of times code has to be written; therefore, less opportunity for error)
- Potential for commonality of code to be reduced, making the database footprint smaller
- Data retrieval can be made simpler
- Lends well to generic types and optimization of the retrieval of data

Generic types within the helper class

While it is always useful to have, say, a method to obtain messages and another for contacts, the reality is that most of the time, when data is being requested it is going to be based on a single parameter (such as `id` or `parent_id`) and a `List`, or single type returned. Now, if you consider how many methods there will be to obtain data, it soon becomes obvious that there will potentially be a very large number of methods essentially doing the same work.

In this case, the use of generic types can be used. The best way to think of a generic type is like saying to a child, "Can you get me a drink from the thing please?". We have a definite property to retrieve, but the object we obtain that from could be anything. There is also a secondary issue that may not be so obvious. While you or I know what an apple is, if we're using a generic type to say where the apple is held, how does the application know that there is an apple in that type? The simple answer is that it doesn't, and this is down to how the compiler deals with generic types.

The problem with a generic type is that the compiler doesn't know what it is and because of that, the compiler has to create a virtual method for every particular type. That is fine as long as the type being compiled actually contains some form of definition for the apple type. If there is no definition for the apple type, the compiler is unable to create a method for that particular type. In other words, the developer has to include a guarantee that the type itself will contain that definition. That task is, thankfully, very simple.

Interfacing with the data classes

The first step for the construction of the helper class is the construction of the data classes that we covered in *Chapter 1, In the Beginning...*. You will notice that each class has two properties in common: id and __createdAt (these are supplied by Azure, so all data objects on the server are guaranteed to have them).

To create the guarantee that the compiler needs, if we create an interface class containing those two properties and ensure that all the classes the database needs inherits them, then not only can we use the classes as a generic class in the database helper, but we can also use them anywhere else within the code base as a generic.

Creating the helper class

The helper class contains four elements: the connection, table creation and destroy, insert and update, and retrieval.

The database connection

It is customary in any application requiring database connections to create one, use it, and then close it; it cuts down on the potential for database corruption (remember, SQLite is effectively just a file giving the random access requirements that a database needs), which is always a useful thing to have. The problem is having to open and close the connection every time, and having to pass the connection database method. That is not really an issue; however, opening and closing takes time.

The alternative is having a permanent connection string to the database and calling the database methods using a pointer set in the singleton class (for iOS, that is within the AppDelegate class and Android needs one to be created). While this does mean that we have a permanent connection, the actual part that does the database work only does something when connected. As with anything else, when the application exits or the method is out of scope, the connection is lost and the database stays.

The connection to the database is as simple as the following code:

```
public DBManager(string dbName)
{
  SQLite3.Config(SQLite3.ConfigOption.Serialized);
  dbLock = new object();
  string documents = Environment.GetFolderPath(Environment.
SpecialFolder.Personal);
  pConnectionString = Path.Combine(documents, string.
IsNullOrEmpty(dbName) ? "default.db" : dbName);
  connectionString = string.Format("{0}; New=true; Version=3;PRAGMA
locking_mode=EXCLUSIVE; PRAGMA journal_mode=WAL; PRAGMA cache_
size=20000; PRAGMA page_size=32768; PRAGMA synchronous=off",
pConnectionString);
}

private string pConnectionString, connectionString;
private object dbLock;

public string DBPath
{
  get { return pConnectionString; }
}

public string ConnectionString
{
  get { return connectionString; }
}
```

The code is nothing difficult. The following line creates the connection string used for the database. At this point, the database is neither created nor connected to:

```
connectionString = string.Format("{0}; New=true; Version=3;PRAGMA
locking_mode=EXCLUSIVE; PRAGMA journal_mode=WAL; PRAGMA cache_
size=20000;PRAGMA page_size=32768; PRAGMA synchronous=off",
pConnectionString);
```

Setting up the database

With the connection in place, it's time to create the tables to be used within the database. This is achieved with the SQLite `CreateTable` method. This simply creates a table based on the format within the class that is passed in.

SQLite is a very primitive database system; it can only handle base types (such as `string`, `bool`, `int`, `double`, and `float`), and cannot handle arrays and generic collections natively (it is possible to store them, but it requires the creation of yet another table containing the data, the data id, and the id that it came from. A full list of supported types can be found on the SQLite website). Therefore, the types to be included within the database table must also only be of those types. That is not to say that you can't have generic collections within the database class; you can. They just need to precede the property with `[Ignore]` as the following code shows:

```
public string id {get;set;}
[Ignore]
public List<string> ids {get {// do something } }
```

The class can still handle the generic collection and do what it asks, but the database ignores the collection:

```
public bool SetupDB()
{
  lock (dbLock)
  {
    try
    {
      using (var sqlCon = new SQLiteConnection(ConnectionString))
      {
        sqlCon.CreateTable<PushServices>();
```

Here, the connection is made and the table created. Once the creation of the table has been completed, the connection goes out of scope and is closed.

The next stage in the process is getting the data into the tables.

Data, data everywhere...

Adding data to an SQLite database though the helper class is a simple affair:

```
public void AddOrUpdateSomeClassData(List<SomeClass> someClass)
{
  foreach (var c in someClass)
  AddOrUpdateSomeClassData (c);
}
```

```
public void AddOrUpdateSomeClassData (SomeClass sC)
{
  lock (dbLock)
  {
    using (var sqlcon = new SQLiteConnection(ConnectionString))
    {
      sqlcon.Execute(Constants.DBClauseSyncOff);
      sqlcon.BeginTransaction();
      try
      {
        if (sqlcon.Execute("UPDATE SomeClass SET id=?, " +
          "name=?, description=?, parentcatagory_id=?, updated_by=?,
__updatedAt=?, is_deleted=? WHERE id=?",
          sC.id, sC.name, sC.description, sC.parentcatagory_id,
sC.updated_by,
          sC.__updatedAt, sC.is_deleted, sC.id) == 0)
        sqlcon.Insert(sC, typeof(SomeClass));
        sqlcon.Commit();
      }
      catch (Exception ex)
      {
        sqlcon.Rollback();
      }
    }
  }
}
```

Or, if you prefer the `async` way:

```
private async Task<string> AddOrUpdateSomeClassData (SomeClass sC)
{
  lock (dbLock)
  {
    using (var sqlcon = new SQLiteConnection(ConnectionString))
    {
      sqlcon.Execute(Constants.DBClauseSyncOff);
      sqlcon.BeginTransaction();
      try
      {
        if (await sqlcon.ExecuteAsync("UPDATE SomeClass SET id=?, " +
          "name=?, description=?, parentcatagory_id=?, updated_by=?,
__updatedAt=?, is_deleted=? WHERE id=?",
          sC.id, sC.name, sC.description, sC.parentcatagory_id,
sC.updated_by,
          sC.__updatedAt, sC.is_deleted, sC.id) == 0)
        sqlcon.InsertAsync(sC, typeof(SomeClass));
        sqlcon.Commit(); )
        return "Single data file inserted or updated";
```

```
      }
      catch (SQLiteException ex)
      {
        return ex.Message;
      }
  }
```

There is nothing wrong with using this form of structure, but it is somewhat wasteful having to create exactly the same code time and again for each class where data has to be entered or updated. It also seems, given the power of the .NET Framework, a perfect opportunity to use reflection.

The code bit

Let's take a look at the code first:

```
private readonly Dictionary<Type, Func<Object, String>> queryBuilders
= new Dictionary<Type, Func<object, string>>();

public string GetInsertQuery(Object entity)
{
  var type = entity.GetType();
  if (!queryBuilders.ContainsKey(type))
  {
    var param = Expression.Parameter(typeof(Object), "entity");
    var typedObject = Expression.Variable(type, "obj");
    var stringBuilder = Expression.Variable(typeof(StringBuilder),
"sb");
    var appendString = typeof(StringBuilder).GetMethod("Append",
    new[] { typeof(String) });
    var objectToString = typeof(Object).GetMethod("ToString");
    var code = new List<Expression>();
    code.Add(Expression.Assign(typedObject, Expression.Convert(param,
type)));
    code.Add(Expression.Assign(stringBuilder, Expression.
New(typeof(StringBuilder))));
    code.Add(Expression.Call(stringBuilder, appendString, Expression.
Constant(string.Format("INSERT INTO {0} (", type.Name))));

    var properties = type.GetProperties();
    for (int i = 0; i < properties.Length - 1; ++i)
    {
      if (properties[i]. GetCustomAttributes(typeof(IgnoreAttribute),
        false).Length > 0)
      next;
      code.Add(Expression.Call(stringBuilder, appendString,
Expression.Constant(properties[i].Name)));
```

```
            code.Add(Expression.Call(stringBuilder, appendString,
    Expression.Constant(", ")));
        }
        code.Add(Expression.Call(stringBuilder, appendString, Expression.
    Constant(properties[properties.Length - 1].Name)));

        code.Add(Expression.Call(stringBuilder, appendString, Expression.
    Constant(") VALUES (")));

        for (int i = 0; i < properties.Length - 1; ++i)
        {
            code.Add(Expression.Call(stringBuilder, appendString,
    Expression.Constant("'")));
            code.Add(Expression.Call(stringBuilder, appendString,
    Expression.Call(Expression.Property(typedObject, properties[i]),
    objectToString)));
            code.Add(Expression.Call(stringBuilder, appendString,
    Expression.Constant("', ")));
        }

        code.Add(Expression.Call(stringBuilder, appendString, Expression.
    Constant("'")));
        code.Add(Expression.Call(stringBuilder, appendString, Expression.
    Call(Expression.Property(typedObject, properties[properties.Length -
    1]), objectToString)));
        code.Add(Expression.Call(stringBuilder, appendString, Expression.
    Constant("', ")));

        code.Add(Expression.Call(stringBuilder, appendString, Expression.
    Constant(");")));

        code.Add(Expression.Call(stringBuilder, "ToString", new Type[] {
    }));

        var expression = Expression.Lambda<Func<Object,
    String>>(Expression.Block(new[] { typedObject, stringBuilder }, code),
    param);
        queryBuilders[type] = expression.Compile();
    }

    string f = queryBuilders[type](entity);
    return f;
}
```

Simple!

Um...

Yeah...

Essentially, all this does is take the class and go through every parameter one by one (unless it has the [Ignore] attribute set), construct the query, and insert the data. The clever part is right at the start:

```
private readonly Dictionary<Type, Func<Object, String>> queryBuilders
= new Dictionary<Type, Func<object, string>>();
```

Getting funky with Func

A Func delegate is a very useful type as it allows for method-like working (so it may be considered an anonymous method), resulting in a type.

The basic Func syntax is given as follows:

```
Func<inputType>
Func<inputType, returnType>
Func<inputType1, inputType2, returnType>
```

To call a Func, it requires an invoke call with the parameters included:

```
Func<double> sinFunc = () => Math.Sqrt(Math.PI/2);
Func<double, string> cosFunc = (x) => string.Format("{0}", Math.
Cos(x));
sinFunc.Invoke();
cosFunc.Invoke(12);
```

By using this fairly complex looking method, not only has the amount of code to be entered been greatly reduced, so have the chances of error. The only down point is that if you don't understand the code, then debugging is a nightmare.

Getting data back out

This is where generic classes really show their usefulness.

If you consider any database, for every data entry, there has to be a data recall; what is the point in having data if you can never see it? Most often, when we want data, we will want either a single instance, a class, or a List array of the class, and these will usually be based on an ID. As we have already said that each class will have inherited the common properties via an interface, we can do something along these lines:

```
private string GetName(string name)
{
  var list = name.Split('.').ToList();
  return list.Count > 1 ? list[list.Count - 1]:list[0];
}
```

```
public List<T> GetListOfObjects<T>(string id) where T:IIdentity, new()
{
  lock (dbLock)
  {
    using (var sqlCon = new SQLiteConnection(ConnectionString))
    {
      sqlCon.Execute(Constants.DBClauseSyncOff);
      sqlCon.BeginTransaction();
      string sql = string.Format("SELECT * FROM {0} WHERE id=\"{1}\"",
GetName(typeof(T).ToString()), id);
      var data = sqlCon.Query<T>(sql);
      return data;
    }
  }
}
```

This simply gets the unqualified name of the class (this means you just get the name of the class rather than namespace and class), and inserts it into a string that is then used for the query. The code returns a List array of whatever T is.

Single object retrieval would be like the following code:

```
public T GetSingleObject<T>(string id) where T:IIdentity, new()
{
  lock (dbLock)
  {
    using (var sqlCon = new SQLiteConnection(ConnectionString))
    {
      sqlCon.Execute(Constants.DBClauseSyncOff);
      sqlCon.BeginTransaction();
      string sql = string.Format("SELECT * FROM {0} WHERE id=\"{1}\"",
GetName(typeof(T).ToString()), id);
      var data = sqlCon.Query<T>(sql).ToList();
      return data[0];
    }
  }
}
```

These methods are by their very nature generic, but they can be made more specific by passing in other parameters to the call. For example:

```
public List<T> GetListOfObjects<T>(string para1, string op1, string
val1, string para2,string op2, string val2) where T:IIdentity, new()
{
  lock (dbLock)
  {
```

```
    using (var sqlCon = new SQLiteConnection(ConnectionString))
    {
      sqlCon.Execute(Constants.DBClauseSyncOff);
      sqlCon.BeginTransaction();
      string sql = string.Format("SELECT * FROM {0} WHERE {1}
{2}\"{3}\" AND {4}{5}\"{6}\"", GetName(typeof(T).ToString()), para1,
op1, val1, para2, op2, val2);
      var data = sqlCon.Query<T>(sql). ToList();
      return data.Count != 0 ? data : new List<T>();
    }
  }
}
```

This could be further refined to the following code:

```
public List<T> GetListOfObjects<T>(params string[] vals) where
T:IIdentity, new()
{
  lock (dbLock)
  {
    using (var sqlCon = new SQLiteConnection(ConnectionString))
    {
      sqlCon.Execute(Constants.DBClauseSyncOff);
      sqlCon.BeginTransaction();
      string sqlQuery = "";
      if (vals.Length != 0)
      {
        for(int i = 0; i < vals.Length; ++i)
        {
          if (vals[i].ToUpper() == "AND" || vals[i].ToUpper() == "OR")
            sqlQuery += " " + vals[i] + " ";
          else
            sqlQuery += vals[i];
        }
      }
      string sql = string.Format("SELECT * FROM {0} WHERE {1}",
  GetName(typeof(T).ToString()), sqlQuery);
      var data = sqlCon.Query<T>(sql). ToList();
      return data.Count != 0 ? data : new List<T>();
    }
  }
}
```

The data retrieval method is possibly as flexible as it can be without becoming inflexible. It is possible to send over the full SQL string as a single string, but then it could be argued that this would potentially give rise to a broken SQL, or make the use of the helper class redundant.

Too much information!

Using * within the SQL query has an unfortunate drawback. It retrieves everything based on the parameters passed into the query. This could mean hundreds of objects returned to List.

As previously discussed, help is at hand. That help is in the form of LINQ.

Getting Linq'd

It should become apparent that LINQ is a powerful addition to the programmer's arsenal. To quote the grandfather of telesales, Billy Mays—but wait, there's more!

Finding data with LINQ

There are six ways of finding data within a collection:

- Where
- First and FirstOrDefault
- Single and SingleOrDefault
- Select
- SelectMany
- Last and LastOrDefault

Where

Where allows searching a collection based on any parameter within the collection. This will result in List<T> or IEnumerable<T>. If .ToList() is omitted, IEnumerable is generated:

```
var demoList = otherList.Where(t=>t.something == "foo");
var demoList = otherList.Where(t=>t.something == "foo").ToList();
```

First and FirstOrDefault

These two LINQ methods are similar insofar as they return the first instance of whatever is being searched for. The difference is that FirstOrDefault will return the default value if the search parameter can't be found. First, by itself, will return null if the search itself is null; it should only be used when you know that the answer can be found:

```
var demoList = otherList.First(t=>t.something == "exist");
var demoList = otherList.FirstOrDefault(t=>t.something == "exist");
var demoList = otherList.FirstOrDefault(t=>t.something == "notexist");
```

The preceding example would return null.

Single and SingleOrDefault

These will return a single instance (or null if SingleOrDefault is used) of an object. This is not the same as First (or FirstOrDefault). Single should be used to return a single instance from List, based on some search parameters:

```
var demo = otherList.Where(t=>t.id == 5).Single(t=>t.something == "foo");
var demo = otherList.Where(t=>t.id == 5).SingleOrDefault(t=>t.something == "bar);
```

Select

Select typically selects a single parameter from a collection and returns either a List, or IEnumerable. It can also be extended to create new objects based on the old objects:

```
var demoList = otherList.Select(t=>t.something).ToList();
var demoList = otherList.Select(t=>t.something);
```

Creating a new List based on the old list can be achieved in one of two ways: iteration in a for type loop or directly.

As a loop

This creates a new List that generates a new class based on the old class:

```
var newList = (from ot in otherList
   Select new {MyName = ot.Name, MyId = ot.id, MySomething =
something}).ToList();
```

Inline

An inline version of the preceding loop would look like the following code:

```
var newList = otherList.Select(e=>new {MyName = e.Name, MyId = e.Id,
MySomething = e.something).ToList();
```

SelectMany

`SelectMany` is similar to `Where` in that it returns `List` or `IEnumerable`, but the similarity stops there. `SelectMany` selects a number of elements into a single collection that will be of a type different type than the original:

```
var otherList = new List<int>{1,2,3,4,5};
var demoList = otherList.SelectMany(t=>t.ToString()).ToList();
```

The result will be `List<string>` rather than `List<int>`.

Last and LastOrDefault

This is the reverse of `First` (and `FirstOrDefault`) in that the `Last` instance of the object is returned from a collection.

Ordering data

Data can be ordered in either forward (`OrderBy`), or backward (`OrderByDescending`) order:

OrderBy

The following code orders the data in ascending order:

```
var intList = new List<int>{2,4,6,3,5,7};
var newList = intList.OrderBy(t=>t).ToList();
```

In the end, `newList` will contain the values 2, 3, 4, 5, 6, and 7, in that order.

t=>t?

This is known as a parameterless query. If a list contains only a single type (such as a `List<string>` or `List<double>`), then there is no parameter property to compare with. So the only object type that can be compared is the object type itself.

OrderByDescending

The following code will order the data in a descending order:

```
var intList = new List<int>{2,4,6,3,5,7};
var newList = intList.OrderByDescending(t=>t).ToList();
```

At the end, `newList` will contain the values 7, 6, 5, 4, 3, and 2, in that order.

ToList, ToArray, ToDictionary, and ToLookup

When a collection is manipulated without a single return value (for example, when using `Where` or `OrderBy`), `IEnumerable` can be changed to `List`, `Array`, `Dictionary`, or `Lookup`.

`ToList` and `ToArray` creates just that: `List<T>` or `T[]`. Whereas, `ToDictionary` creates a `Dictionary` object from the `List` object:

```
var intList = new List<int>{1,2,3,4,5,6};
var dict = intList.ToDictionary(t=>t, t=>t % 2 == 0 ? true : false);
foreach(var output in dict)
  Console.WriteLine(output);
```

The following code will create `Dictionary<int, bool>`. `ToLookup` creates a structure that allows indexing:

```
var stringList = new List<string>{"paul","chris", "harry", "roy"};
var lookup = stringList.ToLookup(t=>t.Length);
for(int i = 3; i < 5; ++i)
{
  foreach(var item in lookup[i])
    Console.WriteLine("Name with {0} characters = {1}", i, item)
}
```

Filters and mutables within LINQ

There are a number of LINQ methods that allow filtering or mutating the collection. The following table should do a good job of explaining them:

LINQ method	Explanation
AsEnumerable	This method will cast a type to the `IEnumerable` equivalent.
AsParallel	Typically, a query will run from a to b to c to d and so on; in other words, in a linear fashion. `AsParallel` will allow queries to operate in parallel to another query. It has advantages when using a multicore processor in terms of speed. If the processor has a single core, there is little advantage to using `AsParallel` in terms of speed.

LINQ method	Explanation

Cast	This casts one collection to another, as given in the following code:
	
	``
	var list = await DBManager.
	GetListOfObjects<AnimalMobs>().Where(t => t.id
	== id).ToListAsync();
	if (list.Count != 0)
	{
	    IEnumerable<AnimalMobs> fooList = list.
	Cast<AnimalMobs>();
	``

Concat	This concatenates two `IEnumerables` of the same type to a single collection:
	
	``
	int[] array1 = {1,5,9};
	int[] array2 = {2,6,10};
	var result = array1.Concat(array2);
	``

Contains	Returns `true` or `false` depending on whether something exists in a collection or not:
	
	``
	var animalList = new List<string>{"dog", "cat",
	"gibbon"};
	var result = animalList.Contains("horse"); //
	returns false
	``

DefaultIfEmpty	If a collection is empty, the collection will have a single object of the collection inserted.

Distinct	This removes duplicates from a collection:
	
	``
	var intList = new List<int>{1,1,1,2,3,4,5};
	var distList = intList.Distinct();
	``
	This returns 1, 2, 3, 4, 5.

ElementAt (and ElementAtOrDefault)	This gets an element at a particular index (or 0 if OrDefault is used). Effectively, this would be the same as using an index element on an array. If OrDefault is not used and the element goes over the end point of the collection, `System.ArgumentOutOfRangeException` is raised.
	
	``
	var intList = new List<int>{1,3,5,6,7};
	var sinInt = intList.ElementAt(2); // returns 5
	var sinInt = intList.ElementAtOrDefault(5); //
	returns 1
	``

LINQ method	Explanation

GroupBy	This transforms a collection into a group or a number of groups. Each group has a key, so it can be considered similar to Dictionary:
	
	``csharp
	var intList = new List<int>{1,2,3,4,5,6,7,8,9};
	var res = intList.GroupBy(a=>a % 2 == 0);
	``
	
	This creates two groups: one where a % 2 == 0 (the value is even) and one for the odd numbers.

GroupJoin	This groups a collection by a key, and joins them to other groups with another collection of objects with keys.
	
	``csharp
	public class people
	{
	   public int number {get;set;}
	   public string name {get;set;}
	}
	public class cars
	{
	   public int carnumber {get;set;}
	   public string make {get;set;}
	}
	public class results
	{
	   public string fullname {get;set;}
	   public IEnumerable<cars> vehicles {get;set;}
	   public results(string name, IEnumerable<cars> vehicle)
	   { fullname = name; vehicles = vehicle }
	}
	var peeps = new List<people>{new people{number=1, name="tom"}, new people{number=2, name="dick"}, new people{number=3, name="harry"}};
	var movers = new List<cars> {new cars{carnumber=1,make="Renault"}, new cars{carnumber=2,make="Citroen"}, new cars{carnumber=1, make="Renault"}};
	var res = peeps.GroupJoin(movers, t=>t.number, u=>u.carnumber), (t, result)=>new results(c.name, result));
	``
	
	This joins the number from movers to the carnumber and passes this into the results class to return a collection back into res.

LINQ method	Explanation
Intersect	This returns a collection of objects where something is found from two collections: ```\nvar intList1 = new List<int>{1,4,6,8};\nvar intList2 = new List<int>{4,6,8,9};\nvar res = intList1.Intersect(intList2); //\nreturns 4,6,8\n```
Join	As the name suggests, this joins two collections based on a condition.
OfType	This performs a search based on the type: ```\nobject[] testObj = new object[3];\ntestObj[0] = "hello";\ntestObj[1] = (float)3.1415;\ntestObj[2] = "john";\nvar res = testObj.OfType<string>(); // returns\nhello and john\n```
Reverse	This reverses the order of a collection: ```\nvar intList = new List<int>{2,5,6};\nvar res = intList.Reverse(); // 6,5,2\n```
Union	Generates a mathematical union on collections of the same type: ```\nvar intList1 = new List<int>{1,2,3};\nvar intList2 = new List<int>{2,3,4};\nvar res = intList1.Union(intList2); // 1,2,3,4\n```
Zip	This is a handy way to perform an operation on two arrays or lists: ```\nvar intArray1 = new int[]{1,3,5,7,9};\nvar intArray2 = new int[]{2,4,5,8,10};\nvar res = intArray1.Zip(inArray2, (a, b) => (a\n* b));\nres = 2, 12, 25, 56, 90\n```

Skipping and taking data

LINQ allows taking or leaving data from a collection.

Skip and SkipWhile

Skip allows ignoring of data from the start of the collection. SkipWhile skips data matching a condition:

```
var intList = new List<int>{1,2,3,4,5,6,7,8};
var resSkip = intList.Skip(3); // 4,5,6,7,8
var resSkipWhile = intList.SkipWhile(t=>t % 2 == 0); // 1,3,5,7
```

Take and TakeWhile

`Take` takes the first *x* number of objects in a collection. `TakeWhile` takes objects from a collection where a condition is met:

```
var intList = new List<int>{1,2,3,4,5,6,7,8};
var resSkip = intList.Take(3); // 1,2,3
var resSkipWhile = intList.TakeWhile(t=>t % 2 == 0); // 2,4,6,8
```

Other LINQ methods

There are eight more methods: `Aggregate`, `All`, `Any`, `Average`, `Count`, `SequenceEqual`, `Sum`, `Max`, and `Min`. `Average`, `Count`, `Sum`, `Max`, and `Min` do exactly what you would expect them to do. `Aggregate`, `All`, `Any`, and `SequenceEqual` need a small amount of explanation.

Aggregate

This applies a method to each element and a function to each successive element. If you consider the following, the first part is to multiply `intList[0]` by `intList[1]`. The second is to take the answer, then multiply by `intList[2]`, and continue until there is no more data:

```
var intList = new List<int>{1,2,3,4,5};
var res  = intList.Aggregate((a, b) => b * a);
// 1 * 2 = 2
// 2 * 3 = 6
// 6 * 4 = 24
// 24 * 5 = 120
```

All

`All` returns `true` or `false` from a collection depending on the condition:

```
var intList = new List<int>{5,10,15};
bool res1 = intList.All(t=>t >=10); // false
bool res2 = intList.All(t=>t <= 20); // true
```

Any

This returns a `bool` value, depending on a condition. For example, if a list contains odd numbers, `Any` will return `false` if the list is tested for even numbers.

SequenceEqual

This compares two collections and tests for the collections being exactly equal. If they are, `SequenceEqual` returns `true` otherwise it returns `false`.

Summary

This chapter has covered a lot of ground. It has taken a relatively simple topic and turned it on its head! Not only have we found the use of a database helper class, but have also shown how simple it is to come up with a helper class that is very flexible and extensible with the use of generic types, classes, collections, and functions.

This chapter has also looked at the power behind LINQ, one of the most useful libraries within .NET for data manipulation outside of an SQL database framework.

For more examples of using LINQ, I recommend the Microsoft 101 LINQ examples at `https://code.msdn.microsoft.com/101-LINQ-Samples-3fb9811b`.

6
A View to a Kill

Before I go any further, this chapter has a tenuous link to the James Bond movie of the same name. You'll see why shortly. This chapter concentrates on the user interface and how to ensure that you are able to create the same application for all the supported platforms with minimum fuss.

In this chapter, we will:

- Create a Xamarin.Forms application that functions on all the three supported platforms based on an application that only runs on one
- Extend the user interface on all three platforms
- See how the choice of graphics heavily influences how the end user feels about the application

Touch-a-touch-a-touch me

There is an awful lot to be said about how Apple approached the user interface and something known as user experience. I'm not an Apple fanboy by any stretch of the imagination (not that you'd guess if you've seen my desk recently!), and designing for iOS can be torturous at times, but I doff my cap to them on how it feels.

A former colleague of mine (who was an Android advocate) once said that he would be buying his parents an Apple iPhone 5S over the latest Samsung phone. The reason was that while Android is extremely powerful, for the end user, Apple wins every time. *It just works.*

When you examine any iOS application from start to finish, everything is designed to follow a familiar and friendly style; even in some of the more poorly designed and constructed apps, this familiarity and friendliness is still there. The graphics are bright, buttons all have soft edges; everything is designed so that the end user has the best possible experience, irrespective of the application.

This is not by accident, but by design. Apple makes the experience you have so enjoyable that it makes you think that perhaps the high price you paid was worth it. It doesn't matter what you think of Apple as a developer; the end user experience is what counts at least for the end user.

Android is different. It is *more bang for the buck*. The number of apps on Google Play knocks those on the App store. However, the quality ranges grossly from apps that don't work at all to those that work and look and feel great. This is the problem with Android in general. As there is little in the way of restrictions (and testing by Google), when you submit the app, some apps feel that the design seemed like a good idea at the time or when they developed the user interface; it made sense to have a bright blue button in the middle of the screen (it was tested on a Nexus 9 tablet and looked fine there, but on a bottom-end small screened HTC, all you can see is the button).

In some respects, this is actually a good thing; the ability to allow the developer to go wild and implement something free and easy should never be discouraged. It should also be recognized that a fair number of developers are clueless when it comes to design. What is a good idea to a developer rarely translates into a good idea in terms of the end user.

Finally, we come to the one and only Windows Phone. I will be clear here; I actually love Windows Phone as a developer. As the end user, it has a big problem; in my opinion, Metro on mobile is terrible! It looks nice enough, but in terms of getting things to play nicely on all the devices, it's awful. Fortunately, this is neither the time nor the place to look into the whys and wherefores on this.

With this in mind, in this chapter, we will see how to make a cross-platform app that looks and feels good on all the platforms.

Wanted... dead or alive

Before writing code for a living, I used to teach forensic science at one of my local colleges. To try to make the experience more real for students, I wrote an Android app called **Time of Death**. This is based on the Henssge's nomogram, which allows a fairly accurate estimation on when a body died for given states. If you're interested in how this works, refer to `http://what-when-how.com/forensic-sciences/time-since-death/` for a start.

 The source code for the original version of this app is in Chapter 6/ Original Version.

When you build the app and run it, after the splash screen, you will see the basic user interface, as shown in the following screenshot:

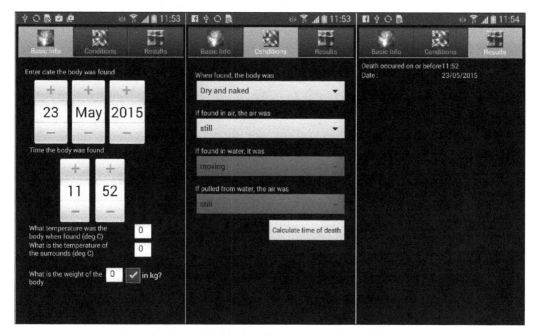

A very basic user interface to gather some very simple information

Here are a few points to note:

- The app uses a tabbed page interface
- The tabs include images that are colored differently depending on whether the tab is in use or not
- The images are solid
- The final tab contains a great deal of dead space

Knowing me, knowing you

The tabbed page interface is a very common paradigm used on iOS applications (not so much on Android or Windows Phone). The reason why it's not seen as much on Android is due to the way Android works.

As you are (no doubt) aware that each new view on Android (unless it is a popup or modal window) requires a new activity, and each activity can only inherit information from the previous activity if you send it through using `PutExtra` when you create the new intent.

This information has to then be read using `base.Intent.GetStringExtra("name")` or any of the other `GetExtra` methods. You will not be able to pass information in the class constructor as simply. This doesn't mean that you can't have something similar to the following line of code:

```
var t = new MyNewView(a, b, c);
```

In `MyNewView.cs`, we have something similar to the following code:

```
public class MyNewView
{
    public class MyNewView(int a, string b, Context c)
    {
        static_a = a;
        static_b = b;
        c.StartActivity(typeof(MyNewViewActivity);
    }
}
```

Here, `static_a` and `static_b` are in some sort of a static variable class. The activity then only needs to reference `static_a` and `static_b` within the code.

> There is nothing wrong with using this sort of code; it will help with keeping your code portable between iOS and Android, but it's somewhat messy.

A tabbed page app on Android is no different than a nontabbed page, in which each page is an activity that also leads to the same issue of passing information between tabs. The difference though is that each tab is a child of the tab page itself. The tab only occupies the top of the page with the child always being placed under the tab. In this case, the tab page can be considered as a container page.

iOS handles tabs differently. Each tab is normally linked to a specific method in the class (although it can also launch a new class), so the problem of passing information between tabs is negated.

A secondary reason why tabs are popular on iOS is that iOS, unlike Android and Windows Phone, does not have a back button (unless you're using a navigation control at the top), so moving between grouped actions on a view can be a problem. It is for this reason that iOS also allows multiple views in a single view controller.

This difference is important to know because tabbed pages under Xamarin Forms act in a sort of a halfway house between the platforms. Each page is considered its own entity (Android), code can be passed through the constructor (iOS/Windows Phone), and each page is held in a page container (Android).

Start all over

Before we code anything, we need to look at the original code to see how it is put together. There are three clear parts:

- The static class for data
- Calculation
- The UI

 The source for this section is in `Chapter6/Time Of Death`, and `Chapter6/TabView`.

The static class and calculations do nothing special and can be copied directly. However, the UI is a different matter.

Little boxes made of ticky-tacky

Creating a tab page with Xamarin Forms is very simple, as shown in the following code:

```
public class TabPage : TabbedPage
{
  readonly Page BasicInfo, Conditions, Results;

  public TabPage()
  {
    // create the links to the pages
    // Rather than use the ItemSource, we shall create Children to the
page.
    // Remember, a tabbedpage is a container with each page associated
with it
    // being a child from it

    Children.Add(new BasicInfo() { Title = "Basic info", Icon =
"cross.png" });
    Children.Add(new Conditions() { Title = "Conditions", Icon =
"weather.png" });
    Children.Add(new Results() { Title = "Results", Icon = "clock.png"
});

    // Current page is the tabbedpage property denoting which of the
child pages you're on
    CurrentPage = Children[0];
  }
```

In this example, `BasicInfo`, `Conditions`, and `Results` are just empty content pages.

When the application is compiled and run, you will see that the graphics don't show on Android. This is not a problem with the code, but the images on tabs are not currently supported with Xamarin Forms. You will see the following screenshot as the output:

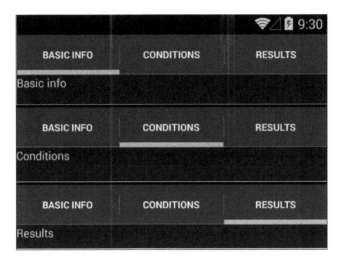

On iOS, the images will show something similar to the following screenshot:

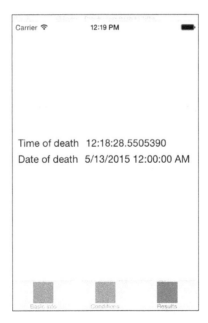

Windows Phone displays a carousel (again without images). The following screenshot displays the carousel as a single image. Tapping on a title (or sweeping the screen) alters the tab in the view:

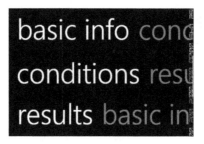

It's functional, but in terms of the user experience, it looks terrible (at least on iOS). On iOS, the problem is the graphics on the tab bar.

The second problem is that on the `BasicInfo` page, you will see something similar to the following screenshot:

Basic info   12:38 PM

Neither of these are big issues to fix, and with a small amount of code and changes to the images, we can alter the view.

Can we fix it? Yes we can!

Xamarin Forms allows tweaks to be made that are specific to a platform. In the case of the top bar being overwritten, the problem only shows on iOS. To remove the problem, we need to add some padding:

```
if (Device.OS == TargetPlatform.iOS)
   Padding = new Thickness(0, 20, 0, 0);
```

This platform-specific tweaking allows (for example) you to set the background color to white on Android and Windows Phone, as shown in the following code:

```
if (Device.OS != TargetPlatform.iOS)
    BackgroundColor = Color.White;
```

The padding alters the UI on iOS to now look like the following screenshot:

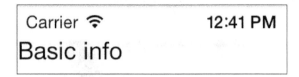

The image on the tab bar currently looks similar the one shown in the following screenshot (the original Android image is shown on the right-hand side of the screenshot):

iOS does not handle solid images well on the tab bar, so you need to alter the image from the solid ones used in the original-to-line images. You have the choice of paying for a graphic artist or using the vast number of images available from Google (which are free), as shown in the following screenshot:

I'm sure you'd agree that the preceding screenshot looks better than a solid blob.

Back to basics

The basic Android UI looks similar to the following screenshot:

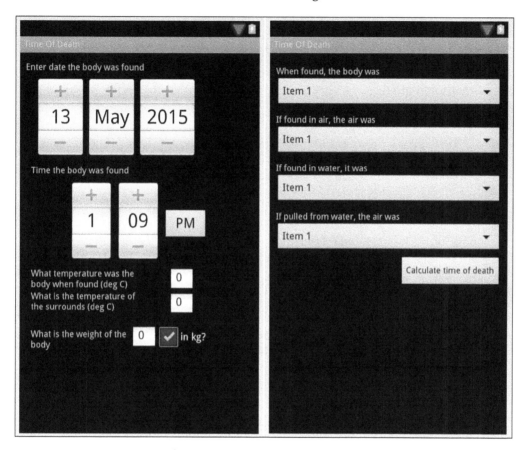

The UI consists of (from top to bottom) DatePicker, TimePicker, three numeric EditText boxes, and one CheckBox, and on the right-hand side, it has four Spinners and one Button. All text are just TextViews. The only element that is not available in Xamarin.Forms is the checkbox. In this case, we will replace this with a picker.

Thankfully, these can be simply replicated and placed in a StackView class.

1. First, we will create the date and time pickers and set the values to be the current date and time:

```
var datePicker = new DatePicker()
{
  Date = DateTime.Now,
  HorizontalOptions = LayoutOptions.CenterAndExpand
};
```

```
var timePicker = new TimePicker()
{
   Time = DateTime.Now.TimeOfDay,
   HorizontalOptions = LayoutOptions.CenterAndExpand
};
```

2. Next, we will create the text entry. Unlike on Android, `Entry` acts more like the iOS `UITextView`, and in effect, the keyboard decides on what the `Entry` method will take:

```
var editBodyTemp = new Entry()
{
   Keyboard = Keyboard.Numeric
};
var editTempSurrounds = new Entry()
{
   Keyboard = Keyboard.Numeric
};
var editWeight = new Entry()
{
   Keyboard = Keyboard.Numeric
};
```

3. Creating the `Picker` method for weight is little more involved. Here, we have to add the items using the following method. Unfortunately, you cannot bind the `Item` property, and there isn't an `AddRange` property that you may expect for an `IList` object:

```
var pickWeightUnits = new Picker();
pickWeightUnits.Items.Add("in Kg");
pickWeightUnits.Items.Add("in lbs");
```

If there were more options than this, use something similar to the following code:

```
var myList = new List<string>{/* put your strings in here */};
foreach(var s in myList)
pickWeightUnits.Items.Add(s);
```

4. Then, we need to do something with the `Entry` gadgets. The important aspect in the conversion is whether the picker for the weight has been changed, as follows:

```
editBodyTemp.TextChanged += (object sender, TextChangedEventArgs
e) => CommonVariables.BodyTemperature = !string.
IsNullOrEmpty(editBodyTemp.Text) ? Convert.ToDouble(editBodyTemp.
Text) : 0;
editTempSurrounds.TextChanged += (object sender,
TextChangedEventArgs e) => CommonVariables.SurroundTemperature
= !string.IsNullOrEmpty(editTempSurrounds.Text) ? Convert.
ToDouble(editTempSurrounds.Text) : 0;
editWeight.TextChanged += (object sender, TextChangedEventArgs e)
=>
{
    var weight = !string.IsNullOrEmpty(editWeight.Text) ? Convert.
ToDouble(editWeight.Text) : 0;
    weight *= pickWeightUnits.SelectedIndex == 0 ? ow * 6.35029318 :
1;
    CommonVariables.BodyWeight = weight;
};
```

5. Now, record the date selected:

```
datePicker.DateSelected += (object sender, DateChangedEventArgs e)
=>
{
    CommonVariables.DateOfDeath = e.NewDate;
};
```

6. The time picker has to be handled differently because there is no equivalent of `DateSelected`. In this case, we will use the `PropertyChanged` event:

```
timePicker.PropertyChanged += (sender, e) =>
{
    var date = CommonVariables.DateOfDeath;
    var time = timePicker.Time;
    CommonVariables.DateOfDeath = new DateTime(date.Year, date.
Month, date.Day, time.Hours, time.Minutes, time.Seconds);
};
```

7. The spinner on the conditions page is also set up in a similar way. Building and testing it shows the following screenshot:

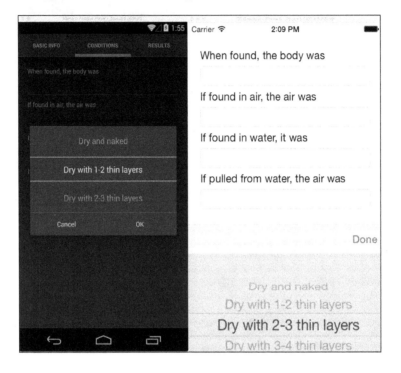

Way to go!

Uncle Tommy, there's more at the door...

The next issue can be seen in the Android version:

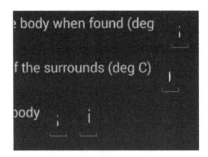

 The code for this part is in Chapter6/Time Of Death2.

We have a problem: the weight `Picker` and the `Entry` points are too small. We can fix this issue using the `WidthRequest` property. The problem is that we want to fix the size of the Label to be a proportion, and this is not something that is available straight off from Xamarin Forms.

To be able to find the size, we need to use the platform-specific code.

Size matters

The question here is why does Xamarin not provide sizes that abstract down to the platform? The abstraction has to work on every Android, iOS, and a Windows Phone device. There are so many different sizes, resolutions, and form factors that finding a *one size fits all* solution is not simple. Xamarin Forms provides a `Size` property for the screen size.

 Despite the name, the Xamarin Forms `Size` property is not the same as the one found in `System.Drawing`. Don't get them confused!

By adding the following code to the entry point of the PCL, we will be able to access the `Size` property on the platform to store the screen size:

```
public class App : Application
{
  public static Size ScreenSize { get; set; }

  public static App Self { get; private set; }

  public App()
  {
    Self = this;
```

Setting up the screen size depends on the platform. In the following code snippets, `App.ScreenSize` is set after the `Forms.Init()` call has been made:

- **iOS**: In **AppDelegate.cs,** this is set:

  ```
  App.ScreenSize = new Size(UIScreen.MainScreen.Bounds.Width,
  UIScreen.MainScreen.Bounds.Height);
  ```

- **Android**: In your launch activity, this is set:

  ```
  App.ScreenSize = new Size(Resources.DisplayMetrics.WidthPixels
  / Resources.DisplayMetrics.Density, Resources.DisplayMetrics.
  HeightPixels / Resources.DisplayMetrics.Density);
  ```

- Windows Phone: In `MainPage.xaml.cs`, this is set:

```
var content = Application.Current.Host.Content;
var scale = (double)content.ScaleFactor / 100;
var height = (int)Math.Ceiling(content.ActualHeight * scale);
var width = (int)Math.Ceiling(content.ActualWidth * scale);

timeofdeath2.App.ScreenSize = new Xamarin.Forms.Size((double)
width, (double)height);
```

To set `WidthRequest`, which is a specific proportion, we can use the `App.ScreenSize.Width` property. We want to make `Label` to be three quarters of the screen width, with `Entry` being one quarter of the width:

```
var twentyFivePC = App.ScreenSize.Width / 4;

var editBodyTemp = new Entry()
{
  Keyboard = Keyboard.Numeric,
  HorizontalOptions = LayoutOptions.CenterAndExpand,
  WidthRequest = twentyFivePC
};

Content = new StackLayout
{
  Orientation = StackOrientation.Vertical,
  VerticalOptions = LayoutOptions.FillAndExpand,
  HorizontalOptions = LayoutOptions.FillAndExpand,
  Padding = new Thickness(20),
  Children =
  {
    new Label { Text = "Enter the date the body was found",
WidthRequest = twentyFivePC * 3 };
```

The result of this modification is shown in the following screenshot:

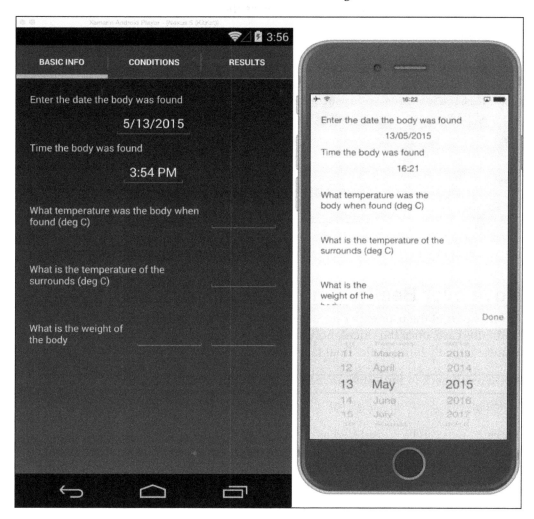

Much better!

And then she cried out – more

If you look carefully at the iOS version, you'll see that the Entry for the weight label is larger than the other Entry boxes, as shown in the following screenshot:

As we are concentrating on ensuring that the user experience is as high as possible, the height needs to be altered to be the same as the other `Entry` boxes:

```
var editWeight = new Entry()
{
   Keyboard = Keyboard.Numeric,
   HorizontalOptions = LayoutOptions.CenterAndExpand,
   VerticalOptions = LayoutOptions.Center,
   WidthRequest = twentyFivePC
};
```

```
What is the
weight of the
body
```

The `Entry` gadget now looks more in place, rather than just placed on the view.

Move over Beethoven

Another part of the user experience is to reduce the amount that the end user has to do. In this case, once the calculation has been performed, we want the user interface to automatically jump to the final tab.

If you recall back in the `TabPage.cs` file, we had the following line:

```
CurrentPage = Children[0];
```

`CurrentPage` can be considered as a bookmark that the app uses in order to know the child page that is currently being used. The problem is similar to what is experienced by Android users who have created a `TabPage` activity (something I referred to at the start of this chapter). `CurrentPage` belongs to the parent. It is accessible, but the method is not obvious.

Xamarin Forms provides a `Parent` property that allows access to the `Parent` view. We will create a local variable that is equal to `Parent` and is cast as a `TabbedPage` property. The `CurrentPage` property is then available, and so are the `Children` pages:

```
var masterPage = Parent as TabbedPage;
masterPage.CurrentPage = masterPage.Children[2];
```

Now you see me, now you don't

The final tab on this application is a waste of a tab. There are two lines of text on it. This looks bad, and the tab can be viewed at any point, giving a false reading as to when the body died. A much cleaner solution is to employ a modal view.

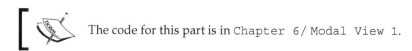

The code for this part is in Chapter 6/ Modal View 1.

There is a fair amount of confusion as to what a modal view actually is. In true terms, it is a supplementary view that sits between two real views and what end users think of modal is really a popup dialog.

The code for Modal View 1 shows the difference, which can be summed up as follows; the test was run on Android (rather than iOS) and the result is similar:

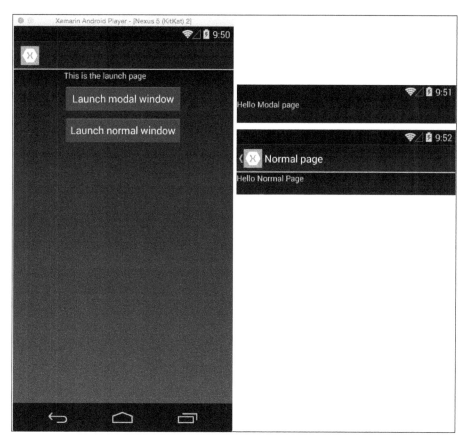

The modal window (when used with a navigation bar) does not show the back button. For iOS, this causes an issue. As there is no back button, which will, of course, be a problem, we will need to put a button on the modal, but only if we are using an iOS device.

Typically, when we create the likes of a stack layout on a page, it will come in the form of the following code:

```
Content = new StackLayout
{
  Orientation = StackOrientation.Vertical,
  HorizontalOptions = LayoutOptions.CenterAndExpand,
  VerticalOptions = LayoutOptions.FillAndExpand,
  Children =
  {
    new Label { Text = "This is the launch page" },
    btnModal,
    btnNormal
  }
};
```

This is fine. However, if we need to start adding additional gadgets to StackLayout when it is in this form, we need to start drilling down the Content to add. This means that if we need to add a conditional button, it becomes messy.

A simple way to structure the additional code of StackLayout is to create a variable, assign StackLayout to the variable, and access the Children list through this:

```
var stackLayout = new StackLayout
{
  Children =
  {
    new Label { Text = "Hello Modal page" }
  }
};

if (Device.OS == TargetPlatform.iOS)
{
  var btn = new Button()
  {
    Text = "Close",
    VerticalOptions = LayoutOptions.End,
    HorizontalOptions = LayoutOptions.End,
    Command = new Command(async () => await Navigation.
PopModalAsync())
```

```
    };

    stackLayout.Children.Add(btn);
}

Content = stackLayout;
```

Although the modal will replace the third tab, it is still a lot of wasted space. A popup is probably more similar to what we need. The problem is that popups are usually only needed for warnings, and so on. What we need is a popup that we can put the data in, as shown in the following screenshot:

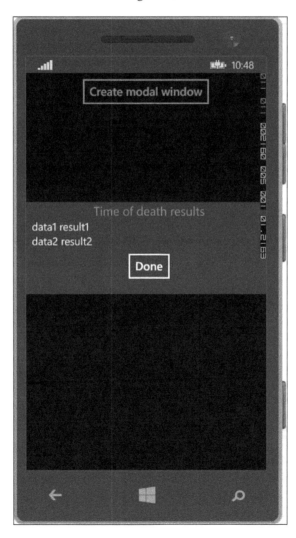

Here we go again...

Creating a pop up for the three different platforms poses four different sets of issues:

1. Communicating with the PCL
2. Creating the Android popup
3. Creating the Windows Phone popup
4. Creating the iOS popup

While these last three platforms are essentially the same, each of them come with their own issues.

 The code for this section is in `Chapter 6/ Modal 2`.

Problem 1 – talking with the PCL

As soon as the PCL passes control to the platform, the platform is in control until the control is passed back. Thankfully, when we create a new custom view renderer, the PCL will hang on an event: `ElementChangedEventArgs<T> e`. As we are hanging on an event, we can look at the properties that the event has provided with it.

For the popup, we will look at `e.OldElement` and `e.NewElement`:

```
protected override void OnElementChanged(ElementChangedEventArgs<Moda
lDialog> e)
{
  base.OnElementChanged(e);
  if (e.OldElement == null)
  {
    var dialog = e.NewElement;
    dialog.HorizontalOptions = LayoutOptions.Center;
    dialog.VerticalOptions = LayoutOptions.Center;
    CreateDialog(dialog);
  }
}
```

Problem 2 – the Android approach

Android has an issue when it comes to producing a dialog box, that is, an activity context is needed in order for the application to know what to associate the dialog box with. It is not possible to use `App.Context`, so we need to use a context from somewhere else.

The most obvious place to take it from is the launcher activity that Android uses:

```
public static Activity activity;

protected override void OnCreate(Bundle bundle)
{
  base.OnCreate(bundle);

  activity = this;
```

Then, we will be able to use this activity when we create the dialog box:

```
public void CreateDialog(ModalDialog dialog)
{
  var dispModal = new Dialog(MainActivity.activity, Resource.Style.
lightbox_dialog);
  dispModal.SetContentView(Resource.Layout.ModalView);
```

We also need to create a layout in the resources directory to produce the dialog and then back in the dialog creation, create a variable to interact with the elements in the dialog. There are two ways to do this: create a variable to assign properties to and create a lambda and just associate an action to the event (top line):

```
((Android.Widget.Button)dispModal.FindViewById(Resource.Id.btnDone)).
Click += delegate
{
  dispModal.Dismiss();
};
var txtData1 = dispModal.FindViewById<TextView>(Resource.Id.txtData1);
var txtData2 = dispModal.FindViewById<TextView>(Resource.Id.txtData2);
```

Finally, we will show the dialog using the following line of code:

```
dispModal.Show();
```

The modal window is displayed, and the control is passed back to the PCL once the dialog is closed.

Problem 3 – the iOS approach

For iOS to create the popup, we can either create a UIView in a .xib file or we can create one in the following code:

```
public void CreateDialog(ModalDialog dialog)
{
  var view = new UIView(new CGRect(8, 32, AppDelegate.Self.ScreenX,
120));
```

We then need to put a couple of `UILabel` properties and a `UIButton` property on the view, as given in the following code:

```
var lblTitle = new UILabel(new CGRect(40, 4, 180, 24))
{
  Text = "Time of death results",
};
view.Add(lblTitle);

var c = 0;
foreach (var dta in App.Self.ModalData)
{
  var d = dta.Split(',').ToArray();
  var vw = UICreation.CreateDoubleLabelView(c == 0 ? 36 : 64, d[0],
d[1]);
  c++;
  view.Add(vw);
}

var btnDone = UICreation.CreateButton(new CGRect((AppDelegate.Self.
ScreenX / 2) - 30, 80, 60, 30), UIButtonType.Custom, "Done");
view.Add(btnDone);

btnDone.TouchUpInside += delegate
{
  view.RemoveFromSuperview();
};
```

 `UICreation` is a helper class, which can be found in the iOS source directory.

We now have a problem. All of what has happened up to now for iOS is pretty standard, but we need to add the view to the main view controller. The issue is that we can't get to the view controller through the PCL without a bit of difficulty. Thankfully, we can add the view directly to the underlying view controller with the following piece of code:

```
UIApplication.SharedApplication.KeyWindow.RootViewController.
Add(view);
```

We now have the popup we want.

Problem 4 – Windows Phone

Windows Phone has its lineage firmly based in the way Windows work. In this case, we will use a `CustomMessageBox`. Unlike on Windows that has a message box in the middle of the view, the `CustomMessageBox` is a bit of a misnomer; it is more akin to a stripe across the screen containing the information.

Thankfully, creating the `CustomMessageBox` only requires a few text blocks, one `Button`, and one `StackLayout` to hold it in. Once created, we just have to show the `CustomMessageBox`, as shown in the following code:

```
var titleBar = new TextBlock
{
  Text = "Time of death results",
  FontSize = 24,
  Foreground = new SolidColorBrush(Colors.Red),
  HorizontalAlignment = System.Windows.HorizontalAlignment.Center
};

var btnDone = new System.Windows.Controls.Button
{
  HorizontalAlignment = System.Windows.HorizontalAlignment.Center,
  Content = "Done"
};

var stackPanel = new StackPanel
{
  Children = { titleBar, resLine1, resLine2, btnDone }
};

var content = new CustomMessageBox
{
  Content = stackPanel,
  Margin = new System.Windows.Thickness(0, 250, 0, 0)
};

content.Show();
```

She's a killer...

Of course, we will leave the popup with the default buttons and backgrounds. It's functional, but in terms of the end user experience, it's not that good to look at. With a small amount of customization, we can make the iOS and Android popups look similar to the following screenshot:

The iOS view can be made opaque with the following code:

```
public static UIView MakePrettyView(UIView vwView, float high = 0,
float x = 16f, float y = 80f)
{
  vwView.Layer.CornerRadius = 4f;
  vwView.BackgroundColor = UIColor.FromRGBA(255, 255, 255, 210);

  var divider = AppDelegate.Self.Retina ? 2 : 1;
  nfloat height = (nfloat)high;
```

```
var width = vwView.Bounds.Width + x > (AppDelegate.Self.ScreenX /
divider) ? vwView.Bounds.Width - (x * 2) : vwView.Frame.Width;
   if (high == 0f)
      height = vwView.Bounds.Height + y > (AppDelegate.Self.ScreenY /
divider) ? vwView.Bounds.Height - (y * 2) : vwView.Frame.Height;

   if (!AppDelegate.Self.IsIPhone)
   {
      x = (float)AppDelegate.Self.ScreenX - ((float)width / 2);
   }
   vwView.Frame = new CGRect(8, y, AppDelegate.Self.IsIPhone ?
AppDelegate.Self.ScreenX - 16 : width, height);
   vwView.Layer.BorderWidth = 1.4f;
   vwView.Layer.ShadowColor = UIColor.DarkGray.CGColor;
   vwView.Layer.ShadowOpacity = 0.75f;
   return vwView;
}
```

Modifying on Windows Phone

With Android and iOS, a button is an object in itself. However, with Windows
Phone, we will have to treat the button as a canvas with a child of the control and
the control as well. To start with, we will clear the canvas where the button is placed.
This doesn't destroy the button, but allows the canvas to be manipulated, as shown
in the following code:

```
[assembly: ExportRenderer(typeof(NewButton),
typeof(NewButtonRenderer))]
namespace WinPhone
{
   class NewButtonRenderer : ButtonRenderer
   { protected override void OnElementChanged(ElementChangedEventArgs<X
amarin.Forms.Button> e)
      {
         base.OnElementChanged(e);
         if (Control != null)
         {
            Children.Clear();
```

Next, we will create the new background. It is here that we will alter the button so
that the edges become rounded:

```
var border = new Border
{
   CornerRadius = new System.Windows.CornerRadius(10),
   Background = new SolidColorBrush(System.Windows.Media.Color.
FromArgb(255, 130, 186, 132)),
```

```
    BorderBrush = new SolidColorBrush(System.Windows.Media.Color.
FromArgb(255,45,176,51)),
    BorderThickness = new System.Windows.Thickness(0.8),
    Child = Control  // this adds the control back to the border
};
```

Finally, we will alter the button itself and add the button back to the canvas as follows:

```
Control.Foreground = new SolidColorBrush(Colors.White);  // make the
text white
Control.BorderThickness = new System.Windows.Thickness(0); // remove
the button border that is always there
Children.Add(border); // add the border to the canvas. Remember, this
also contains the Control
}
```

Let's see what's left

We now have a two tab UI with a popup for the result. The application will start to look much better. We still have a problem. When we create a tab page, the app creates the code for all the views, so if a `Label` has some text associated with it (such as `DateTime`), when you access the view with that label, the `DateTime` at the time the application was executed is the time that is displayed.

This is a bit of a pain to say the least!

 The code for this section is in `Chapter 6/ Time of death 3`.

The code to display the information is simple enough:

```
void CreateModalAnswer()
{

  App.Self.ModalData = new List<string>
  { string.Format("Death occured on or around,{0}", App.Self.
commonVariables.GetTime),
    string.Format("on the,{0}", App.Self.commonVariables.GetDate)
  };
  var cv = new ModalDialog()
  {
    IsClippedToBounds = true
  };
  theStack.Children.Add(cv);
}
```

This will only show the time and date at the time of execution. To stop this from taking place, we need to add a `PropertyChanged` event in the static class used for the variable storage:

```
public class CommonVariables : INotifyPropertyChanged
{
  public event PropertyChangedEventHandler PropertyChanged;

  protected virtual void OnPropertyChanged(string propertyName)
  {
    if (PropertyChanged == null)
      return;

    PropertyChanged(this, new PropertyChangedEventArgs(propertyName));
  }
```

We will only display `Date` and `Time`, so we only need to act on these properties:

```
public string GetDate
{
  get
  {
    var split = DateOfDeath.ToString().Split(' ');
    OnPropertyChanged("CommonVariables");
    return split.Length == 0 ? string.Empty : split[0];
  }
}

public string GetTime
{
  get
  {
    var split = DateOfDeath.ToString().Split(' ');
    OnPropertyChanged("CommonVariables");
    return split.Length == 0 ? string.Empty : string.Format("{0}
{1}", split[1], split.Length > 2 ? (!string.IsNullOrEmpty(split[2]) ?
split[2].ToLower() : "") : "");
  }
}
```

If the DateOfDeath property alters, the GetDate and GetTime events are fired and raised. When compiled and some data is entered, we have our new application, as shown in the following screenshot:

The UI is different, the user experience is much better, and the general friendliness of the app alters. This is the difference between an app and a popular app.

Summary

This has been a very long chapter, but it is a chapter that takes you from an okay looking app to an app that looks far more professional. We looked at the problems of how to create a custom view across the three main mobile platforms, how to take the code meant for just one platform, and how leveraging Xamarin Forms can create three applications with very little in the way for developers. Having said that, anything more than a basic UI requires customization on the platform level.

In the next chapter, we'll look at how to connect to various types of web services.

References

http://www.zdnet.com/article/ios-versus-android-apple-app-store-versus-google-play-here-comes-the-next-battle-in-the-app-wars/

7
Connect Me to Your Other Services

While Azure provides a very powerful mobile service, you may decide to connect to another type of service, such as one employing a RESTful interface or using the **Windows Communications Framework (WCF)**. Both are very different. In this chapter, we will look at both.

In this chapter, we will:

- Use a RESTful interface for a web service
- Look at a WCF interface for a web service

Let's take a REST

Before we look at the interface, we need to understand what REST is. In its simplest terms, REST is a set of six constraints, which when applied to an architecture (such as a web service) gives the basis of the RESTful style.

While it is outside the scope of this book to look at the architecture, there are many very good websites that cover what REST is. As far as we're concerned, we are interested in communicating with the web service.

REST services are typically transmitted using HTTP's GET and POST methods and return data in plain XML.

POST and GET

The best way to think about the difference between POST and GET is to consider a standard mail. If you have something to send, you POST it. If you receive something, you GET it.

So far, it's easy

When we receive the information from the server, it is typically in XML. This is a plain text format in a serialized format (which is a form of formatting that takes the objects being sent by the server and creates a plain text inline list). The exact form of the serialized data depends on the objects being serialized.

The most common format used for RESTful interfaces is known as **JSON (JavaScript Object Notation)**.

A JSON code looks like the following:

```
{
  "glossary": {
    "title": "example glossary",
    "GlossDiv": {
      "title": "S",
      "GlossList": {
        "GlossEntry": {
          "ID": "SGML",
          "SortAs": "SGML",
          "GlossTerm": "Standard Generalized Markup Language",
          "Acronym": "SGML",
          "Abbrev": "ISO 8879:1986",
          "GlossDef": {
            "para": "A meta-markup language, used to create markup
languages such as DocBook.",
            "GlossSeeAlso": ["GML", "XML"]
          },
          "GlossSee": "markup"
        }
      }
    }
  }
}
```

The XML representation of the preceding code will appear as follows:

```
<!DOCTYPE glossary PUBLIC "-//OASIS//DTD DocBook V3.1//EN">
 <glossary><title>example glossary</title>
  <GlossDiv><title>S</title>
```

```
    <GlossList>
     <GlossEntry ID="SGML" SortAs="SGML">
      <GlossTerm>Standard Generalized Markup Language</GlossTerm>
      <Acronym>SGML</Acronym>
      <Abbrev>ISO 8879:1986</Abbrev>
      <GlossDef>
       <para>A meta-markup language, used to create markup
languages such as DocBook.</para>
        <GlossSeeAlso OtherTerm="GML">
        <GlossSeeAlso OtherTerm="XML">
       </GlossDef>
       <GlossSee OtherTerm="markup">
      </GlossEntry>
     </GlossList>
    </GlossDiv>
   </glossary>
```

Transferring JSON to something we can use

One of the reasons why C# and JSON go so well together is that everything is an object, so if the example was sent over, it can be deserialized into container classes of that object type. The preceding example will break up into the following classes:

```csharp
public class GlossDef
{
  public string para { get; set; }
  public List<string> GlossSeeAlso { get; set; }
}

public class GlossEntry
{
  public string ID { get; set; }
  public string SortAs { get; set; }
  public string GlossTerm { get; set; }
  public string Acronym { get; set; }
  public string Abbrev { get; set; }
  public GlossDef GlossDef { get; set; }
  public string GlossSee { get; set; }
}

public class GlossList
{
  public GlossEntry GlossEntry { get; set; }
}

public class GlossDiv
```

```
{
  public string title { get; set; }
  public GlossList GlossList { get; set; }
}

public class Glossary
{
  public string title { get; set; }
  public GlossDiv GlossDiv { get; set; }
}

public class RootObject
{
  public Glossary glossary { get; set; }
}
```

We don't have to pass in every object when you deserialize, just the `RootObject` class.

It's a bit messy, isn't it?

The answer here is that it depends. Yes, it can be a problem when you deserialize to classes, in which unless you know the API, you need to rely on a service, such as **JSON2CSharp**, to generate the classes. This can result in quite a few problems because depending on the calls to the service may result in different classes being generated.

There are packages available that can decode the JSON dynamically (such as Newtonsoft's Json.NET, which is available on NuGet), so we'll look at both systems to decode the incoming data.

The practicalities

In order to use a web service, we need to have one first. The service that will be used for the examples are available at `openweathermap.org`; a very good weather system that aggregates national, local, and independent weather stations from any one particular area. To use this service, you will first need to register (for free) on the website and obtain an API ID code.

 The code for the next section is available in `Chapter 7/Weather`.

Let's make a start

As with all our examples, this will also be a Xamarin Forms project. You will recall that a PCL supports only a subset of the full .NET libraries, so some parts are missing.

For example, the following code will not work in a PCL:

```
string responseContent;
try
{
  using (var response = request.GetResponse() as HttpWebResponse)
  {
    using (var reader = new StreamReader(response.
GetResponseStream()))
    {
      responseContent = reader.ReadToEnd();
    }
  }
  var deserial = Deserialize<WeatherData>(responseContent);
  return deserial;
}
```

The problem is that the `GetResponse` method is not supported in the subset of the .NET libraries in a PCL.

The following code is the PCL version:

```
var Weather = new WeatherData();
string responseContent;
try
{
  var asyncResult = request.BeginGetResponse(new AsyncCallback(s =>
  {
    var response = (s.AsyncState as WebRequest).EndGetResponse(s);

    using (var reader = new StreamReader(response.
GetResponseStream()))
    {
      responseContent = reader.ReadToEnd();
    }
    Weather = Deserialize<WeatherData>(responseContent);
  }), request);
  return Weather;
}
```

The call to the web service is as follows:

```
var param = string.Format("lat={0}&lon={1}&APPID={2}", App.Self.
Latitude, App.Self.Longitude, App.Self.WeatherID);
var request = WebRequest.Create("http://api.openweathermap.org/
data/2.5/forecast?" + param) as HttpWebRequest;
request.Method = "GET";
request.Accept = "application/json";
request.ContentType = "application/json";
```

The request (if expressed as a URL) would translate to be as follows:

```
http://api.openweathermap.org/data/2.5/forecast?lat=-
2.956&lon=53.431&APPID=MY_APP_ID
```

 This may look familiar to you; you will see something similar when you use any form of a search engine or a parameterized call on a website (for example, Packt Publishing returns `https://www.google.co.uk/#q=Packt+publishing`).

The `WeatherJSON.cs` file contains the deserialized classes for the API. The application also needs a latitude and longitude for the map. The code to perform this is platform-specific. I won't go into details here (mainly because I do so in *Chapter 10, This is the World Calling…*). It is sufficient to say that it does what it needs to do.

When you build the app in the code examples that come with this book, you'll hit a problem; it doesn't work. The weather object contains nothing, so when we come to any line that requires looking at an array, the code crashes.

Why is this? The answer is that the object is returned before the data has been downloaded. To fix this, we need to change the code that grabs the data from the service. Let's look at what we have:

```
var asyncResult = request.BeginGetResponse(new AsyncCallback(s =>
{
  var response = (s.AsyncState as WebRequest).EndGetResponse(s);

  using (var reader = new StreamReader(response.GetResponseStream()))
  {
    responseContent = reader.ReadToEnd();
  }
  Weather = Deserialize<WeatherData>(responseContent);
}), request);
return Weather;
```

We cannot move the return statement to the body of the callback (the callback returns `void`), but we can use another method. We know that we have to await the call to the service, so rather than doing everything in one step, we can break it down and use `Task.Factory` to help us, as shown in the following code:

```
try
{
  var response = (HttpWebResponse)await Task.Factory.
FromAsync<WebResponse>(request.BeginGetResponse, request.
EndGetResponse, null);
  if (response.StatusCode == HttpStatusCode.OK)
  {
    using (var reader = new StreamReader(response.
GetResponseStream()))
    {
      responseContent = reader.ReadToEnd();
    }
    Weather = Deserialize<WeatherData>(responseContent);
  }
  return Weather;
}
```

This time, the weather information is returned and the UI displays the following information:

Using Json.NET

After creating the new project, install **Json.NET** from NuGet, as shown in the following screenshot:

 The code for this section is available in `Chapter 7/WeatherJSONNET`.

If you look at the `WeatherJSON.cs` file and compare it with the version in the previous project, you'll notice two changes:

1. The `Deserialize` method has been removed.

2. We will now use the following code to perform the deserialization:

```
Weather = (WeatherData)JsonConvert.DeserializeObject(responseConte
nt, typeof(WeatherData));
```

3. When compiled and executed, we will get something similar to the following screenshot:

Which is better?

This all depends on what you want to do. If you have no need for serialization and the other facilities, then Json.NET may be overkill and add size to the final binary that isn't required. Having said that, Json.NET is faster compared to the standard .NET deserialization.

The Windows Communication Framework

To use the WCF, you must first have a file known as a generated client class. This class for use with a PCL must be created using the Silverlight Svsvcutil binary that comes as part of the Silverlight SDK. A similar named binary (svcutil) comes as part of the Windows SDK. Do not use this binary because the client class produced cannot be used in the PCL. The client class can only be generated on a Windows machine (or on a virtualized Windows machine).

 The code for this section is available in Chapter 7/WCF.

For this, I've chosen to use Microsoft's VirtualEarth service. To use this, you will also need to generate a temporary key. This key is similar to a Google Maps key or the OpenWeatherMap API key, which is needed when communicating with the service to authenticate who you are. The key is free. When you create the key, ensure that the key is a trial key and the type is **Other Public Mobile App**. Copy the generated key and store it in the `public readonly string` API key variable in the `WCF.cs` file.

In the PCL, there is a file called `GeocodeService.cs`. This is the generated client class from the web service. It is through this that the service is accessed.

Using the web service

The first stage is to authenticate with the service. To do this, we need to set an instance to the WCF class in the same way as you would for any other class, as shown in the following code:

```
var geocodeRequest = new GeocodeRequest
{
  Credentials = new GeocodeService.Credentials
  {
    ApplicationId = "MY_KEY"
  }
};
```

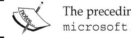 The preceding example is based on `https://msdn.microsoft.com/en-us/library/dd483215.aspx`.

Believe it or not, the hard part is over. The WCF has done the hard work for you and communicated with the server. This is done to the WCF that contains a large number of endpoints as well as the IP address of the service being used (in this case, Bing Maps). Bing provides a large number of facilities to the user. Using the WCF service, these facilities are simple to access.

One of the issues with WCF is that although they have `async` in the method name, the call doesn't require an `await` because `await` is performed in the background in the proxy (the `GeocodeService.cs` file). This causes a bit of an issue as the flow of the application won't `await` on a background, so to catch the return, an event is thrown, which we can listen in.

As with any event, we can create its own method or we can do it inline:

```
geocodeService.GeocodeCompleted += async (object sender,
GeocodeCompletedEventArgs e) =>
{
  if (e.Error == null)
  {
    var res = e.Result;
    if (e.Result.Results.Length > 0)
      if (e.Result.Results[0].Locations.Length > 0)
      {
        myLoc = e.Result.Results[0].Locations[0];
        var uri = await Map.GetMapUri(myLoc.Latitude, myLoc.Longitude,
2, "HYBRID", 300, 300);

        await Navigation.PushAsync(new Map(uri));
      }
  }
};
```

Alternatively, we can use this:

```
geocodeService.GeocodeCompleted += GeocodeCompletedEvent;

void GeocodeCompletedEvent(object sender, GeocodeCompletedEventArgs e)
{
    ...
}
```

Adding a web reference

An alternate method of using WCF is to add a service reference to the application.
This attaches the application to the service directly and is simple enough to perform.

 The code for this part can be found in `Chapter 7/WCF`.

In the PCL part of the application, highlight the WCF (master) file on the solution explorer window. Now, perform the following steps:

1. Click on the menu and scroll down to **Add | Add Web Reference**:

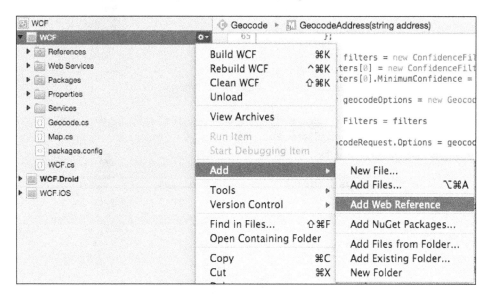

2. When you select the **Add Web Reference**, a new window will be displayed:

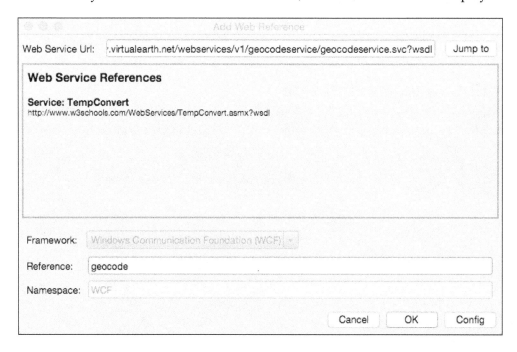

3. Copy and paste the web service URL in the top box, give the service a reference name, and click on **OK**. Once done, the service reference will be displayed in the **Solution Explorer** window, as shown in the following screenshot:

Unlike the previous method, the namespace being used is now the reference name (so, in the case of `http://dev.virtualearth.net/webservices/v1/geocodeservice/geocodeservice.svc?wsdl`, the namespace is `WCF.geocode`).

The advantage of using this over creating your own proxy is that the service in use will always be the most up-to-date service (as long as you remember to update the service references).

The code has a couple of small changes from the original non-web service version, but at the end, when you run the application, you should see the following screenshot:

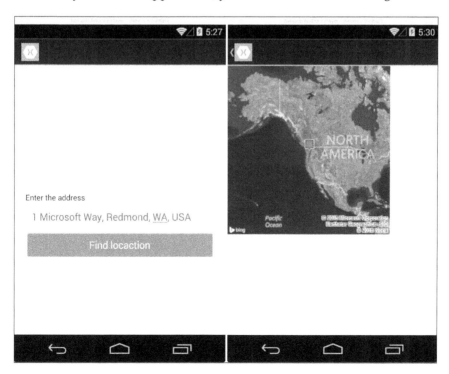

The degree of zoom can be altered in the `public static string GetMapUri` method via the call to the method in the `var uri = Map.GetMapUri(myLoc.Latitude, myLoc.Longitude, 2, "HYBRID", 300, 300);` line.

We can also change the size of the map by altering the two `300` parameters at the end of the call.

Summary

There isn't anything difficult in connecting to the other types of service available, be it RESTful, WCF, or anything else available (within reason). The difficulty typically comes with setting up the interface for the outside world.

In the next chapter, we'll look at one of the most powerful aspect of the forms development: data binding. It's not as bad as you'd think and is incredibly powerful.

References

- `http://json.org/example`
- `http://json2csharp.com`

8
What a Bind!

In terms of a messenger app, to make it of any use at all, we will need to display data; this can be the message thread, the message itself, or any other part of the application (such as our contacts held). This can be very time consuming. Thankfully, we are able to leverage the `BindingProperty` of most UI elements. This means that we can cut down on the code required to generate what we need.

In this chapter, we will:

- Learn how to use binding
- Understand how binding makes life simpler
- Implement binding to our data to create our UI

 Before carrying on, it may be worth familiarizing yourself with an example message data structure (a copy is available in `Chapter8/Message`).

A bit of a history lesson

Data binding is nothing new. In many ways, it has been around in computing for decades; a simple example is that of mail merge. Here, you have a master document with a number of parameter fields inserted and a data file with matching fields. The software would take the master file as the template and sequentially read through the data file, insert the matched fields, and generate a new document (which could either be saved or disposed of) containing the newly created documents.

The issue here is that if you make a mistake on the master document, each newly created document will have the same error, and if you need to add more names to the data file, you will either have to create all the letters again or tell the software to use a third data file and then generate the letters that way, but then remember to merge the two data files together to cut down on the time required later on.

As time moved on, so did software; data binding moved to desktop applications. It may not seem to be the case, but quite a lot of software relies on data binding in some form or another; pretty much anything that takes data from a source and displays it on a screen uses data binding; this is how a spinner can be created once and called from anywhere.

Consider the following pseudo code:

```
public static void MakeMySpinner(this Spinner mySpinner, string
filename, string menuOpts, EventHandler handle = null)
{
  Create holding list for spinner menu names
    try
  {
    Open the file (no need to load it in)
    Search file for instances of menuOpts
      Store in the list
    Once done and the list has data add to mySpinner
    If handle != null
    Attach the handler to mySpinner
  }
  catch (Exception ex)
  {
    Handle exception gracefully
  }
}
```

The preceding code can be invoked from anywhere in the application. Once the data has been read, it is added to the spinner. It doesn't matter where the spinner is in the application, this small method can be used time and again to bind the data from the files to the element.

Binding the mobile arena

Standard UI elements for iOS and Android do not directly allow data binding. This means that if we want to display a large amount of data, we need to use either `ListView` (Android) or `UITableView` (iOS). Depending on what you want to display will depend on whether this actually is a good plan. Consider the following two messages:

> Hi, do you fancy a beer tonight?

> Sure, I have got to pick up the kids first from football practice and then drive the wife home. 8 pm ok with you?

The first difference is the size of the speech bubbles. As the amount of text increases, so does the size of the bubble. The messenger doesn't use standard SMS protocols (if it did, Apple would not allow it in the store). So, in theory, we can send as much text as we want as a message.

This causes issues for `UITableView`. Although we can define `UITableCell` to be what we want, we still have the problem of resizing the bounds and then wrapping the speech bubble around. There is nothing to say that the third message is as simple as a smiley reply or something closer to a chapter in War and Peace!

Android has a similar issue. It needs to use a patched image to ensure that it covers the size. There is no problem with the amount of text the list layout can handle, but there is a different problem: adding the data.

Normally, the `ListView` adapter needs the data to be filled. This means that the template needs to be filled, which in turn requires even more code.

For Android, there is another way to perform the task without the `ListView` adapter. For this, you need to have a `ScrollView`, add a table row, inflate the message holder, fill it, add the table row to the `ScrollView`, and let it render.

The problem with all of these methods is that they require processing time, and this makes the app slow (even using a powerful phone, such as the iPhone 6+ or Sony Z3, and rendering large amounts of constantly changing formatted data can slow things down greatly). If we add more to this, and should a new message come in while we're viewing the thread, it will need to be added to the bottom of the table, which would require a redraw. We also have the problem of code size with this.

Binding allows a property in the element to be bound to a value. For example, if we have a `Label` element in a `Xamarin.Forms` application, we can bind `Label.TextProperty` to the element in our list containing the message, and if we use a custom rendered, we can add the background text bubble as well.

Looks useful? Well, it is!

A simple binding project

To start with, let's create a `List<string>` of random text (in this case, a random song lyrics):

```
// set up a list of data
var dataList = new List<string>
{
   "Ding dong, the witch is dead",
   "When you walk through a storm",
   "I love rock and roll",
   "D'oh!",
   "People say on the day of victory, no fatigue is felt\n" +
   "Garbo, it's you that has the power that makes ev'ry man's heart
melt\n" +
   "They say that, when the heart is a fire sparks fly out of the
cage\n" +
   "But beauty is like a good wine, the taste is sweeter with age",
   "No man can guess in cold blood what he might do in passion\n" +
   "But the things that he deplores today are tomorrow's latest
fashion\n" +
   "Serving one's own passion is the greatest slavery\n" +
   "But if in wanting you I become your slave, I intend no bravery",
     "Remember you're a womble"
};
```

The source for this part can be found in `Chapter8/SimpleBindingProject`.

Some of the strings in the list are large, some are small; this is fine, as we want to emulate a real message list.

Now, we will create the `ListView` container (it's not really an element because it holds many replicated templates). The `ListView` container needs a data source (the list of strings) as well as a template to fill in, as shown in the following code:

```
var listView = new ListView()
{
  ItemsSource = dataList,
  ItemTemplate = new DataTemplate(typeof(LyricViewCell))
};
```

`ItemTemplate` has to be a cell (`TextCell`, `ViewCell`, `SwitchCell`, or `ImageCell`). For this example, a class has been created that inherits `ViewCell`. This allows you to use any UI element, position it the way you want, and make it look the way you wish.

The `LyricViewCell` class looks like the following code:

```
public class LyricViewCell : ViewCell
{
  public LyricViewCell()
  {
    var label = new Label()
    {
      Text = "lyric",
      Font = Font.SystemFontOfSize(NamedSize.Default),
      TextColor = Color.Blue
    };
    label.SetBinding(Label.TextProperty, new Binding("."));

    View = new StackLayout()
    {
      Orientation = StackOrientation.Vertical,
      VerticalOptions = LayoutOptions.StartAndExpand,
      Padding = new Thickness(12, 8),
      Children = { label }
    };
  }
}
```

The hard work for the binding is held in the following line:

```
label.SetBinding(Label.TextProperty, new Binding("."));
```

Here, we will tell the label to set the `Text` property to a binding. As we will only use a list of strings for the `ItemsSource`, "." can be thought of as *whatever the element in the list is.*

Compile and run the code, and you'll see that something isn't right, as shown in the following screenshot:

This is not unexpected and is something that we need avoid with messages. Thankfully, `ListView` has a property called `HasUnevenRows`. If this is set to true, then we should see the UI as we would expect. To make the change, go to the following code:

```
var listView = new ListView()
{
  ItemsSource = dataList,
  ItemTemplate = new DataTemplate(typeof(LyricViewCell))
};
```

Alter the preceding code to the following code:

```
var listView = new ListView()
{
  HasUnevenRows = true,
  ItemsSource = dataList,
  ItemTemplate = new DataTemplate(typeof(LyricViewCell))
};
```

Compile and run the preceding code, and you will see the following screenshot:

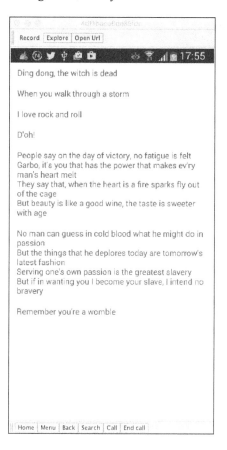

Everything shows, and better still, the cells are in the correct size for the text.

Let's step it up a notch

Although it's great that we can bind to a list of strings easily enough, it rarely happens. It is more likely that there will be a list of a class containing the data, in which we need to bind a particular class member (or members depending on what we are doing).

Consider the following `Message` class:

```
public class Message
{
  [PrimaryKey]
  public string id { get; set; }
```

```
        public string parent_id { get; set; }

        public string message { get; set; }

        public DateTime datestamp { get; set; }

        public bool is_reply { get; set; }

        public bool has_attachments { get; set; }

        public string attachment_id { get; set; }
    }
```

We will need to bind the message text to the message with the position change, depending on the value of is_reply. As this is stored in a SQLite database, it's safe to assume that the data will be held in a List<> container.

LINQ, anyone?

There is nothing wrong in creating a List<string> container that contains the message text and order on the datestamp member. The problem comes in doing it this way. This means that there isn't anything obvious to say, whether it is a reply or whether or not there is anything attached to the message.

How about creating a Dictionary using a subset of the Message class with the is_reply and has_attachments messages? This too would work, but then we will be creating a copy of the data that we already have, so we will end up with pretty much duplicate objects taking up twice the space. Not a big problem if the message list is small, but a big issue if the list isn't small. Also, if you have the data once, why make duplicate copies?

How to perform the binding

Of course, the first step is to create List and add some data to it. The data isn't from a database in the example, but it will be by the time we reach the end of the book.

Take a look at the following code:

```
    void FillMessageList()
    {
      var lyrics = new List<string>
      {
        "Ding dong, the witch is dead",
        "When you walk through a storm",
        "I love rock and roll",
```

```
      "D'oh!",
      "People say on the day of victory, no fatigue is felt\n" +
      "Garbo, it's you that has the power that makes ev'ry man's heart
melt\n" +
      "They say that, when the heart is a fire sparks fly out of the
cage\n" +
      "But beauty is like a good wine, the taste is sweeter with age",
      "No man can guess in cold blood what he might do in passion\n" +
      "But the things that he deplores today are tomorrow's latest
fashion\n" +
      "Serving one's own passion is the greatest slavery\n" +
      "But if in wanting you I become your slave, I intend no bravery",
        "Remember you're a womble"
   };
   var rand = new Random();
   foreach (var l in lyrics)
   {
      messageList.Add(new Message
      {
        id = Utils.NewID,
        parent_id = Utils.NewID,
        message = l,
        datestamp = DateTime.Now.AddDays((double)rand.Next(0, 10)),
        is_reply = rand.Next(0, 10) >= 5 ? true : false,
        has_attachments = rand.Next(0, 10) >= 5 ? true : false,
        attachment_id = Utils.NewID // just fill it for now
      });
   }
}

public static class Utils
{
  public static string NewID
  {
    get
    {
      return new Guid().ToString();
    }
  }
}
```

 The source for this section can be found in Chapter8/
ComplexBinding.

The `ListView` still points to the list of messages for `ItemsSource`, so nothing has really changed here. The difference comes in `ViewCell`, where we bind the message to `Label.TextProperty`, as shown in the following code:

```
label.SetBinding(Label.TextProperty, new Binding("message"));
```

When built and executed, the following screenshot is displayed. The `messageList` container had sort applied to it, so it won't display the lyrics in the order that it had been inserted in the list:

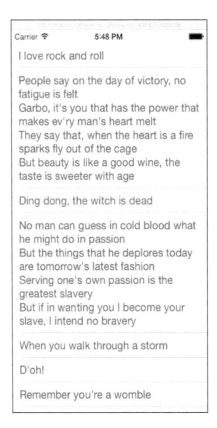

Can we do anything else with the bindings?

Good question. Let's try and do two more things. First, if it's a reply, put it in the right-hand side corner. Second, change the text color to check whether it's a reply. These can all be done in `ViewCell` as our `BindingContext` (what the cell is bound to) is each instance of the `Messenger` class within `List` in turn.

Let's start with the position. The most obvious place to set the position will be in `StackLayout`, and to set `HorizontalOptions`. The question is how?

The obvious solution here will be to have something similar to the following code:

```
var isReply = new Binding("is_reply");
```

Right? No!

isReply here is a binding variable, not bool. It just so happens that what isReply is bound to is a Boolean variable. It could equally be any other type.

Remember, a binding has to bind to something. How about we use the following line of code:

```
View.SetBinding(View.HorizontalOptionsProperty, new Binding("is_
reply"));
```

Well, this is getting closer, but all we're doing is binding HorizontalOptionsProperty to Boolean; we're not actually telling the layout to be on either side of the screen. Surely the code will compile, but there isn't a change.

This puts us in a bit of a dilemma; how do you perform an operation based on the value of a binding that you can't easily access?

The answer is to use a class that inherits the IValueConverterinterface.

IValueConverter

BoolToColor is a class that inherits IValueConverter. This implements the following two methods required by the interface itself:

- public object Convert(object value, Type targetType, object parameter, CultureInfo culture)
- public object ConvertBack(object value, Type targetType, object parameter, CultureInfo culture)

The idea is that the conversion is a two-way process, although the reverse is not going to be used in our example.

Using IValueConverter is simple. Take a look at the following code:

```
label.SetBinding(Label.TextColorProperty, new Binding("is_reply",
converter: new BoolToColor()));
```

The conversion is handled by the instance of BoolToColor(); it is important to use the converter that precedes the new BoolToColor() method. If it is omitted, the conversion fails.

The `BoolToColor` class looks similar to the following code:

```
public class BoolToColor : IValueConverter
{
  #region IValueConverter implementation

  public object Convert(object value, Type targetType, object
parameter, CultureInfo culture)
  {
    Color col;
    var b = value.ToString();
    col = b.ToLower() == "true" ? Color.Blue : Color.Red;
    return (Color)col;

  }

  public object ConvertBack(object value, Type targetType, object
parameter, CultureInfo culture)
  {
    var col = (Color)value;
    return col == Color.Red ? false : true;
  }

  #endregion
}
```

Setting the horizontal position

A similar solution for the horizontal position can also be used. We can't use the `BoolToColor` class, but we can use something very similar to position the text. Remember that it's not `StackView` that is being acted on, but the `Label`, so the following code will work:

```
label.SetBinding(Label.HorizontalOptionsProperty, new Binding("is_
reply", converter: new BoolToHPos()));
```

However, the following code will not result in what you would think should happen:

```
View.SetBinding(View.HorizontalOptionsProperty, new Binding("is_
reply", converter: new BoolToHPos()));
```

Once run, you will see something similar to the following screenshot:

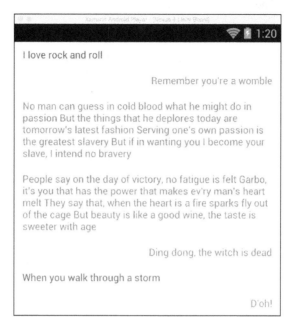

Any other alternatives?

To quote one of my former physical chemistry lecturers, and a longtime friend, Dr. Alex Woods (formerly of Liverpool John Moores University) – *"you can skin a cat a thousand ways, but at the end you have a skinned cat"*. In other words, there are usually far more than a single way to solve an issue.

We can always use a trigger (refer to *Chapter 3, Making It Look Pretty and Logging In,* for details), or we can use the `BindingContextChanged` event. Here, we will cast the event sender to the underpinning class (in this case, `Messenger`) and access the members directly, as shown in the following code:

```
label.BindingContextChanged += (object sender, EventArgs e) =>
{
  var m = (Message)BindingContext;
  App.Self.IsReply = m.is_reply;
};
```

To the next level, we will go!

At the start of this chapter, I showed you some sort of graphic around the text. We will implement the background in this part because again, it will use another `IValueConverter`.

The source to this section can be found in `Chapter8/TextAndGraphics`.

With all `Xamarin.Forms` apps, the graphics being referenced need to be placed in `Resource/Drawable/*` (Android), `Resources` (iOS), and `Toolkit.Content` (Win Phone).

The source comes with two new graphics. These will be used as the backdrop for the messages, as shown in the following image:

The issue here is that neither `Label` nor `StackLayout` have a background image, so we will need to implement a custom renderer to add the background, which also leads to another issue, that is, we don't know the height to expand around the text.

Android

Android needs some work to figure out the size of the text and the size of the background. Without changing or calculating the size of the text, the UI looks similar to the following screenshot:

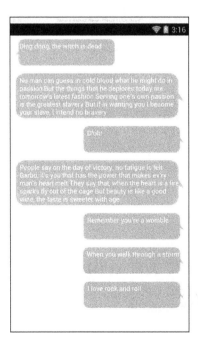

There is nothing wrong in having the same size image backgrounds all the time, but it is a waste of screen real estate. Finding the text height is not that simple. Android devices come in a vast array of shapes, sizes, and pixel densities. This makes finding physical sizes not as simple as you would imagine.

There are three aspects that need to be addressed:

- The bubble height
- The bubble width
- Resizing the bubble

As I've said, Android screens are widely varied. Thankfully, there are a couple of ways to make calculation values agnostic of the device hardware:

```
public static float ConvertDpToPixel(this float dp)
{
  var metrics = Application.Context.Resources.DisplayMetrics;
  return dp * ((float)metrics.DensityDpi / 160f);
}

public static float ConvertPixelToDp(this float px)
{
  var metrics = Application.Context.Resources.DisplayMetrics;
  return (px * 160f) / (float)metrics.DensityDpi;
}
```

Extension methods

The preceding two examples may look slightly odd because they contain float as the parameter in the braces. This is an example of an extension method. This means that the code can be used in the following way:

```
var imageSize = someDPvalue.ConvertDpToPixel(120f);
```

To create an extension method, the method has to be static and include one parameter in brackets. This parameter is the value being acted upon, so in my example, someDPvalue will be acted upon with the value of the float being used.

The text width and height

Android provides three methods to find the width of a text string:

- GetTextBounds
- MeasureText
- GetTextWidths

MeasureText and GetTextWidths returns the number of pixels. These work well, except when you are dealing with fonts when these two methods may not return the correct width (sometimes by quite a considerable amount).

To this effect, GetTextBounds is more accurate in finding the width and height of the textbox because it takes into account where the font "paints" passed the end of the text. Why is this important? When you look at the text in this book, all the text has a certain size and weight. On Android, some fonts (to make them look nicer) paint past the end of the letter, causing a slight overlap on the next letter.

This looks bad, so the font system pushes the next letter very slightly with the net effect being that everything moves along slightly, making the actual end of the text bounds different to the MeasureText or GetTextWidth values.

Taking into account the text typeface

GetTextBounds does a very good job of calculating the bounds, but it can be further improved to take into account antialiasing and the subpixel text:

```
public static int GetTextHeight(this string text, int maxWidth, float
textSize, Typeface typeface)
{
   var paint = new TextPaint(PaintFlags.AntiAlias | PaintFlags.
SubpixelText)
   {
     TextSize = textSize,
   };
   paint.SetTypeface(typeface);
   int lineCount = 0, index = 0, length = text.Length();
   while (index < length - 1)
   {
     index += paint.BreakText(text, index, length, true,maxWidth,
null);
     lineCount++;
   }
   var bounds = new Rect();
   paint.GetTextBounds("Py", 0, 2, bounds);
   return (int)Math.Floor(lineCount * bounds.Height());
}
```

We now have a way to work out the width and height accurately. The next step is to create the image for the background. At this point, it is worth mentioning that Android has a problem: memory management. Thankfully, this has reduced with successive versions of the operating system. Essentially, you need to be careful with bitmaps and drawables, to ensure that if you're doing anything with them, you need to free up the memory as soon as you're done.

To help with this, encapsulate any processing you perform in the `using (...) {}` construct. As soon as the processing reaches the end of the construct, the garbage collector is called and memory freed.

Converting a drawable image to a bitmap image

Images on Android have an associated resource ID (`int`). The following code is what you use when you see:

```
myImageView.SetBackgroundResource(Resource.Drawable.mypic);
```

This does not make `mypic` a drawable; it could be the same as our `RoundedButton` example (the XML file defining the button). It is not difficult to convert a drawable to a bitmap image. The following line of code does the work for us:

```
var myBitmap = BitmapFactory.DecodeResource(Resources, resourceId);
```

What we then need to do is scale the bitmap to the correct size. For this, we will create a bitmap, set the required size and height (with some padding), and return the bitmap image, as shown in the following code:

```
public static Bitmap DrawableToBitmap(int resourceId, int height, int width)
{
  var bitMap = Bitmap.CreateBitmap(width + 24, height + 16);
  var drawable = Resources.System.GetDrawable(resourceId);
  using (var bitmap = BitmapFactory.DecodeResource(Resources, resourceId))
  {
    using (var myBitmap = Bitmap.CreateScaledBitmap(bitmap, width + 24, height + 16, false))
    {
      using (var canvas = new Canvas(myBitmap))
      {
        drawable.SetBounds(0, 0, width + 24, height + 16);
        drawable.Draw(canvas);
        bitMap = myBitmap;
      }
    }
  }
  return bitMap;
}
```

Another way to perform the scaling is to use the following code:

```
public static Drawable ResizeDrawable(int resourceId)
{
  var drawable = Application.Context.Resources.
GetDrawable(resourceId);
  var bitmap = ((BitmapDrawable)drawable).Bitmap;
  var sizeX = (int)System.Math.Round((double)drawable.IntrinsicWidth *
.25);
  var sizeY = (int)System.Math.Round((double)drawable.IntrinsicHeight
* .5);
  var resizedBitmap = Bitmap.CreateScaledBitmap(bitmap, sizeX, sizeY,
true);
  drawable = new BitmapDrawable(Application.Context.Resources,
resizedBitmap);
  return drawable;
}
```

If you use this method, we can cut down on the calculations (all of which take time), but it does result in the following screenshot for the UI:

This may look good, but take a look at the corner:

This is just an issue with scaling. Android has thought of this and allows something known as a `Patch9` file. These allow scaling of images in certain places. The `draw9patch` application comes as part of the Java SDK (which is installed when you install `Xamarin.Android`). Find this on your hard drive (for example, on Mac, it's in `~/Library/Developer/Xamarin/android-sdk-mac_x86/tools`). Perform the following steps:

1. Start the `draw9patch` application and drop in the `Resources/drawable/bubblesolidleft.png` file.

2. To select the area that you want to allow to expand or contract, move to just outside the left (or right) of the bubble and click and drag the mouse down. A black line will appear.

3. Do the same up or down. You have now created a bubble scalable on the X and Y axis and added some padding as well.

4. To see the area left from the scaling, click on the **Show Patches** checkbox. You will see something similar to the following screenshot:

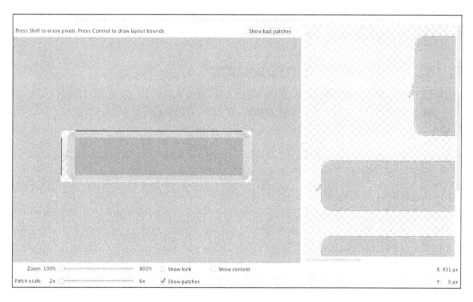

5. Saving this will result in a 9patch file (this will be called something as bubblesolidleft.9.png).

The 9 patch file is the same as a normal image, but it can be scaled. There is an issue though, that is, ResizeDrawable cannot be used (the image is not a true PNG, but a PNG with some additional information added to the end).

Adding to your list

Although it's great that we can do a number of different things to make our UI look good, this is just a messaging app. This means that we need to constantly add to the bottom when a new message comes in. Let's see how we can do this.

 The source code for this section can be found in Chapter8/ AddingMore.

Before we implement this, there is a simple aspect to consider. If you think of any messenger style application, the last message received is always at the bottom of the list. Moreover, lists are always generated from the top.

This will mean two things when it comes to the UI—either we have to constantly refresh the view to add the new message (this will mean that the view reverts to the top and we have to physically move the view to the bottom, which is not a good plan as far as the user is concerned), or we come up with some form of a cunning method.

In reality, we don't need to do anything because ListView comes with a method called ScrollTo. This allows the view to scroll to the position we want (Center, End, or Start).

Simulating to add a message

To simulate the addition of a new message, we first need to add a button that says Add. The simplest way to do this is to have the main page become a NavigationPage and add a ToolbarItem to it, as shown in the following code:

```
this.ToolbarItems.Add(new ToolbarItem(){ Text = "Add", Command = new
Command(o => AddAnotherItem()) });
```

The second change required is to change List<Message> to ObservableCollection<Message>. An ObservableCollection is similar to List, except that ObservableCollection implements INotifyCollectionChanged, which ItemSource is bound to. LINQ also deals with ObservableCollection differently, so the sorting based on time needs to be altered.

One thing that may strike you is the second parameter in `ToolbarItem; Command = new Command(o=>AddAnotherItem())`. All this will do is act as a `Clicked` event on `ToolbarItem`, but it does not use the standard `object sender, EventArgs e`, instead it allows you to send whatever parameters you want via the `CommandParameter` property.

The `AddAnotherItem` method is a very simple affair. Take a look at the following code:

```
void AddAnotherItem()
{
  var moreLyrics = new List<string>
  {
    "Hey, hey we're the Monkees",
    "Power from the needle to the plastic, AM FM I feel so extatic,",
    "Peu dormi, vidé, et brimé - J'ai du dormir dans la gouttière -
j'ai eu un flash - Hou! Hou! Hou! Hou! - En quatre couleurs",
    "What'sa matta you, hey - Gotta no respect, whatta you think you
do - Why you looka so sad? - It's-a not so bad, it's-a nice-a place -
Ah, shaddap you face",
    "Amadeus, Amadeus, Oh Oh Oh, Amadeus",
    "Don't dream it, Be it",
    "Taumatawhakatangihangakoayauo-Tamateaturipukakapikimaungahoro-
Nukypokaiwhenuakitanatahu",
    "Always look on the brightside of life",
    "Tie my kangaroo down sport",
    "Waltzing Matilda, Waltzing Matilda, You'll come a Waltzing
Matilda with me",
    "Who are you?",
    "You're the one that I want, one that I want",
    "Hello shoes, I'm sorry I'm going to have to stand on you
again.... euw!",
    "Chalkdust!"
  };
  var rand = new Random();

  messageList.Add(new Message
  {
    id = Utils.NewID,
    parent_id = Utils.NewID,
    message = moreLyrics[rand.Next(0, moreLyrics.Count)],
    datestamp = DateTime.Now.AddDays((double)rand.Next(0, 10)),
    is_reply = rand.Next(0, 10) >= 5 ? true : false,
    has_attachments = rand.Next(0, 10) >= 5 ? true : false,
    attachment_id = Utils.NewID
```

```
    });

    listView.ScrollTo(messageList.Count - 1, ScrollToPosition.End,
true);
}
```

All we will do is create another `Message` object and add it to `messageList`. As this is an `ObservableCollection` though, the `INotifyCollectionChanged` interface does its magic and the view is updated, as shown in the following screenshot:

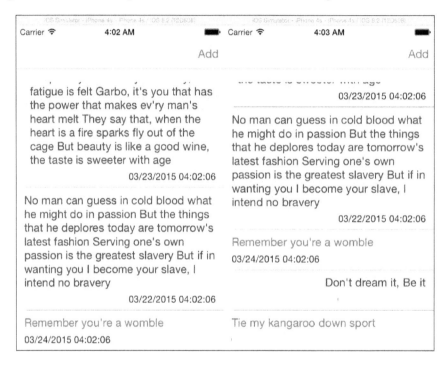

Summary

Binding is a very powerful tool when it comes to creating a user interface, but with such power comes a few problems. However, these are not problems that cannot be sorted with a bit of lateral thinking.

In the next chapter, we will look at how to use some of the more platform-specific parts of the application, how to connect to social media, and touch a bit on the app security.

9
Addressing the Issue

It would not be expected that Xamarin Forms would have access to the device-specific capabilities and facilities, such as the camera, audio, and GPS. Why would it? Xam. Forms is (as it has been said) a UI abstraction layer. The thing about any UI abstraction layer is that from time to time, it needs to render information from the platform to the user.

In this chapter, you will learn how to incorporate the system-specific address book in our app.

Addressing issues

There are two typical modes of operation for a messenger application:

- Use only the contacts on your device
- Use only the contacts on the service being used

The reasons for this are never clear, and with the exception of privacy concerns, there really should be no reason why you cannot have access to both.

As far as we're concerned, we have to consider that we have to use something very platform-specific in terms of the address book, and for social media, we need to use various web services as well as some form of an authenticator system.

Xamarin does have a number of components available, which will help with most aspects, and we can certainly make use of them. There are also the likes of `Xamarin.Forms.Labs` that will help. There is little point in reinventing the wheel, so I will show you how to use these components as well. `Xamarin.Forms.Labs` is an extension library designed to fill the gaps not supported by Xamarin Forms. It is free and available via NuGet.

Irrespective of the method used, we will still need some form of local storage with an identifier to tell the application the type of service that will be needed to send the message.

The address storage class

The address storage class is simple enough. Take a look at the following code:

```
public class AddressStorage
{
  [PrimaryKey]
  public string id { get; set; }

  public string name { get; set; }

  public string service_type { get; set; }

  public string internal_number { get; set; }

  public List<string> external_contact { get; set; }

  public DateTime last_used { get; set; }

  public bool inapp_invite_sent { get; set; }

  public DateTime date_invite_sent { get; set; }
}
```

Some of these properties won't always be filled with the last two being used to invite people to download the messenger app. We don't need an `invite_accepted` or `date_accepted` property because once they have been accepted, the `last_used` property will be set to a `DateTime` not equal to January 1, 1971 at midnight.

The `service_type` property will be Phone, Facebook, Twitter, Google+, or Messenger. These could equally be an `int` rather than a `string`, but for ease, keeping the service as a string will be used.

The issue with this storage class is that we have `List<string>`. This cannot be used with SQLite as it isn't supported. The work around is simple; we will create a secondary storage class to store the `external_contact` details. This will be accessed through an ID. To save time, we can keep `List<string>` in the storage class, but we can alter it, as shown in the following code:

```
public string external_contact_id { get; set;}

[Ignore]
```

```
public List<string> external_contact { get {return App.Self.DBManager.
GetListOfObjects<AddressExternalsContacts>("id", external_contact_
id);} }
```

The `AddressExternalContacts` class contains an ID and a string for the contact type. This is an example of a one-to-many relationship (`id` is linked to many feeder classes). Although this may give a small performance hit (remember that every call to the SQLite service requires some sort of processing time), it does mean that when we retrieve the `AddressStorage` class, the `external_contact` list will be filled at the same time.

Accessing the internal address book

The approach I will take here is to get a list of contacts, display it, and allow the user to select whom to add to the app. I'll deal with the native implementation first and then with how to use the `Xamarin.Mobile` component.

> The code for this section can be found in
> `Chapter 9/AddressBook`.

In either case, the following interface will be used:

```
public interface IAddress
{
   Dictionary<string, string>ContactDetails();
}
```

The first string is the name, and the second string is the contact number.

The native implementation

The main mobile platforms have their own methods to obtain data from their contacts system. This is fine because we don't need all the information held, just the name and phone number.

The native implementation for Android

The Android application will need the `ReadContacts` permission setting in the manifest, as shown in the following screenshot:

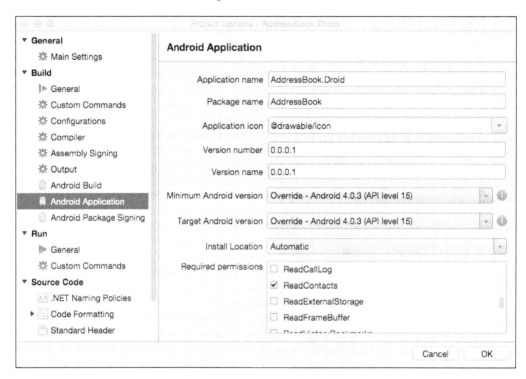

Android stores contacts in a database that is accessed through `ContactsContract.Contacts.ContentUri`; its contents are queried through `Cursor` (via the `ICursor` interface), `ManagedQuery`, or (as is the case here) through the `ContentResolver.Query` method. As we are outside of an activity, we have to specify how we will obtain the `Query` method. Take a look at the following code:

```
var resolver = Application.Context.ContentResolver;
var cursor = resolver.Query(addressUri, null, null, null, null);
```

Here, the parameter after `addressUri` is an interesting one. If we leave it as null, then in effect, we are saying that we want everything from the query that returns the equivalent of `Select * From AddressUri` on a database. We can also specify a list of what to return by creating a string array and passing it instead of null:

```
string[] query = { ContactsContract.Contacts.InterfaceConsts.Id,
ContactsContract.Contacts.InterfaceConsts.DisplayName };
```

```
var cursor = resolver.Query(addressUri, query, null, null, null);
```

To obtain the number, we next need to interrogate the returned data in `cursor`. Remember that this is a database table returned in a cursor, so we need to find the data stored in the `ContactsContract.CommonDataKinds.Phone.Number` column.

However, there is an added complication here in that the phone can store many different types of numbers (mobile, landline, secondary contacts, and so on). Additionally, we can have multiple contacts with the same name. The type of number (primary, secondary, and so on) is found by looking in the cryptically named `DATA2` column.

The cursor will hold a data table. This means that it may contain any number of entries, so we will need to iterate it to fill our `Dictionary` object. Thankfully, this is made simple because the table is stored in a `List` style object, so that the `Count` property can be used.

The issue with using any table is that in a database, tables are often linked, and this is certainly the case with Android. This necessitates the need for a secondary `Query` in the first `Query` loop with the `Id` from the primary search.

This is how the final code looks:

```
public Dictionary<string,string> ContactDetails()
{
  var addressUri = ContactsContract.Contacts.ContentUri;
  var contactDict = new Dictionary<string,string>();

  var resolver = Application.Context.ContentResolver;
  var cursor = resolver.Query(addressUri, null, null, null, null);


  if (cursor.Count !=0)
  {
    while (cursor.MoveToNext())
    {
      var name = cursor.GetString(cursor.
GetColumnIndex(ContactsContract.ContactsColumns.DisplayName));
      var id = cursor.GetString(cursor.GetColumnIndex(BaseColumns.
Id));
      if (cursor.GetInt(cursor.GetColumnIndex(ContactsContract.
ContactsColumns.HasPhoneNumber)) == 1)
      {
        var numberCursor = resolver.Query(ContactsContract.
CommonDataKinds.Phone.ContentUri, null, "CONTACT_ID = " + id, null,
null);
        while (numberCursor.MoveToNext())
        {
```

```
        var number = numberCursor.GetString(numberCursor.
GetColumnIndex(ContactsContract.CommonDataKinds.Phone.Number));
        contactDict.Add(name, number);
      }
    }
   }
  }

  return contactDict;
}
```

 To know what is held in the columns, refer to the Android documentation at http://developer.android.com/ reference/android/provider/ContactsContract. CommonDataKinds.Phone.html.

The native implementation for iOS

As with anything Apple, the user must first give permission for the contacts to be requested before they can be accessed. The best time to request the permission is within AppDelegate:

```
public bool IsAuthorised { get; private set;}
public static AppDelegate Self { get; private set;}
public override bool FinishedLaunching(UIApplication app, NSDictionary
options)
{
  AppDelegate.Self = this;

  IsAuthorised = RequestAccess;
  // rest of method
}

bool RequestAccess
{
  get
  {
    bool rv = false;
    NSError err;
    var addressBook = ABAddressBook.Create(out err);
    if (err != null || addressBook == null)
      ShowInstructions();
    else
    {
```

```
      if (ABAddressBook.GetAuthorizationStatus() !=
ABAuthorizationStatus.Authorized)
        {
          addressBook.RequestAccess(delegate(bool allowed, NSError
error)
          {
            if (allowed && error == null)
              rv = true;
            else
              ShowInstructions();
          });
        }
        else
          rv = true;
      }
    return rv;
  }
}

void ShowInstructions()
{
  var alert = new UIAlertView("Contacts access denied", "Please add
the permission in Settings->Privacy->AddressBook", null, "OK", null);
  alert.Show();
}
```

Once the permissions are granted, we can create the interface code. It is good practice to include the check for authorization:

```
public Dictionary<string,string> ContactDetails()
{
  if (!AppDelegate.Self.IsAuthorised)
    return new Dictionary<string,string>();
```

Obtaining the entries is quite simple from here. We will create an instance of the ABAddressBook object. This contains a number of ABRecord entries that can then be iterated with the final name and number coming in the form of a Dictionary style object:

```
public Dictionary<string, string> ContactDetails()
{
  var contactsDict = new Dictionary<string, string>();
  if (!AppDelegate.Self.IsAuthorised)
    return contactsDict;

  NSError err;
```

```
    var addressBook = ABAddressBook.Create(out err);
    if (err == null)
    {
      foreach (var item in addressBook)
      {
        if (item.Type == ABRecordType.Person)
        {
          var person = item as ABPerson;
          var name = string.Format("{0} {1}", person.FirstName, !string.
IsNullOrEmpty(person.LastName) ? person.LastName : "");
          Console.WriteLine("name = {0}", name);
          var phones = person.GetPhones(); // phones type is a
ABMultiValue<string>
          if (phones.Count != 0)
          {
            var number = phones[0].Value;
            if (!string.IsNullOrEmpty(number))
              contactsDict.Add(name, number);
            Console.WriteLine("{0} : {1}", name, number);
          }
        }
      }
    }

    return contactsDict;
}
```

Using the Xamarin mobile component

Xamarin recognized well before `Xamarin.Forms` that by having a common language with common facilities on all devices it should be possible to create a component that gives a common library to these features. Essentially, it's the same model as Xamarin forms, but for platform-specific features.

`Xamarin.Mobile` can be accessed through nuget or the component store. Either method will require the installation of the correct packages in the correct project.

Installing through the component store

In all the Xamarin applications, you will see a folder called **Components**, as shown in the following screenshot:

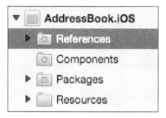

Let's proceed with the following steps:

1. First, click on the **Components** folder and look for the drop-down menu button on the right-hand side of the screen:

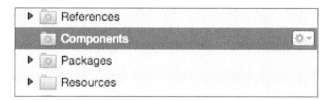

2. Then, click on the menu button on the right-hand side and a menu will appear:

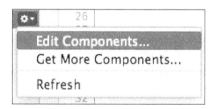

3. Clicking on **Get More Components...** will take you to the Xamarin component store. Here, type `Xamarin Mobile` in the search box. The result is shown in the following screenshot:

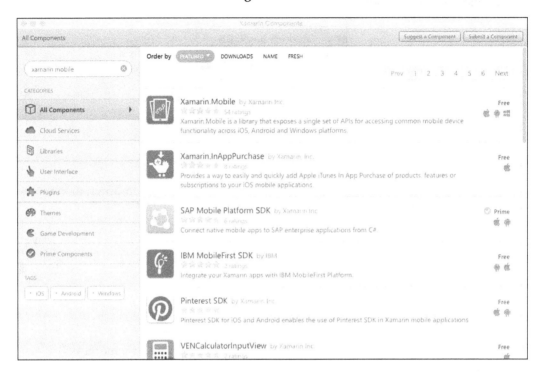

4. Double-click on the **Xamarin.Mobile** component to install.

Installing through NuGet

Installing through NuGet is a similar process to installing through the component store. It does have the advantage that if there is an update to a package, a message next to the **Packages** folder is displayed, and you can select it to update all the packages at once:

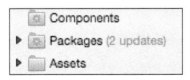

Similarly, to add from the components, highlight the **Packages** folder on the directory structure and select **Add Packages** from the menu. The nuget interface window will now appear. Type `xamarin mobile` in the search box:

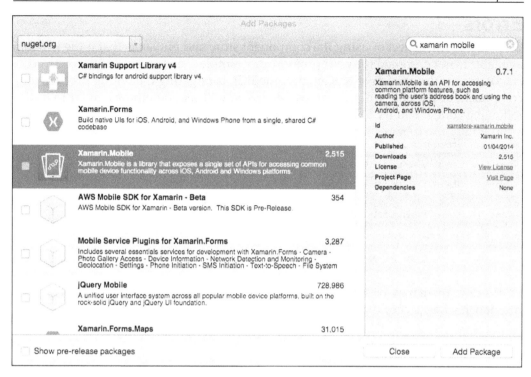

Should the installation go according to plan, you will see something similar to the following screenshot when you expand the **Packages** directory:

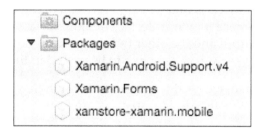

Mixing components and packages

Mixing components and packages with the same name should not be an issue, but it could be an issue on different platforms (for example, using Xamarin Mobile from NuGet for Android and Xamarin Mobile from the component store for iOS should not result in any issue).

On the same platform, you cannot install the package and component with the same name.

Errors

One very useful aspect of using the component store and NuGet is that if the version available is not designed for your project (for example, your version of `Xamarin.iOS` is too new for the version of NuGet, or if the PCL is targeting the wrong profile), the component or package will not get installed. You will see something similar to the following code if you try to grab from NuGet:

```
Adding xamstore-xamarin.mobile...
Installing 'xamstore-xamarin.mobile 0.7.1'.
Added file 'xamstore-xamarin.mobile.props' to folder 'xamstore-xamarin.mobile.0.7.1/build/monoandroid'.
Added file 'xamstore-xamarin.mobile.props' to folder 'xamstore-xamarin.mobile.0.7.1/build/monotouch'.
Added file 'README.txt' to folder 'xamstore-xamarin.mobile.0.7.1'.
Added file 'xamstore-xamarin.mobile.0.7.1.nupkg' to folder 'xamstore-xamarin.mobile.0.7.1'.
Successfully installed 'xamstore-xamarin.mobile 0.7.1'.
Adding 'xamstore-xamarin.mobile 0.7.1' to AddressBookComponent.iOS.
Could not install package 'xamstore-xamarin.mobile 0.7.1'. You are trying to install this package into
a project that targets 'Xamarin.iOS,Version=v1.0', but the package does not contain any assembly
references or content files that are compatible with that framework. For more
information, contact the package author.
```

In this case, there may be a preview release. To check for this, select the **Show preview packages** checkbox.

Xamarin Mobile

As with Xamarin Forms, Xamarin Mobile is an abstraction layer. It covers contacts, geolocation, and media picker facilities of the platform in a set of very handy classes. For our example here, we will use the `Xamarin.Contacts` namespace.

This contains a very handy class called `AddressBook`. We can utilize this class anywhere so that we can use it in the interface definition class. The only real difference between Android and the other two supported platforms is that Android needs an instance of `Application.Context` to be passed in the class.

As with the native version, we need to set the permission first. This is performed in `FinishedLoading`. We will also declare an extra property:

```
public static Xamarin.Contacts.AddressBook ContactList { get; private
set;}
```

The `IsAuthorised` variable is now set:

```
ContactList.RequestPermission().ContinueWith (t =>
{
  if (!t.Result)
  {
    IsAuthorised = false;
    var alert = new UIAlertView ("Permission denied", "User has denied
this app access to their contacts", null, "Close");
```

```
    alert.Show();
  }
  else
  {
    IsAuthorised = true;
  }
}, TaskScheduler.FromCurrentSynchronizationContext());
```

To obtain the `Dictionary` class to be passed back to the PCL, we will use the following code:

```
public Dictionary<string, string> ContactDetails()
{
  var contactsDict = new Dictionary<string, string>();
  if (!AppDelegate.Self.IsAuthorised)
    return contactsDict;

  var list = AppDelegate.ContactList.OrderByDescending(t =>
t.FirstName).ToList();

  if (list.Count != 0)
  {
    foreach (var item in list)
    {
      var name = string.Format("{0} {1}", item.FirstName, item.
LastName);
      var number = item.Phones.Select(t => t.Number).ToString();
      if (!contactsDict.ContainsKey(name) && !string.
IsNullOrEmpty(number))
        contactsDict.Add(name, number);
    }
  }

  return contactsDict;
}
```

For Android, the code can be handled completely in the interface class:

```
public static readonly AddressBook ContactsList = new AddressBook
(Application.Context) { PreferContactAggregation = true };
...
public Dictionary<string,string> ContactDetails()
{
  var contactDict = new Dictionary<string,string>();

  ContactsList.RequestPermission().ContinueWith (t =>
```

```
   {
     if (!t.Result)
     {
       // A UIAlert could be used here if you want
       // the user to see the alert on the device
       Console.WriteLine("Permission denied - check your manifest
permissions");
       return contactDict;
     }
     foreach (var contact in ContactsList.OrderByDescending(w=>w.
FirstName))
     {
       var name = string.Format("{0} {1}", contact.FirstName, !string.
IsNullOrEmpty(contact.LastName) ? contact.LastName : "");
       var number = contact.Phones.Select(w=>w.Number).ToString();
       if (!contactDict.ContainsKey(name) && !string.
IsNullOrEmpty(number))
         contactDict.Add(name, number);
     }
   }, TaskScheduler.FromCurrentSynchronizationContext());

   return contactDict;
}
```

Viewing the address book

We have completed what we need from the platforms. Now, we can move back to the PCL.

The first thing we need to do is grab the data from the platform and run a quick check to make sure that there is something there to display:

```
IAddress addresses = DependencyService.Get<IAddress>();
var addressList = addresses.ContactDetails();
if (addressList.Count == 0)
{
  await DisplayAlert("No contacts", "Your phone has no contacts stored
on it", "OK");
  return;
}
```

Remember that `addressList` is going to be `Dictionary<string,string>`; we therefore have two equal-sized lists of keys and values. Our UI will have the name at the top, with the number under it:

```
var myList = new ListView()
{
  ItemsSource = addressList,
  ItemTemplate = new DataTemplate(typeof(MyLayout))
};

public class MyLayout : ViewCell
{
  public MyLayout()
  {
    var label = new Label()
    {
      Text = "name",
      Font = Font.SystemFontOfSize(NamedSize.Default),
      TextColor = Color.Blue
    };
    label.SetBinding(Label.TextProperty, new Binding("."));

    var numberLabel = new Label()
    {
      Text = "number",
      Font = Font.SystemFontOfSize(NamedSize.Small),
      TextColor = Color.Black
    };
    numberLabel.SetBinding(Label.TextProperty, new Binding("."));

    View = new StackLayout()
    {
      Orientation = StackOrientation.Vertical,
      VerticalOptions = LayoutOptions.StartAndExpand,
      Padding = new Thickness(12, 8),
      Children = { label, numberLabel }
    };
  }
}
```

We have the basics here, but we have the problem of extracting the values of `Key` and `Value`. While the `MyLayout` class will have `BindingContext` from `ListView`, we can't access it directly because the constructor for the `BindingContext` class is null, so we cannot cast `BindingContext` to be `KeyValuePair<string,string>`.

Thankfully, we can obtain `KeyValuePair` with the `BindingContextChanged` event as follows:

```
this.BindingContextChanged += (object sender, EventArgs e) =>
{
  var item = (KeyValuePair<string,string>)BindingContext;
  label.SetBinding(Label.TextProperty, new Binding(item.Key));
  numberLabel.SetBinding(Label.TextProperty, new Binding(item.Value));
};
```

Unfortunately, viewing the data is not yet sorted.

The data is certainly there, but the binding is not correct, as shown in the following screenshot:

```
Binding: 'Trevor — Work' property not found on '[Trevor — Work, ▒▒▒▒▒4]', target property: 'Xamarin.Forms.Label.Text'
Binding: 'Trevor — Work' property not found on '[Trevor — Work, ▒▒▒▒▒4]', target property: 'Xamarin.Forms.Label.Text'
Binding: '▒▒▒▒▒▒' property not found on '[Trevor — Work, ▒▒▒▒▒]', target property: 'Xamarin.Forms.Label.Text'
Binding: '▒▒▒▒▒▒' property not found on '[Trevor — Work, ▒▒▒▒▒]', target property: 'Xamarin.Forms.Label.Text'
```

The issue is that we will use Key and Values directly, rather than key and value. Once we use the correct binding property, we will get the following output on the UI:

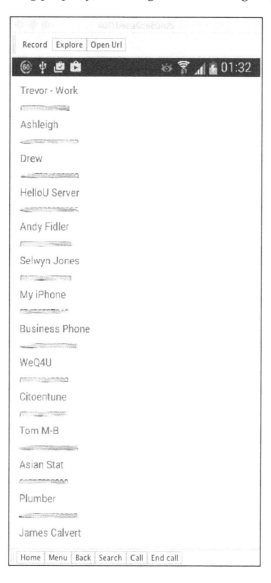

We have the first part done; the contacts from the device are now being displayed. What we next need to do is select the `ListView` item and store the name and phone number.

The `ItemSelected` event is assigned to `ListView`, as shown in the following code:

```
var myList = new ListView()
{
  ItemsSource = addressList,
  ItemTemplate = new DataTemplate(typeof(MyLayout))
};
myList.ItemSelected += MyList_ItemSelected;

void MyList_ItemSelected (object sender, SelectedItemChangedEventArgs
e)
{

}
```

The problem is that under normal circumstances, we could cast the sender to either `UITableCell` or an element in `ListView`. Xamarin Forms has neither, so how can we obtain the data from the cell?

There are two ways: via `WeakReference` or `BindingContext`.

What is WeakReference?

In any .NET application, memory is handled using something known as the **Garbage Collection (GC)**. While an object is *in scope*, the GC cannot touch this object, to free the memory used by it.

For example, take a look at the following code:

```
void myExample()
{
    var myList = new List<string>{"a","b", "c"};
    // do something to myList
    Console.WriteLine("third character = {0}", myList[2]);
}
```

Once `myExample` has been executed, what happens to `myList`? The answer is that it goes out of scope, and the GC frees the memory allocated for the object. This is known as **Strong Reference**.

A weak reference can be thought of as a time-limited rights access. At the end of the method, the GC still collects the object that has gone out of scope, but still allows the application access to the object for a time-limited period.

There are two types of weak references: short (the default) and long:

Short Weak Reference	Long Weak Reference
This is managed by the object and subject for the GC (as for any object).	This allows the object to be created, but the object state is unpredictable (you will need to test it before using).
This becomes `null` when reclaimed by the GC.	This reference is retained after the `Finalize` method is called. If the object type does not have the `Finalize` method, it is treated as a weak reference.

To use the weak reference in our code, we need to make a couple of simple changes.

1. We will first set up a class called `PhoneDetails`:

```
public class PhoneDetails
{
    public string Text {get;set;}
    public WeakReference<MyLayout> Layout {get;set;}
    public PhoneDetails(string text) { Text = text; }
}
```

2. `IAddress` will need to be altered to the following code:

```
Public interface IAddress
{
    Dictionary<string,Address> ContactDetails();
}
```

3. In `MyLayout`, the event needs altering, as shown in the following code:

```
this.BindingContextChanged += (object s, EventArgs e) =>
{
    var item = (KeyValuePair<string, Address>)BindingContext;
    label.SetBinding(Label.TextProperty, new Binding("Key"));
    numberLabel.SetBinding(Label.TextProperty, new Binding("Value.
Text"));
    item.Value.Layout = new WeakReference<MyLayout>(this);
}
```

4. Finally, the event handler for the item selected will be as follows:

```
void myList_ItemSelected(object s, SelectedItemEventArgs e)
{
    var kvp = (KeyValuePair<string,Address>)e.SelectedItem;
    var item = kvp.Value;
    MyLayout cell;
    item.Layout.TryGetTarget(out cell);
    // then do as we wish
}
```

As we now have an instance to the actual `ViewCell`, rather than purely the data, we can access the `View` properties themselves. If we have `View`, we can interrogate whatever is in there and obtain the values directly. This is great if we have a complex object in the cell.

Using BindingContext

As you should know by now, when we create anything in `ListView`, whatever `ItemsSource` provides `BindingContext` for `DataTemplate` gets created in `ItemsTemplate`. In our example, `BindingContext` becomes available in the raised event. The `ItemSelected` handler is also an event, so `BindingContext` in this cell is available to the handler.

Therefore, to obtain `Key` and `Value`, we just cast `e.SelectedItem` to be `KeyValuePair<string, string>` (the same as we did in the `MyLayout` class) and access the details directly.

Weak reference versus BindingContext

There really isn't a *versus* here. Both can be used, and it's really just a matter of preference at the end of the day. While we can use `WeakReference` and do what we need to the View once we have `ViewCell`, this does require a number of extra steps and may lead to confusion in the code (it shouldn't, but it may). As we also have to interrogate `View` for specific objects, we have to create the code for it. This also increases the size.

A `BindingContext` is useful because all the properties are accessible once the `BindingContext` that has been cast can be accessed. We are therefore dealing simply with the data object, not the UI layer around it. This makes the code much simpler to see; therefore, there is less potential for confusion. Having said that, it may not always be obvious what goes where.

In either case, once we have our data, we need to store it. The storage can be via the likes of SQLite (refer to *Chapter 5, Data, Generics, and Making Sense of Information*) or in the XML file (refer to *Chapter 11, A Portable Settings Class*). To demonstrate how the casting of `e.SelectedItem` works, a `DisplayAlert` has been put in place, as shown in the following screenshot:

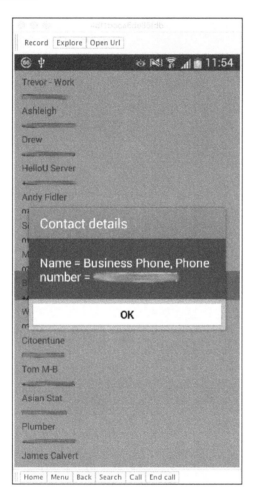

Summary

Using your own address book in the messenger app is not difficult. Certainly, gathering the information from the device is not difficult either. In this chapter, we looked at the different ways of how to access and use the address book.

In the next chapter, we will expand on this and look at how to implement maps, GPS, and push notifications.

10
This is the World Calling…

An application that sits will just do that. It has no idea about the outside world, no idea about anyone trying to contact them, and moreover, no idea about where it is. In the last chapter, we looked at how to use the address book. In this chapter, we will expand on this, use some of the hardware facilities, and communicate with the outside world via push notifications.

In this chapter, we will:

- Learn how to implement push notifications
- Incorporate maps and GPS with your app

Using GPS and push notifications

One useful feature of a messenger app would be to find people who are also using the application. In order to do this, we will need to talk from the PCL to the app and then send this up to the server.

The server then transmits a push notification to alert the user that there are so many users within the same area as you.

 The code for this section can be found in Chapter10/GPSPush.

Setting up the iOS provisioning profile

Neither iOS nor Android allows you to just use push notifications without a bit of set up. There is nothing difficult in setting up the provisioning profile for iOS; it's just a bit involved. Perform the following steps:

1. To start with, log in to your Apple developer and create a new application ID for this section:

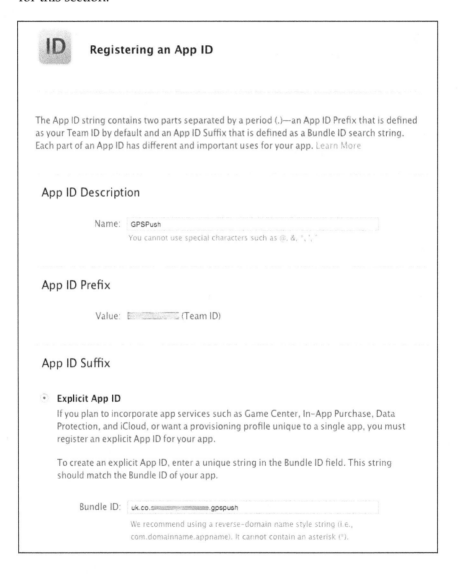

ID   **Registering an App ID**

The App ID string contains two parts separated by a period (.)—an App ID Prefix that is defined as your Team ID by default and an App ID Suffix that is defined as a Bundle ID search string. Each part of an App ID has different and important uses for your app. Learn More

App ID Description

Name: GPSPush

You cannot use special characters such as @, &, ', ', "

App ID Prefix

Value: ▨▨▨▨▨▨ (Team ID)

App ID Suffix

⦿ **Explicit App ID**

If you plan to incorporate app services such as Game Center, In-App Purchase, Data Protection, and iCloud, or want a provisioning profile unique to a single app, you must register an explicit App ID for your app.

To create an explicit App ID, enter a unique string in the Bundle ID field. This string should match the Bundle ID of your app.

Bundle ID: uk.co.▨▨▨▨▨▨▨.gpspush

We recommend using a reverse-domain name style string (i.e., com.domainname.appname). It cannot contain an asterisk (*).

2. Enter the description for **App ID** and **Bundle ID**. Do not use a wildcard ID for push notifications; it's not a good idea.

3. Once this has been filled, scroll down and select the **Push Notifications** option in services:

4. Next, you need to create a profile. Click on the provisioning profile option and then on the **+** button, as shown in the following screenshot:

5. Then, create a new development profile as follows:

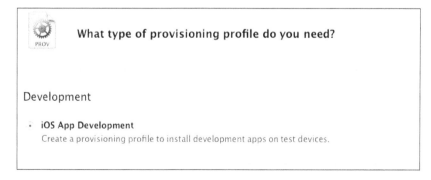

6. Now, select the **App ID** to associate with this profile.

7. Select the certificate to associate with this profile:

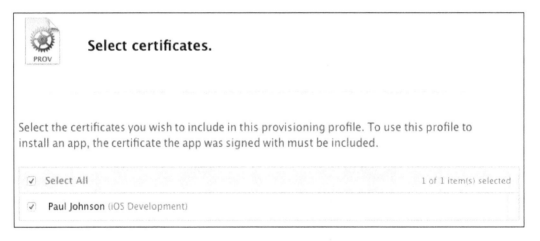

8. Now, select the devices allowed for this profile.

9. Finally, give the profile a name, generate it, and once downloaded, double-click on the file to install the profile:

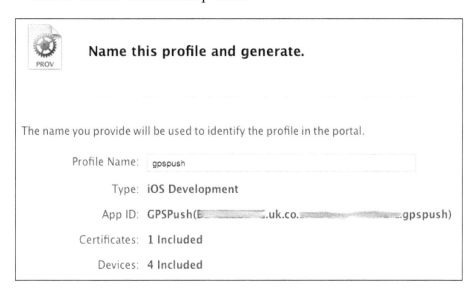

10. Now that this has been created, restart Xamarin Studio. Once done, reload the application and go to the **Options** menu:

11. Ensure that **iOS Bundle Signing** is set as follows:

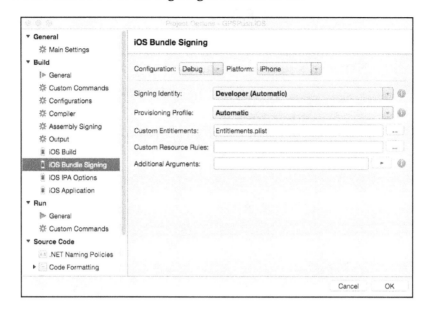

12. The last step is to select the **iOS Application** menu and set up the application name (this needs to be the same as the one you created for the provisioning profile):

13. Scroll down and select **Enable Background Modes** and **Remote notifications**:

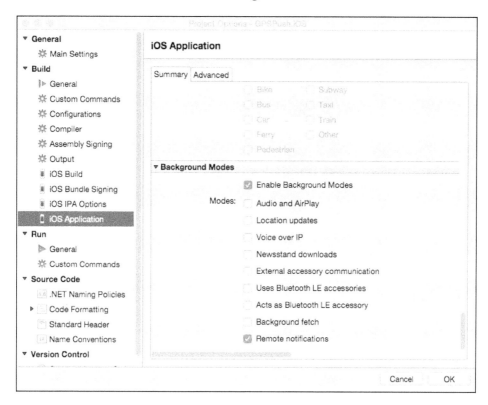

Setting up push notifications in the app

Push notifications are now almost complete. The final step is to create the code required by the application. This needs to be created in the `AppDelegate.cs` file.

In `FinishLaunching`, add the following code:

```
using (var settings = UIUserNotificationSettings.GetSettingsForTy
pes(UIUserNotificationType.Alert | UIUserNotificationType.Badge |
UIUserNotificationType.Sound, new NSSet()))
{
  UIApplication.SharedApplication.RegisterUserNotificationSettings(se
ttings);
}
UIApplication.SharedApplication.RegisterForRemoteNotifications();
```

This code alerts the application that it will need to register for remote notifications. As with the address book used earlier, the Apple rule states that the user has to give permission for notifications. This code will ask for the permission.

The preceding code is only the beginning. Remote notifications require another three overridden methods:

- `RegisterForRemoteNotification`
- `FailedToRegisterForRemoteNotification`
- `ReceivedRemoteNotification`

Next, you have to perform the actual listening, as shown in the following code:

```
public override void RegisteredForRemoteNotifications(UIApplication
application, NSData deviceToken)
{
  var trimmedDeviceToken = deviceToken.Description;
  if (!string.IsNullOrWhiteSpace(trimmedDeviceToken))
  {
    trimmedDeviceToken = trimmedDeviceToken.Trim('<');
    trimmedDeviceToken = trimmedDeviceToken.Trim('>');
  }

  DeviceToken = ftrackData.myPushToken = trimmedDeviceToken;
}

public override void FailedToRegisterForRemoteNotifications(UIApplicat
ion application, NSError error)
{
  Console.WriteLine("Failed to register for notifications : {0}",
error.ToString());
}

public override void ReceivedRemoteNotification(UIApplication
application, NSDictionary userInfo)
{
  NSObject objType = null, objId = null;
  var outObjType = userInfo.TryGetValue((NSString)"object_type", out
objType);
  var outObjId = userInfo.TryGetValue((NSString)"object_id", out
objId);

  if (outObjId && outObjType)
  {
    string objectid = (NSString)objId;
    string objecttype = (NSString)objType;
  }
}
```

The iOS application is now good to go for remote notifications. The service will still require the set up (refer to *Chapter 14, Bringing It All Together* for details on how to perform this).

Setting up Android for push notifications

As with iOS, setting up notifications requires setting it up on the Android console website and setting up the application.

The website set up is easy enough. Perform the following steps:

1. Log in to your developer account and select to create a new project:

2. Select the newly created project and select the **APIs & Auth** option from the drop-down menu:

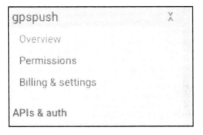

3. Select the cloud menu option by clicking on **Cloud messaging for Android**:

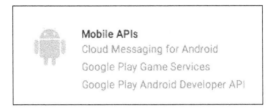

4. Then, select the **Enable API** button:

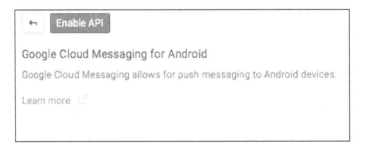

5. You will be presented with the following screen when push is set up with Google:

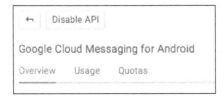

Setting up the Android push notifications in the app

For push notifications to work, the permissions have to be enabled first. Perform the following steps:

1. Select **Options** from the application context menu:

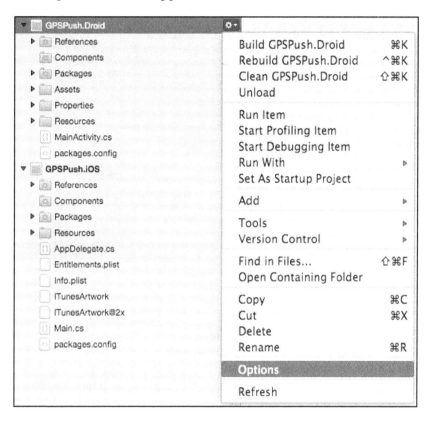

2. Next, the **GetAccounts**, **Internet**, and **WakeLock** permissions needs to be selected:

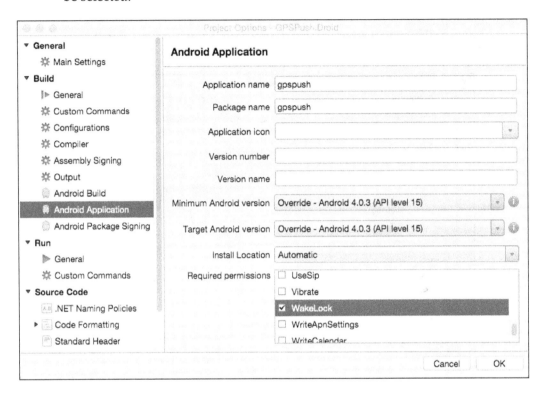

The problem now is that despite the permission being set, working with push notifications requires additional permissions, a broadcast receiver (this listens for broadcasts from a push server), `IntentService`, and the code handler itself.

Additional permissions

Inside the `Properties/AndroidManifest.xml` file, you will need to add the following permissions, as shown in the following code:

```
<uses-permission android:name="com.google.android.c2dm.permission.
RECEIVE" />
<uses-permission android:name="@PACKAGE_NAME@.permission.C2D_MESSAGE"
/>
```

These will need to be entered manually as they are not available via the standard UI permission settings window.

The broadcast receiver

This is a special piece of code that enables the app to listen for information from the Google Cloud Message service. The information comes as an Intent.

When we set up the receiver, we also have to set up filters to receive, register, and retry when notifications fail. We can also set up a filter to listen for notifications when the app is closed. Perform the following steps:

1. To create the file, from the project drop-down menu, select the **Add** menu item and then the **New File...** option:

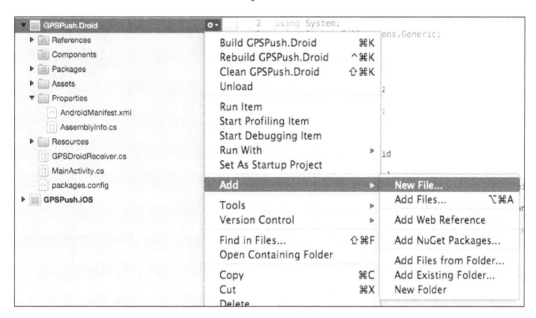

2. A new file window will appear. Select the **Broadcast Receiver** option and give the file a name, as shown in the following screenshot:

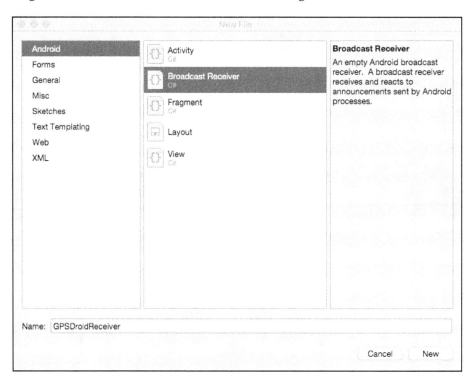

3. We now need to add the filters and complete the receiver as follows:

```
namespace GPSPush.Droid
{
    [BroadcastReceiver(Permission = "com.google.android.c2dm.
permission.SEND")]
    [IntentFilter(new string[]{"com.google.android.c2dm.intent.
RECEIVE"}, Categories = new string[]{"@PACKAGE_NAME@"})]
    [IntentFilter(new string[]{"com.google.android.c2dm.intent.
REGISTRATION"}, Categories = new string[]{"@PACKAGE_NAME@"})]
    [IntentFilter(new string[]{"com.google.android.gcm.intent.
RETRY"}, Categories = new string[]{"@PACKAGE_NAME@"})]
    [IntentFilter(new string[]{Android.Content.Intent.
ActionBootCompleted})]
    public class GPSDroidReceiver : BroadcastReceiver
    {
```

4. If we use `ActionBootCompleted` `IntentFilter`, the `ReceiveBootCompleted` permission will also need to be set in the same way as the other permissions are set.

5. We need only one method in `BroadcastReceiver` — `public override void OnReceive(Context context, Intent intent):`

```
public override void OnReceive(Context context, Intent intent)
{
    GPSDroidService.RunIntentInService(context, intent);
    SetResult(Result.Ok, null, null);
}
```

6. The application is now set to listen. To get it to perform something, **Service** needs to be created.

The Android service

We need to create a new file to deal with the code. The simplest way is to create a new `Activity` file and locate the following line:

```
[Activity(Label = "GPSDroidService")]
```

Then, replace it with the following line:

```
[Service]
```

We also need to not inherit `Activity`, but inherit `IntentService`.

It is important to ensure thread safety (we can have multiple messages delivered at any point, which may mean that the handler code may not have completed before a new call is made). This is achieved using lock. For the service, the lock is needed if the application is being woken up from the broadcast receiver.

Outside the lock, we can acquire `wakeLock`, set an intent, and start the service. The complete code looks similar to the following code:

```
[Service]
public class GPSDroidService : IntentService
{
    static PowerManager.WakeLock wakeLock;
    static object LOCK = new object();

    static void RunIntentInService(Context context, Intent intent)
    {
        lock(LOCK)
        {
            if (wakeLock == null)
            {
                var pm = PowerManager.FromContext(context);
```

```
            wakeLock = pm.NewWakeLock(WakeLockFlags.Partial, "Woken
    lock");
        }
    }

    wakeLock.Acquire();
    intent.SetClass(context, typeof(GPSDroidService));
    context.StartService(intent);
}
```

The next stage in the service is to handle the intent action code sent by the broadcast receiver. This is not the data, but the action.

There are three actions that must be handled: `Register`, `Unregister`, and `Receive`.

The Register action

This action registers the application sender with the Google Cloud messaging system and is performed by sending an intent. The intent requires two parameters: app and sender. The app is known as `PendingIntent`. It allows the Google services framework to obtain information from the app for registration. The sender is a comma-separated string that holds the sender IDs and sends the messages to the app. The IDs can be found on the Android developers console.

The Unregister action

This is the opposite of the `Register` action.

Listening for a return

When the action is used, a return value will come back from the GCM, as shown in the following table:

Error code	What it means
ACCOUNT_MISSING	This specifies that no Google account is held on this device
AUTHENTICATION_FAILED	This denotes that the password or e-mail address used is incorrect or invalid
INVALID_PARAMETERS	This specifies that you have made a request to the server that has not been recognized, or the parameters expected are incorrect
INVALID_SENDER	This denotes that the ID sent was incorrect
PHONE_REGISTRATION_ERROR	This specifies that the phone does not support GCM
SERVICE_NOT_AVAILABLE	This denotes that the server gave an error, or the device doesn't understand the data sent back to it

Receive

This is the actual data and is also a string.

Handling the actions in code

This is handled in the service as part of the overridden `OnHandleIntent` method, as shown in the following code:

```
protected override void OnHandleIntent(Intent intent)
{
  try
  {
    var context = ApplicationContext;
    var action = intent.Action;

    switch(action)
    {
      case "com.google.android.c2dm.intent.REGISTRATION":
      var senders = "MySenderID";
      var regIntent = new Intent("com.google.android.c2dm.intent.
REGISTER");
      regIntent.SetPackage("com.google.android.gsf");
      regIntent.PutExtra("app", PendingIntent.GetBroadcast(context, 0,
new Intent(), 0));
      regIntent.PutExtra("sender", senders);
      context.StartService(regIntent);
      break;
      case "com.google.android.c2dm.UNREGISTER":
      var unregIntent = new Intent("com.google.android.c2dm.intent.
UNREGISTER");
      unregIntent.PutExtra("app", PendingIntent.GetBroadcast(context,
0, new Intent(), 0));
      context.StartService(regIntent);
      break;
      case "com.google.android.c2dm.intent.RECEIVE":
      // do something with the string here
      break;
    }
  }
  finally
  {
    lock(LOCK)
    {
```

```
      if (wakeLock != null)
        wakeLock.Release();
    }
  }
}
```

Handling the messages

The problem we have with the likes of push notifications is that the PCL is totally unaware of them. They are purely handled on the platform. We can certainly pass information to the PCL, but how do we get the PCL to react?

The simplest way to do this is to broadcast an event from the platform code and have the PCL listen to it. The event itself has to be created in the PCL as follows:

```
namespace GPSPush
{
  public class ChangedEventArgs : EventArgs
  {
    public ChangedEventArgs(string name="", string id = "")
    {
      ModuleName = name;
      Id = id;
    }

    public readonly string ModuleName;
    public readonly string Id;
  }

  public class ChangedEvent
  {
    public event ChangeHandler Change;

    public delegate void ChangeHandler(object s,ChangedEventArgs ea);

    protected void OnChange(object s, ChangedEventArgs e)
    {
      if (Change != null)
        Change(s, e);
    }

    public void BroadcastIt(string message, string id)
    {
      if (!string.IsNullOrEmpty(message) && !string.IsNullOrEmpty(id))
```

```
        {
            var info = new ChangedEventArgs(message, id);
            OnChange(this, info);
        }
      }
    }
  }
}
```

We also need a static variable that allows you to access the `BroadcastIt` method. This should be created in the method that contains the start code, as shown in the following code:

```
public class App : Application
{
  public static App Self { get; private set;}

  public ChangedEvent ChangedClass { get; set; }

  public App()
  {
    App.Self = this;
    ChangedClass = new ChangedEvent();
```

In the platform code, we need to broadcast the message. For example, the Android code will be as follows:

```
public class App : Application
{
  public static App Self { get; private set;}

  public ChangedEvent ChangedClass { get; set; }

  public App()
  {
    App.Self = this;
    ChangedClass = new ChangedEvent();
```

In the PCL, we need a handler for the event. However, let's pause for a moment. As you look at the broadcast, the question why we're not passing the object to the PCL needs to be asked.

The answer is that the broadcast can be for anything, so we could have a tiny object (plain text) or an image, sound clip, or pretty much anything. If we pass `eventname` and `eventid`, the PCL can intercept this event and download the object. If we have a listener in the UI pages, we can also issue a redraw, so the UI is refreshed at the same time.

What about GPS and maps?

In Xamarin Forms, maps are supported via an additional NuGet package, but only as a subset of the full mapping facility of the native platform. On the other hand, GPS isn't supported at all because it is a platform-specific facility. To obtain this data, we need to grab the position from the device. As with anything where we have to obtain data from the device, we will construct an interface to obtain the data:

```
public interface IGPSData
{
    double[] GetLatLongData();
}
```

Then, as before, we will implement this natively.

Why bother?

This is a good point. We already have the event system set up—why not just use this? We could always have geodata and send this back to the PCL in the `id` field as a comma-separated value. Then, in the PCL, use `string.Split` to obtain the geolocation coordinates. As the change of location generates an event, we will actually have a simple and effective way to gather the data; add the event to the location change event, and this should work.

Adding the geolocation events to the code

Geolocation is handled without any further libraries natively on each platform. Android will need the `AccessCoarseLocation` and `AccessFineLocation` permissions setting. iOS needs the following code added to the `info.plist` file:

```
<key>NSLocationAlwaysUsageDescription</key>
<string>Can we use your location</string>
<key>NSLocationWhenInUseUsageDescription</key>
<string>We are using your location</string>
```

Adding the geolocation events to Android

Android relies on `LocationManager`, `LocationProvider`, and `ILocationListener`. This will need to be created in `Activity`. As we will use very few facilities from the native platform, we should place this in the `MainActivity` code.

To initialize `LocationManager`, we will create a class-wide variable and then instantiate this in `MainActivity`:

```
using Android.Locations;
public class MainActivity : global::Xamarin.Forms.Platform.Android.
FormsApplicationActivity
{
  LocationManager location;
  public override void OnCreate(Bundle bundle)
  {
    location = GetSystemService(Context.LocationService) as
LocationManager;
```

To obtain the location updates, we need to implement the `OnResume` method:

```
protected override void OnResume()
{
  base.OnResume();

  var provider = LocationManager.GpsProvider;
  if (location.IsProviderEnabled(provider))
    location.RequestLocationUpdates(provider, 2000, 1, this);
}
```

`RequestLocationUpdates` uses the (`provider`, `minTime`, `minDistance`, and `ILocationListener`) format.

For the updates, we need to implement `ILocationListener`. Of all the methods `ILocationListener` provides, we're only interested in the `OnLocationChanged` method. Here, we just need to issue the event as follows:

```
public void OnLocationChanged(Location location)
{
  var loc = string.Format("{0},{1}", location.Longitude, location.
Latitude);
  App.Self.ChangedClass.BroadcastIt("location", loc);
}
```

Adding the geolocation events to iOS

Once the additional dictionary entries have been added to the `info.plist` file, we can implement the location code in the application. To start with, this should be done in the `FinishedLaunching` method. Locations are handled with `CoreLocation`, as shown in the following code:

```
public partial class AppDelegate : global::Xamarin.Forms.Platform.iOS.
FormsApplicationDelegate
{
  private CLLocationManager locationManager;
```

This is instantiated in `FinshedLaunching`, as shown in the following code:

```
locationManager = new CLLocationManager
{
  DesiredAccuracy = CLLocation.AccuracyBest
};
```

Once `locationManager` has been instantiated, we can start to monitor updates. Then, we need to handle `Failed` and `LocationsUpdated`:

```
locationManager.Failed += (object sender, NSErrorEventArgs e) =>
{
  var alert = new UIAlertView{ Title = "Location manager failed",
Message = "The location updater has failed" }.Show();
  locationManager.StopMonitoring();
};


locationManager.LocationsUpdated += (object sender,
CLLocationsUpdatedEventArgs e) =>
{
  var newloc = string.Format("{0},{1}", e.Locations[0].Coordinate.
Longitude, e.Locations[0].Coordinate.Latitude);
  App.Self.ChangedClass.BroadcastIt("location", newloc);
};
```

In the PCL

We need to make a small adjustment to the `App` code, as shown in the following code:

```
public double Longitude { get; private set;}
public double Latitude { get; private set;}
```

Also, we need to make a small adjustment in the `App()` method:

```
// we need give the co-ordinates an initial value
Longitude = 53.431;
Latitude = -2.956;

this.ChangedClass.Change += (object s, ChangedEventArgs ea) =>
{
  if (ea.ModuleName == "location")
  {
    var locdata = ea.Id.Split(',').ToArray();
    Latitude  = double.Parse(locdata[0]);
    Longitude = double.Parse(locdata[1]);
  }
};
```

We now have the data for our initial position. Until the application receives a position update, we will use the default location.

Creating the Xamarin Forms map

We need to start by installing the `Xamarin.Forms.Maps` package from NuGet. The maps package needs to be initialized in `MainActivity` (Android) and `FinishedLoading` (iOS) on Android:

```
global::Xamarin.FormsMaps.Init(this, bundle);
```

For iOS, use the following line:

```
global::Xamarin.FormsMaps.Init();
```

In the Android code, you will also need to obtain the Google Maps API v2 key and add it to the AndroidManifest.xml file as follows:

```
<meta-data android:name="com.google.android.apps.v2.API_KEY"
android:value="MY_API_KEY" />
```

Also, allow the following methods; they are required for the Maps package:

- `AccessLocationExtraCommands`
- `AccessMockLocation`
- `AccessNetworkState`
- `AccessWifiState`

Adding the map

The map is simple to add, as shown in the following code:

```
public class MapPage : ContentPage
{
  public MapPage()
  {
    var myMap = new Map(MapSpan.FromCenterAndRadius(new Position(App.
Self.Longitude, App.Self.Latitude), Distance.FromMiles(0.3)))
    {
      IsShowingUser = true,
      HeightRequest = 100,
      WidthRequest = 960,
      VerticalOptions = LayoutOptions.FillAndExpand
    };


    Content = new StackLayout
```

```
        {
            Spacing = 0,
            Children =
            {
                myMap
            }
        };
    }
}
```

When we run the code, we will see the following screenshot (taken on iPhone):

We have a problem though. The UI doesn't update. You can move around as much as you like, but it won't change, so how can we get the UI to update?

An answer to the preceding question is that we can broadcast an event that is listened for and updated to the UI. In the App method, we will create the event. This event is added to the location event, as shown in the following code:

```
ChangedClass.BroadcastIt("updated-location");
```

Then, add the following code to the MapPage method as follows:

```
App.Self.ChangedClass.Change += (object s, ChangedEventArgs ea) =>
{
  if (ea.ModuleName == "updated-location")
    myMap.MoveToRegion(MapSpan.FromCenterAndRadius(new Position(App.
Self.Longitude, App.Self.Latitude), Distance.FromMiles(0.3)));

};
```

Start the application, and after a few minutes, the initial view will change to wherever you are, as shown in the following screenshot:

Map types and pins

There are three types of maps that are available:

- Street (default)
- Satellite
- Hybrid (mix of the preceding two views)

To set a type, add `myMap.MapType = MapType.Hybrid` (for example) to the code. Pins are used to denote a location. To add one to our map, we will add the following code:

```
var myPin = new Pin
{
    Type = PinType.Place,
    Position = new Position(App.Self.Latitude, App.Self.Longitude),
    Label = "my pin",
    Address = "I am here"
};
myMap.Pins.Add(myPin);
```

Two caveats to be aware of

The two issues that can make the user interface unresponsive with the event system being used here are as follows:

1. If the event is being fired from the native platform too often, the page being generated will be created rapidly, causing a slow down and possible crash.
2. When the view is created, the event listener is also created. However, if we change the view to something else, this listener is still there and still responding. While the UI may not be updating, the event will be firing.

As the code stands, we can address both of these issues.

Updating the UI very often

If we set up a couple of dummy variables in `MapPage` to hold the current `Longitude` and `Latitude` and then when the event that is fired checks against them, we can test to see whether there has been any movement. If there has been no movement, we don't need to draw the map.

Deregistering the listener

The event is currently known as `anonymous event`; we're not actually creating a
method for the event. If we create a named method and change the view, we can
deregister this method and remove the listener.

With both of these changes, the code will look similar to the following code:

```
namespace GPSPush
{
  public class MapPage : ContentPage
  {
    double lon, lat;
    Map myMap;

    public MapPage()
    {
      this.ToolbarItems.Add(new ToolbarItem{ Text = "back", Command =
SendBackButtonPressed() });
      lon = App.Self.Longitude;
      lat = App.Self.Latitude;

      myMap = new Map(MapSpan.FromCenterAndRadius(new Position(App.
Self.Longitude, App.Self.Latitude), Distance.FromMiles(0.3)))
      {
        IsShowingUser = true,
        HeightRequest = 100,
        WidthRequest = 960,
        VerticalOptions = LayoutOptions.FillAndExpand
      };

      App.Self.ChangedClass.Change += HandleMapChanged;

      Content = new StackLayout
      {
        Spacing = 0,
        Children =
        {
          myMap
        }
      };
    }

    protected override bool OnBackButtonPressed()
    {
```

```
        App.Self.ChangedClass.Change -= HandleMapChanged;
        this.Navigation.PopAsync();
    }

    void HandleMapChanged(object s, ChangedEventArgs ea)
    {
        if (ea.ModuleName == "updated-location")
        {
            if (lon != App.Self.Longitude || lat != App.Self.Latitude)
            {
                myMap.MoveToRegion(MapSpan.FromCenterAndRadius(new
Position(App.Self.Longitude, App.Self.Latitude), Distance.
FromMiles(0.3)));
                lon = App.Self.Longitude;
                lat = App.Self.Latitude;
            }
        }
    }
}
```

Both problems are solved very easily.

Summary

As you have seen in this chapter, push notifications and maps are simple affairs to implement and understand. We looked at a method to send data to the PCL without using inversion of control and added value to our application with very little work. This is really the whole point of using Xamarin and Xamarin Forms; more value with very little work.

In the next chapter, we will take a look at how to implement user configuration settings.

11
A Portable Settings Class

All the mobile providers allow settings to be stored in an application with their own systems. There is nothing wrong with this, and it works well. The issue with any PCL-based application is that you need to write some form of wrapper around the storage code for entry and retrieval, which also means that you need to know how to use these storage systems.

In this chapter, we will examine:

- How the platforms store their settings
- How to construct an interface for these storage systems
- How to create a unified settings portable class

The native platform storage

Each platform has its own unique way of storing user data and settings. When using a native approach, it is typical for the device to store the individual application settings in the application bundle itself, rather than as a universal settings file. This is primarily not only for security, but also for usability.

Consider a scenario where a user has three messenger applications on their phone. Each of them will have a username and password setting. If there was a universal settings file, there would firstly be no way of knowing which username/password corresponded to which app, and secondly, the other two applications would potentially be able to intercept the incorrect password and use it for nefarious purposes.

The iOS native platform storage

iOS stores settings via a dictionary with the <key><value> format. Here, the type can be of the string, int, bool, or double base types. The data is stored in an app-specific .plist file and may look similar to the following code:

```
<dict>
  <key>Type</key>
  <string>UISlider</string>
  <key>DefaultValue</key>
  <int>10</int>
  <key>MinValue</key>
  <int>0</int>
  <key>MaxValue</key>
  <int>10</int>
  <key>IsEnabled</key>
  <bool>false</bool>
</dict>
```

There is nothing difficult in reading from the plist file:

```
var readValue = NSUserDefaults.StandardDefaults.
IntForKey("DefaultValue");
```

Writing back to the plist file is performed using the following line of code:

```
NSUserDefaults.StandardDefaults["DefaultValue"] = 3;
```

Alternatively, the NSNotificationCenter class can be used. This can be considered as an internal broadcast system that informs the app when something has been changed via the NSUserDefaultDidChangeNotification notification. The advantage of using the notification center over setting NSUserDefaults is that any NSObject class can be set to act as the notification observer.

 The examples of how to use the internal settings can be found in the Chapter 11 source download archive.

The Android native platform storage

Android uses the Android.Content namespace. The preferences file can have a number of permissions set on it when it is created:

- Append: This specifies that if the file already exists, you can carry on adding it to the end of the file

- **Multiprocess**: This denotes that the provider can be launched in the process of the component that started it

- **Private**: This is the default setting and specifies that the file can only be accessed by the application

- **WorldReadable**: This denotes that any application can read the file, but cannot write to it

- **WorldWritable**: This specifies that any application can write to the file

The permissions can also be mixed with the following line of code:

```
prefs = GetSharedPreferences("MyPrefs", FileCreationMode.WorldReadable
| FileCreationMode.WorldWritable);
```

In its simplest form, the following code shows you how the system works:

```
public enum SettingType
{
  Bool,
  Float,
  Int,
  Long,
  String,
  StringSet
}

[Activity(Label = "droidsettings", MainLauncher = true, Icon =
"@drawable/icon")]
public class MainActivity : Activity
{
  ISharedPreferences prefs;

  protected override void OnCreate(Bundle bundle)
  {
    base.OnCreate(bundle);

    prefs = GetSharedPreferences("MyPrefs", FileCreationMode.Private);

    SaveSetting("SliderMinValue", 5, SettingType.Int);
    SaveSetting("SliderName", "MyName", SettingType.String);
    SaveSetting("SomeNumber", (float)Math.PI, SettingType.Float);

    Console.WriteLine("SomeNumber * 3 = {0}", LoadSetting<float>("Some
Number", SettingType.Float) * 3);
  }
```

```
   protected void SaveSetting<T>(string name, T value, SettingType
type)
   {
     var editor = prefs.Edit();
     editor.Remove(name);
     switch ((int)type)
     {
       case 0:
       editor.PutBoolean(name, (bool)(object)value);
       break;
       case 1:
       editor.PutFloat(name, (float)(object)value);
       break;
       case 2:
       editor.PutInt(name, (int)(object)value);
       break;
       case 3:
       editor.PutLong(name, (long)(object)value);
       break;
       case 4:
       editor.PutString(name, (string)(object)value);
       break;
     }
     editor.Commit();
   }

   protected void SaveSetting(string name, List<string>values)
   {
     var editor = prefs.Edit();
     editor.Remove(name);
     editor.PutStringSet(name, values);
     editor.Commit();
   }

   protected T LoadSetting<T>(string name, SettingType type)
   {
     var nv = new object();
     switch ((int)type)
     {
       case 0:
       nv = prefs.GetBoolean(name, false);
       break;
       case 1:
       nv = prefs.GetFloat(name, 0);
```

```
      break;
      case 2:
      nv = prefs.GetInt(name, 0);
      break;
      case 3:
      nv = prefs.GetLong(name, 0);
      break;
      case 4:
      nv = prefs.GetString(name, "");
      break;
    }
    return (T)nv;
}

protected List<string>LoadSetting(string name)
{
  var strList = prefs.GetStringSet(name, null);
  var list = new List<string>();
  if (strList == null)
    return list;
  if (strList.Count == 0)
    return list;
  foreach (var i in strList)
  list.Add(i);

  return list;
}
```

The Windows Phone native platform storage

Last on the list, before we examine how we can construct something that can be used from the PCL that accesses the system preferences method is how Windows Phone performs this task. Although Windows Phone is not supported by Xamarin directly, for this part, it is important that we have an understanding of how the Windows Phone device stores user settings.

Windows Phone uses a key/value dictionary system. This is fairly similar to the one used on iOS and is accessed via IsolatedStorage. The class has four key methods to handle the settings:

- Add: This method adds an entry to the dictionary
- Contains: This method checks whether the dictionary contains the key
- Remove: This method does what it says on the tin
- Save: This method saves the settings to IsolatedStorageSettings

The `settings` dictionary is of the `<string, object>`form, so it is able to store whatever object you wish to send to the `settings` dictionary. In its simplest form, the settings API can be used as follows:

```
var settings = IsolatedStorageSettings.ApplicationSettings;
if (settings.Contains("myData"))
settings.Add("myData", 1234);
else
setings["myData"] = 1234;
settings.Save();

int readout = -1;
if (settings.TryGetValue("myData", out readout))
{
    Console.WriteLine("myData = {0}", settings["myData"] as int);
    settings.Remove("myData"); // save not required
}
```

Data persistence

Data persistence in an application means that should the app crash, hang, or totally mess itself up somehow, then the data will not be lost, a restart or reinstall should sort the issue.

Data persistence does not extend to removal and reinstallation. In this case, all the application settings will be lost.

Constructing a persistent and cross-platform settings system

Let's consider what we know from our previous examples:

- All the system settings use a key and value system to store the names
- The methods of entry and retrieval are different
- Android cannot store all types of primitive (doubles are excluded), but it can store collections

From the PCL side, we need an interface to the main platform code:

```
public interface IUserSettings
{
    void SetSetting<T>(string name, T value);

    T GetSetting<T>(string name);
}
```

Unlike the example used with Android, we will not pass an enumeration as a second or third parameter.

After this, the platform implementations are required. The full source for this can be found in the `Chapter 11` source code archive. I'll demonstrate how the implementation works for Android. To emulate a real setting, I've created the settings file and added some dummy data.

Creating the initial data

To start with, it's a good idea to start with creating a singleton. This is a single point class. This class can act as a base for the storage of variables that may be used across the entire application.

For this example, we will see a very simple piece of code:

```
public class Settings
{
  public static Settings Singleton;
  public static ISharedPreferences Prefs {get;set;}

  public Settings()
  {
    Settings.Singleton = this;
  }
}
```

To access the `Prefs` variable, it is just a case of using `Settings.Prefs`. The data can then be inserted. Note that `GetSharedPrefs` is not in the singleton, but in the initial `OnCreate` method, as shown in the following code:

```
[Activity(Label = "Version1.Droid", Icon = "@drawable/icon",
MainLauncher = true, ConfigurationChanges = ConfigChanges.ScreenSize |
ConfigChanges.Orientation)]
public class MainActivity : global::Xamarin.Forms.Platform.Android.
FormsApplicationActivity
{
  protected override void OnCreate(Bundle bundle)
  {
    base.OnCreate(bundle);

    var l = new Settings();

    Settings.Prefs = GetSharedPreferences("MyPrefs", FileCreationMode.
Private);
```

```
        CreateDummyData();

        global::Xamarin.Forms.Forms.Init(this, bundle);

        LoadApplication(new App());
    }

    void CreateDummyData()
    {
      var editor = Settings.Prefs.Edit();
      editor.Remove("DateToday");
      editor.PutString("DateToday", DateTime.Now.ToShortDateString());
      editor.PutFloat("YouTube", (float)Math.PI);
      editor.PutInt("MyAge", 43);
      editor.PutString("Company","FarmApps Pty Ltd");
    }
  }
}
```

Creating the implementation of the IUserSettings interface – Android

The following section shows you how to implement the UserSettings interface for Android. It is not quite the same for iOS and Windows Phone, but it is still not too bad.

Saving preferences

As described back in *Chapter 4, Making Your Application Portable*, obtaining data from the interface in the platform projects is done through Dependency Injection. Despite not being needed since .NET 4.0, the default constructor for any class is not required, whereas for Xamarin.Forms applications, the default constructor has to be present for injection to work. The implementation also has to be set as being one for injection.

In the following example, I've created the class and had Xamarin.Studio insert the implementations:

```
    [assembly: Xamarin.Forms.Dependency(typeof(SettingsClass))]
    namespace Version1.Droid
    {
      public class SettingsClass: Java.Lang.Object, IUserSettings
      {
        public SettingsClass()
        {
        }
```

```
#region IUserSettings implementation

public void SetSetting<T>(string name, T value)
{
    throw new NotImplementedException();
}

public T GetSetting<T>(string name)
{
    throw new NotImplementedException();
}

#endregion
    }
}
```

The handy aspect here is that the code will now build, although accessing the methods will result in the app giving a NotImplementedException error prior to crashing.

This is because we aren't passing a real type to the implementation and need a primitive to pass to the settings. Thankfully, it is possible to use typeof(T). ToString() == typeof(...).ToString() and that to insert the correct type, as shown in the following code:

```
public void SetSetting<T>(string name, T value)
{
    var editor = Settings.Prefs.Edit();
    editor.Remove(name);
    if (typeof(T).ToString() == typeof(string).ToString())
        editor.PutString(name, (string)(object)value);
    if (typeof(T).ToString() == typeof(bool).ToString())
        editor.PutBoolean(name, (bool)(object)value);
    if (typeof(T).ToString() == typeof(long).ToString())
        editor.PutLong(name, (long)(object)value);
    if (typeof(T).ToString() == typeof(float).ToString() || typeof(T).
ToString() == typeof(double).ToString())
    {
        if (typeof(T).ToString() == typeof(double).ToString())
            editor.PutFloat(name, (float)(double)(object)value);
        else
            editor.PutFloat(name, (float)(object)value);
    }
    if (typeof(T).ToString() == typeof(int).ToString())
        editor.PutInt(name, (int)(object)value);
    editor.Commit();
}
```

Loading preferences

Similar to the save preferences, using `typeof(T)` quickly allows the correct preference to be retrieved, as shown in the following code:

```
public T GetSetting<T>(string name)
{
  var nv = new object();
  if (typeof(T).ToString() == typeof(bool).ToString())
    nv = Settings.Prefs.GetBoolean(name, false);
  if (typeof(T).ToString() == typeof(float).ToString() || typeof(T).
ToString() == typeof(double).ToString())
  {
    if (typeof(T).ToString() == typeof(double).ToString())
      nv = Convert.ToDouble(Settings.Prefs.GetFloat(name, 0));
    else
      nv = Settings.Prefs.GetFloat(name, 0);
  }            if (typeof(T).ToString() == typeof(int).ToString())
  nv = Settings.Prefs.GetInt(name, 0);
  if (typeof(T).ToString() == typeof(long).ToString())
    nv = Settings.Prefs.GetLong(name, 0);
  if (typeof(T).ToString() == typeof(string).ToString())
    nv = Settings.Prefs.GetString(name, "");

  return (T)nv;
}
```

Creating the implementation of the IUserSettings interface – iOS

As described earlier in this chapter, iOS uses the `<key><value>` dictionary style mechanism to store the settings. This makes life simple for the `SetSetting` code. However, the issue here is that the value is not a .NET value, but `NSObject`, so it is the same way as for Android; we need to do a bit of work before we can insert the following code:

```
public void SetSetting<T>(string name, T value)
{
  dynamic insertValue = null;
  if (typeof(T).ToString() == typeof(string).ToString())
    insertValue = (NSString)(string)(object)value;
  if (typeof(T).ToString() == typeof(bool).ToString())
    insertValue = (NSNumber)(bool)(object)value;
  if (typeof(T).ToString() == typeof(long).ToString())
```

```
      insertValue = (NSNumber)(long)(object)value;
    if (typeof(T).ToString() == typeof(float).ToString() || typeof(T).
  ToString() == typeof(double).ToString())
    {
      if (typeof(T).ToString() == typeof(double).ToString())
        insertValue = (NSNumber)(double)(object)value;
      else
        insertValue = (NSNumber)(float)(object)value;
    }
    if (typeof(T).ToString() == typeof(int).ToString())
      insertValue = (NSNumber)(int)(object)value;
    NSUserDefaults.StandardUserDefaults[name] = insertValue;
  }
```

You may have seen here that I've used the `dynamic` type. The `dynamic` type is a bit of an oddball because it can adopt any type you wish to throw at it. To use it, the `Microsoft.CSharp` reference will need to be added to the iOS project.

It is quite handy to use in this instance because we will need to pass `StandardUserDefaults` and `NSObject`, and rather than having multiple copies of this with each of a different value, we can set `dynamic` to be whatever the type needs to be; unbox it, and then pass this because it will already be `NSObject`.

However, the `GetSetting` method will be more of an issue because we will return `T` instead of a definite type, and we will also have to deal with the values not being of a .NET type, rather than the likes of `NSNumber` or `NSString`.

Thankfully, the task of returning a value is not that difficult, as shown in the following code snippet:

```
public T GetSetting<T>(string name)
{
  var value = NSUserDefaults.StandardUserDefaults[name];
  dynamic returnValue = null;
  if (typeof(T).ToString() == typeof(string).ToString())
    returnValue = value.ToString();
  else
  {
    var val = (NSNumber)value;
    if (typeof(T).ToString() == typeof(bool).ToString())
      returnValue = val.BoolValue;
    if (typeof(T).ToString() == typeof(long).ToString())
      returnValue = val.LongValue;
    if (typeof(T).ToString() == typeof(float).ToString() || typeof(T).
  ToString() == typeof(double).ToString())
    {
```

```
      if (typeof(T).ToString() == typeof(double).ToString())
        returnValue = val.DoubleValue;
      else
        returnValue = val.FloatValue;
    }
    if (typeof(T).ToString() == typeof(int).ToString())
      returnValue = val.Int32Value;
  }
  return (T)returnValue;
}
```

The types that we have stored are either NSString or NSNumber. We separate the two again with dynamic to store the result. For NSNumbers, there are a number of very handy extension properties that do the conversion from the NSNumber values to .NET.

Creating the implementation of the IUserSettings interface – Windows Phone

Windows Phone works in .NET and uses a standard .NET dictionary to store the <key><value> pairs, so its implementation should also be straightforward, as shown in the following code:

```
public void SetSetting<T>(string name, T value)
{
  var settings = IsolatedStorageSettings.ApplicationSettings;
  if (!settings.Contains(name))
    settings.Add(name, value);
  else
    settings[name] = value;
  settings.Save();
}

public T GetSetting<T>(string name)
{
  var settings = IsolatedStorageSettings.ApplicationSettings;
  dynamic readout = null;
  if (settings.TryGetValue(name, out readout))
    return (T)readout;
  else
    return default(T);
}
```

Is there an alternative?

What we have here is three different implementations for three different platforms with the same interface name. This is fine and works, but what if we want something that works on all the platforms, but isn't restricted to the limited range that can be loaded and saved. Is this possible?

Yes, it is. It can be performed in one of two ways. The first is an XML-based solution, and the second is part of the SQLite database.

 The source code for both of the following section can be found in the accompanying source code file of this chapter.

The XML-based solution

In my first book, *Xamarin Mobile Application Development for iOS, Packt Publishing,* I mentioned a simple, yet effective XML-based solution (it's in *Chapter 13, User Preferences* if you want to check it out). The issue with anything XML-based is that it will read and write to and from the filesystem. This is not supported in the PCL part of the application, but it is on the platform side.

As with the examples covered here, we can access the settings through an interface, and with inversion of control, obtain the settings data and inject it into the application. The interface in the PCL will be the same as it has been in the previous examples: a single get and set method. The main differences being in the setup of the platform code.

The main interface code is similar for each platform (the following code is from the iOS version):

```
public void SetSetting<T>(string name, T value)
{
  if (typeof(T).ToString() == typeof(string).ToString())
    AppDelegate.Self.GetSetter.SetStringValue(name, Convert.
ToString(value));
  if (typeof(T).ToString() == typeof(double).ToString())
    AppDelegate.Self.GetSetter.SetDoubleValue(name, Convert.
ToDouble(value));
  if (typeof(T).ToString() == typeof(bool).ToString())
    AppDelegate.Self.GetSetter.SetBoolValue(name, Convert.
ToBoolean(value));
}

public T GetSetting<T>(string name)
```

```
    {
        dynamic result = null;
        if (typeof(T).ToString() == typeof(string).ToString())
            result = AppDelegate.Self.GetSetter.GetStringValue(name);
        if (typeof(T).ToString() == typeof(string).ToString())
            result = AppDelegate.Self.GetSetter.GetDoubleValue(name);
        if (typeof(T).ToString() == typeof(string).ToString())
            result = AppDelegate.Self.GetSetter.GetBoolValue(name);
        return result;
    }
```

This is the only code that will need to change between platforms to point to the correct singleton instance (for example, the Android version is called Settings.Singleton.GetSetter). The other required classes can be found in standard C#, so it can be copied between the projects.

The GetSet class

This class contains a number of simple methods that call the main UserData class, which in turn sets or gets data from the XML file.

An example of the GetSet method in the class looks similar to the following code:

```
    public void SetIntValue(string name, int val)
    {
        UserData.SetPropertyValue(this, name, val);
    }

    public int GetIntValue(string valToGet)
    {
        var rv = (int)UserData.GetPropertyValue(this, valToGet);
        return (int)rv;
    }
```

The UserData class

This class is the main engine to store and retrieve data from the XML file. The clever part of the class is shown in the following code:

```
    public static object GetPropertyValue(object data, string
    propertyName)
    {
        return data.GetType().GetProperties().SingleOrDefault(pi => pi.Name
    == propertyName).GetValue(data, null);
    }
```

```
public static void SetPropertyValue<T>(object data, string
propertyName, T value)
{
  data.GetType().GetProperties().SingleOrDefault(pi => pi.Name ==
propertyName).SetValue(data, value);
}
```

These two very small methods take `propertyNames` (the names used in the XML schema), assigns it to them or retrieves the values for them, and returns the value. If the names don't exist, the code will fail with an exception. This can be caught quickly with a `try`/`catch` construct.

The rest of the class is concerned with serializing or deserializing the data through another helper class.

The serializer class

The serializer class serializes or deserializes the data to the XML file as follows:

```
public static T XmlDeserializeObject<T>(string filePath)
{
  using (var sr = new StreamReader(filePath))
  {
    var xmlSer = new XmlSerializer(typeof(T));
    return (T)xmlSer.Deserialize(sr);
  }
}

public static void XmlSerializeObject<T>(T obj, string filePath)
{
  using (var sw = new StreamWriter(filePath))
  {
    var xmlSer = new XmlSerializer(typeof(T));
    xmlSer.Serialize(sw, obj);
  }
}
```

There is a great deal of code reuse going on here, but there is an inherent problem with using this system. Should the application crash while saving the file (remember that the file will only be open for a very small amount of time, so it's unlikely), the file will corrupt and become unusable. When the app fires up, the settings file will be there, but it will be completely empty, so trying to read from it will result in a null exception being thrown.

A simple solution to this is that when the app fires up and if the size of the settings file is 0 (it's empty), delete the file completely and let UserData create a new file. Finding the file size can be performed as follows:

```
var filesize = new FileInfo(filename).Length;
```

The SQLite solution

The SQLite solution is simply a table in the SQLite database (how to set up a helper class and use SQLite in the app is covered in *Chapter 6, A View to a Kill*). The only real caveat to using this method is that on Windows Phone, the SQLite package is installed from NuGet. The interface class will simply look similar to the following code:

```
public void SetSetting<T>(string name, T value)
{
    if (typeof(T).ToString() == typeof(string).ToString())
        AppDelegate.Self.DBManager.AddOrUpdateSettings(name, Convert.
ToString(value));
    if (typeof(T).ToString() == typeof(double).ToString())
        AppDelegate.Self.DBManager.AddOrUpdateSettings (name, Convert.
ToDouble(value));
    if (typeof(T).ToString() == typeof(bool).ToString())
        AppDelegate.Self.DBManager.AddOrUpdateSettings (name, Convert.
ToBoolean(value));
}

public T GetSetting<T>(string name)
{
    dynamic result = null;
    result = AppDelegate.Self.DBManager.GetSingleValue<Settings>(name);
    return result;
}
```

However, the issue here exists in the GetSingleObject method in the DBManager helper class. Although it is possible to search for a name in the table, it's not effective in terms of time (remember that all the calls to the SQLite database will have a performance hit). Therefore, if we box cleverly and have the parameter name as the same as the name we pass, we can use the following code:

```
public T GetSingleObject<T>(string name) where T:IIdentity, new()
{
    lock (dbLock)
    {
        using (var sqlCon = new SQLiteConnection(ConnectionString))
        {
```

```
        sqlCon.Execute(Constants.DBClauseSyncOff);
        string sql = string.Format("SELECT * FROM {0} WHERE
    {1}=\"{1}\"", GetName(typeof(T).ToString()), name);
        var data = sqlCon.Query<T>(sql) ToList();
        return data[0];
      }
    }
  }
```

In other words, we search the table for the name passed and return the value from this search.

The SQLite method is not as likely to become corrupt as the XML solution. It also allows the off-device backup, so should something go wrong, or if the user moves to a different platform, their app settings can be downloaded and applied, thereby improving the final user experience. Having said that, the SQLite access is a slow process compared with a simple XML read/write to a file. At the end of the day, the three possible solutions (using the native system, storage in the XML file, and storage in the SQLite database) to store the app settings are here. If you wish to explore, there may be other ways to store the data.

Summary

User settings and user data are a vital part of any application and the storage. The user needs to be handle it with care. Data persistence is becoming a much bigger topic now than it was a few years back, and while the objective of using a common language across all platforms has meant that it is possible to have a commonality when it comes to creating some form of persistent system, as you have seen in this chapter, it is far from a simple task.

In the next chapter, we will cover all of the aspects that we looked at until now in one application.

12
Xamarin Forms Labs

As we rapidly approach the final chapter of this book, I am sure that, by now, you will have mixed emotions about Xamarin Forms. On one hand, it simplifies the development of applications on all the three platforms, but on the other hand, it is very limited without having to create a custom renderer. Step forward `Xamarin.Forms.Labs`, the open source extension library.

In this chapter, we will examine:

- What Xamarin Forms labs is
- How to create your own extension library

What is Xamarin Forms Labs?

When Xamarin Forms first came out, it was only intended as a means for abstraction of the user interface that allows you a simplified way to create an app. In that respect, it is great. The problem though is that when you start on that track, the development community generally wants more.

Xamarin is not concerned with this because Xamarin Forms is purely for the UI—anything else is outside the remit of the project. Xamarin Forms Labs came about to fill the parts of the UI missed by the main project.

Let's take `CheckBox` as an example.

Installing Xamarin Forms Labs in your project

Xamarin Forms Labs is available via NuGet. Create your application as you would normally.

Perform the following steps:

1. Select the PCL at the top and click on the context menu icon.
2. From the menu, select **Add | Add NuGet Packages....**

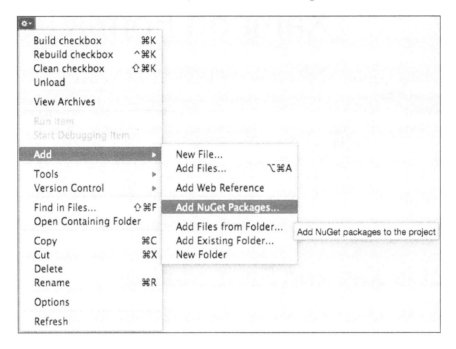

3. A new window will appear. Type `XLabs Forms` in the search box:

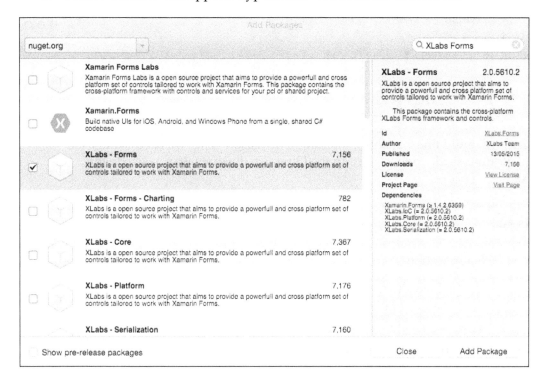

4. Tick the checkbox and click on **Add Package**.

This will install the library in your project and give you the entire library in one swoop. You will need to repeat this for each platform.

Checkboxes

Checkboxes are not supported under Xamarin Forms natively. This is down to iOS not having a checkbox available natively.

 The example code for this section can be found in `Chapter 12/Checkbox`.

Implementing a checkbox is simple enough, as shown in the following code:

```
var chkBox = new CheckBox
{
  DefaultText = "Check box - click it",
  CheckedText = "Check box - clicked",
  TextColor = Color.Blue,
  HorizontalOptions = LayoutOptions.FillAndExpand
};
```

This will build fine, but shows nothing. The reason being we need to alter the platform-specific code to start up the library in the same way as we do for Xamarin Forms.

iOS

`AppDelegate.cs` needs to be changed to allow Xamarin Forms Labs to work with your iOS application. Perform the following steps:

1. We first have to set the inherited class from Xamarin Forms to `XFormsApplicationDelegate`.

2. Then, we need to instantiate the renderers, as shown in the following code:

```
new CheckBoxRenderer();
new CheckBoxCellRenderer();
```

3. Now, let's add the following code:

```
Forms.ViewInitialized += (sender, e) =>
{
  if (!string.IsNullOrWhiteSpace(e.View.StyleId))
    e.NativeView.AccessibilityIdentifier = e.View.StyleId;
};
```

4. Finally, we need to instantiate the library and a resolver as follows:

```
var app = new XFormsAppiOS();
app.Init(this);
var resolverContainer = new SimpleContainer();
resolverContainer.Register<IDevice>(t => AppleDevice.
CurrentDevice)
.Register<IDisplay>(t => t.Resolve<IDevice>().Display)
.Register<IFontManager>(t => new FontManager(t.
Resolve<IDisplay>()))
.Register<IXFormsApp>(app)
.Register<IDependencyContainer>(t => resolverContainer);

Resolver.SetResolver(resolverContainer.GetResolver());
```

Android

Adding Xam.Forms.Labs to your Android app requires only a couple of changes to whatever your main class is (for example, MainActivity.cs):

1. The MainActivity class needs to inherit XFormsApplicationDroid:

```
public class MainActivity : XFormsApplicationDroid
```

2. Next, the resolver needs to be checked. This is performed before the Forms.Init() line, as shown in the following code:

```
if (!Resolver.IsSet)
  SetIoc();
else
{
  var app = Resolver.Resolve<IXFormsApp>() as IXFormsApp<XFormsApp
licationDroid>;
  app.AppContext = this;
} if (!Resolver.IsSet)
  SetIoc();
else
{
  var app = Resolver.Resolve<IXFormsApp>() as IXFormsApp<XFormsApp
licationDroid>;
  app.AppContext = this;
}
```

3. As with the iOS method, the ViewInitialized event has to be intercepted as follows:

```
App.Init();

Forms.ViewInitialized += (sender, e) =>
{
  if (!string.IsNullOrWhiteSpace(e.View.StyleId))
    e.NativeView.ContentDescription = e.View.StyleId;
};
```

 App.Init() can be found in the PCL.

4. Finally, we need to set the resolver, as shown in the following code:

```
private void SetIoc()
{
  var resolverContainer = new SimpleContainer();
```

```
        var app = new XFormsAppDroid();
        app.Init(this);

        resolverContainer.Register<IDevice>(t => AndroidDevice.
CurrentDevice)
            .Register<IDisplay>(t => t.Resolve<IDevice>().Display)
            .Register<IFontManager>(t => new FontManager(t.
Resolve<IDisplay>()))
            .Register<IDependencyContainer>(resolverContainer)
            .Register<IXFormsApp>(app);

        Resolver.SetResolver(resolverContainer.GetResolver());
}
```

Windows Phone

Windows Phone is simple to set up for XLabs. Let's see how it's done:

1. Add the following line to `MainPage.xaml.cs`:

    ```
    App.Init();
    ```

2. We also need to set the resolver. This is in the `App.xaml.cs` file:

    ```
    private void SetIoC()
    {
        var resolverContainer = new SimpleContainer();

        var app = new XFormsAppWP();

        app.Init(this);

        resolverContainer.Register<IDevice>(t => WindowsPhoneDevice.
    CurrentDevice)
            .Register<IDisplay>(t => t.Resolve<IDevice>().Display)
            .Register<IFontManager>(t => new FontManager(t.
    Resolve<IDisplay>()))
            .Register<IDependencyContainer>(t => resolverContainer)
            .Register<IXFormsApp>(app);

        Resolver.SetResolver(resolverContainer.GetResolver());
    }
    ```

3. This code is called from within the `public App()` default constructor.

In the PCL

In the `App` class, the following code needs to be added:

```
public static void Init()
{
    var app = Resolver.Resolve<IXFormsApp>();
    if (app == null)
        return;
}
```

This is called from the `App` default constructor.

Is there anything else, you ask? This should be all you need to do to add the checkbox.

The resolver

As with anything in terms of custom renderers, we need some form of inversion of control (remember that this is where control of the app is passed to the platform instead of the PCL). The resolver creates the holder for the IoC services. You can pass as much or as little as you like.

 A fuller example of how to use this and the other controls can be found on the XLabs website at `https://github.com/XLabs`.

Rolling your own

Earlier in the book (*Chapter 6, A View to a Kill*, to be exact), we created a dialog box where the box could have anything as well as have some buttons in it. We will change this code to be its own standalone library for distribution on the likes of NuGet.

 The code for this can be found in `Chapter 12/DialogLibrary`.

PCL

The biggest difference between the original version and the library is that in the PCL, the only code required is the interface to the platform. However, this time we need to pass more than what we passed previously because we no longer have the abilities to pass code from the the custom view calling class.

The original interface passed `ModalDialog` through the interface. `ModalDialog` is an empty class that inherits `ContentView`. We can still use this in the library. The bigger problem is passing information to the platform class.

In the original, we had `List<string>` that was accessible from the platform through `App.Self.ModalData`. Thankfully, we can pass something similar though the interface.

We can either pass all types of primitive and generic data that is somewhat wasteful, or we can use the generic type: `T`. This means that the interface definition looks slightly different to how it is normally seen:

```
public interface IModalWindow<T>
{
    void CreateModalView(ModalDialog dialog);
    List<T> DataList {get;set;}
    T Data {get;set;}
    Dictionary<T, object> DictData {get;set;}
    string Title {get;set;}
    bool OKButton {get;set;}
    bool OKResult {get;set;}
}
```

The beauty of this form is that we can pass whatever we like as `T`; this includes primitives, classes, and anything else we like.

Once we have created the interface and class for `ModalDialog`, the PCL part is complete. However, this does not tell you the whole story of how this `T` thing works, and it may be worth taking some time to help you understand.

The magical type T

C# owes its history (at least in part) to the C family of languages. Although it is true that it takes a few liberties here and there, on the whole, it fits into the C family far better than (some may say) Objective-C.

One aspect feature that C++ had for many years that C# also implemented was the generic type `T`. This could be absolutely any type the compiler understood. You could replace a large number of methods that replicated the same operation (but only varied in type) just by replacing the type with `T`. The only caveat to using this is that the return type is the same type as the represented one, so you couldn't have an operation on `T x` and `T y` and return `int`. You would need to return `T`. The reason is logical when you think about it.

Let's say that `T` is of the `string` type. You can certainly add strings together, but then you would have to return the product, which will also be a string. You could not, therefore return `float`.

Of course, you can return `void` when you pass `T`.

The devil is in the detail

With this in mind, what is the problem with using `T` for everything? The simple answer is that as `T` can be anything when the compiler creates the code; the code has to cater to all possibilities, and therefore, a method such as the following:

```
private T AddStuff<T>(T a, T b)
{
   return a + b;
}
```

We would have to create as many different instances of the method with all the types the language knows can be added together. In the end, the code, although being five times smaller, ends up being larger to accommodate the `int`, `float`, `double`, `string`, and `bool` addition operations.

 Although this won't necessarily make the code slower in execution, it will increase the overall binary size.

Should it stay or should it go?

This is a difficult call to make, and there really isn't a simple answer. For the example of the interface we're passing, using `T` is good in terms of code brevity and simple to understand. In terms of code size, it will probably be larger than using distinct types.

Having said that, the compiler does a very good job of analyzing the final code and stripping out the code that isn't used. So, for my `AddStuff` example, if there is never a case to add two `bool` and `string` variables in the code, these versions of `AddStuff` will be stripped out. Having said that, as we're creating a library, it is very unlikely that the compiler will strip out any possible code.

As you can see, there is no simple answer.

The general UI considerations

The original version of the code sent over `List<string>`, with each `string` in the `List` being comma-separated. The first part of each string would be on the left-hand side (the title), and the second part goes on the right-hand side.

This was fine for the original example, but we are now passing List<T>, Dictionary<T, object>, and bool to see whether we want an okay button as well as a cancel button.

What have we currently got?

Currently, the UI has four labels and one button. This was fine for what we had, but in terms of making something useful, it's pretty useless. If we had (let's say) more than two members in the List passed, anything after the second item is ignored.

Marrying the interface to the UI

As it stands, the interface allows a great deal of flexibility. We have two collections. These give the largest headaches in terms of UI development. We can handle this in one of two ways: using a web view or using a list.

The web view

This gives a great deal of flexibility as we can style the generated HTML. It is handled in the same way for all platforms. After all, HTML is HTML.

List views

All the three platforms have their own way of displaying a list. Android and Windows Phone uses ListView, and iOS uses UITableView. While Android and Windows Phone have the same name for all the list views, they are greatly different. Windows Phone is much closer to how Xamarin Forms performs ListView. In other words, we have to reinvent the wheel on each device.

What else is there to add?

We need to deal with a title, additional button, and T Data. The title and data are single element variables, so can just have Label assigned to them. An additional button is not a difficulty either. The problem with the additional button is that we need to do something with the event generated. In this case, setting the CancelResult and OKResult properties will do. Leave it to the end user of what to do with it.

We could always pass EventHandler for the buttons via the interface, but this too has its issues, in which we have to create the events in the platform.

Generating the UI

The difficulty of generating the UI is that we can do nothing in the interface properties to all the properties (except the CancelResult and OKResult ones). To keep the dialog flexible, we need to generate one on the fly.

For example, we may need `WebView`, but only if the `List` and `Dictionary` objects are not empty. `T Data` may be empty, so a label isn't needed.

Platform-specific considerations

The main consideration that has to be made is that Android requires a reference to an activity context for the creation of any form of widget and `Dialog`. By far, the simplest way is to have a line like this in the `MainActivity.cs` file:

```
public static Activity activity;
```

Then, in the `OnCreate` method, we will have the following code:

```
activity = this;
```

There is nothing wrong with using this, but it does rely on the end user to add this code. There is a simpler way. Consider the following code (again from the `OnCreate` method):

```
global::Xamarin.Forms.Forms.Init(this, bundle);
```

The first parameter is a pointer to the activity. If we will pass this, can we not retrieve the `Context` somehow? The answer is yes. More specifically, we can access `Xamarin.Forms.Forms.Context`. This property will return the context being used by the Xamarin Forms application.

Android also has to supply the layout and the styles, something that neither the iOS nor Windows Phone versions need to do.

Let's make a start – Android

The first issue is that we have the interface with `<T>`. This causes an issue with `ExportRenderer`. If we have the following line:

```
public class DialogLibrary<T>: ViewRenderer<ModalDialog, Android.
Views.View> ,IModalWindow<T>
```

Then, `ExportRenderer` becomes:

```
[assembly: ExportRenderer(typeof(ModalDialog),
typeof(DialogLibrary<T>))]
```

This is not allowed as `<T>` is unknown.

The answer to this problem is simple: omit T from `typeof(DialogLibrary<T>)`.

The `protected override void OnElementChanged(ElementChangedEventArgs<ModalDialog> e)` method remains essentially the same. The only difference is that we obtain the underpinning context and assign this to a local variable.

The big difference (as you may expect) is in the dialog creation method. Here, we will generate the UI elements and add these to the `LinearLayout`, having first added some layout information to the widgets being used.

For example, when we add `WebView`, we alter the view to match the width of the dialog and wrap the contents before adding it to `LinearLayout`, as shown in the following code:

```
webView.LayoutParameters = new LinearLayout.LayoutParams(LinearLayout.
LayoutParams.MatchParent, LinearLayout.LayoutParams.WrapContent);
```

However, if we need the additional button, we can alter the layout parameters to include a margin between it and the **Cancel** button as follows:

```
using (var lp = new LinearLayout.LayoutParams(LinearLayout.
LayoutParams.WrapContent, (int)ConvertDpToPixel(42f)))
{
    lp.SetMargins((int)ConvertDpToPixel(8f), 0, 0, 0);
    okButton.LayoutParameters = lp;
}
```

The `ConvertDpToPixel` method is a small piece of math that takes the `(DisplayMetrics.Density / 160)` * the dp value passed in.

We should now have everything we need to get this working.

iOS

iOS has a single problem: `UILabel` and `UIWebView` have to be positioned in the code. We can use a simple formula.

To start with, let's take a look at the `Title` property. This needs to be centered, but how can we center something that we don't know the length of?

1. Before we can do this, we need to assign a variable to the size of `ScreenX`:

   ```
   readonly nfloat ScreenX = UIScreen.MainScreen.Bounds.Width;
   ```

2. One aspect that has to be taken into consideration before we go any further is where on the *y* position are the labels, and so on, going to be placed? The simplest is to set a variable to the current *y* position, as shown in the following code:

   ```
   var yPos = 8;
   ```

3. The actual calculation for the position of the label is not difficult, as shown in the following code:

```
if (!string.IsNullOrEmpty(modalWindow.Title))
{
  var lblTitle = new UILabel { Text = modalWindow.Title, Font =
UIFont.BoldSystemFontOfSize(24) };
  var expectedSize = lblTitle.Text.StringSize(UIFont.
BoldSystemFontOfSize(24));

  // we know the size of the screen and that we are in by 8,
therefore the actual size is ScreenX - 8
  var centreOfView = (ScreenX - 8) / 2;
  // we know the length of the label, so divide that by 2
  var halfTextSize = expectedSize.Width / 2;
  // if we subtract the halfTextSize from centreOfView, this
should give us the start point for the x position
  var startPosn = centreOfView - halfTextSize;

  // create the frame size
  lblTitle.Frame = new CGRect(startPosn, yPos, expectedSize.Width,
expectedSize.Height);
  // add to the view
  view.Add(lblTitle);
  // add the size to the yPos + 8
  yPos += expectedSize.Height + 8;
}
```

Adding `UIWebView` is very similar to the Android code. The final aspect to the UI is the buttons. Unlike the Android version, we need to add the buttons dynamically.

4. We have to consider that we have one or two buttons, and these buttons have to be placed as follows:

```
if (modalWindow.OKButton)
{
  var btnCancel = UICreation.CreateButton(new CGRect((ScreenX / 4)
- 30, yPos, 60, 30), UIButtonType.Custom, "Cancel");
  view.Add(btnCancel);

  var btnOK = UICreation.CreateButton(new CGRect(((ScreenX / 4) -
30) * 3, yPos, 60, 30), UIButtonType.Custom, "OK");
  view.Add(btnOK);
  btnOK.TouchUpInside += delegate
  {
    modalWindow.OKResult = true;
    view.RemoveFromSuperview();
```

```
      };
   }
   else
   {
     var btnDone = UICreation.CreateButton(new CGRect((ScreenX / 2) -
   30, yPos, 60, 30), UIButtonType.Custom, "Cancel");
     view.Add(btnDone);

     btnDone.TouchUpInside += delegate
     {
       view.RemoveFromSuperview();
     };
   }
```

Windows Phone

Windows Phone does not have the typical form of dialog, as shown in the following screenshot:

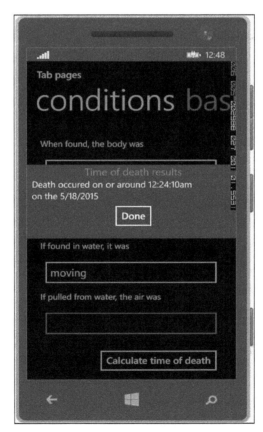

This doesn't mean that we can't use the same approach as with the other dialog boxes. We need to follow the same style for the creation of the UI as we would for a standard Xamarin Forms application, however, we need to construct the stack slightly differently.

As we will need to conditionally add the controls to `StackPanel`, we need to create each object before we assign anything to them. It is then just a case of adding text to the controls, similar to this:

```
var titleBar = new TextBlock
{
  FontSize = 24,
  Foreground = new SolidColorBrush(Colors.Red),
  HorizontalAlignment = System.Windows.HorizontalAlignment.Center
};
if (!string.IsNullOrEmpty(modalWindow.Title))
{
  titleBar.Text = modalWindow.Title;
  stackPanel.Children.Add(titleBar);
};
```

The rest is more or less the same as for iOS and Android.

Creating the library

This can be performed under OS X and Windows. For Windows, I would recommend using the GUI package creator (full instructions can be found at https://docs.nuget.org/Create/using-a-gui-to-build-packages), whereas for OS X, the command-line version needs to be used.

It can be called into life using mono; the only difference to the given instructions is that you will need to precede the NuGet call with mono, so take a look at the following code:

```
nuget spec MyAssembly.dll
```

The preceding code will become:

```
mono nuget spec MyAssembly.dll
```

Summary

As with the other chapters, we've covered a great deal in this chapter. We've seen how we can extend the functionality of the Xamarin Forms application using the well supported and ever expanding XLab Forms. We also looked at how to create our own plugin that can be distributed via NuGet. The opportunities to extend Xamarin Forms are great; it just takes a bit of effort to do it.

In the next chapter, we will see how to incorporate various social media outlets into your app.

13
Social Media into the Mix

Social media (such as Facebook, Google+, and Twitter) forms an ever increasingly important role in a user and developer's life. Adding some form of social media in an app is not difficult, but it does pose a few issues. Add into the mix the networks that are not always possible to connect to, and it can be appreciated that things can become messy quickly.

In this chapter, we will:

- Learn how to test for network connectivity
- Connect to Facebook and Twitter in an app

Connect me up, Scotty

By default, Xamarin Forms has no way of knowing if a phone has a network connection. But then, why should it? Remember that anything hardware-specific has to be handled by the hardware. This means that we need to use injection.

There is a package on NuGet that allows you to check on connectivity, but it is more interesting to see how we can do it without relying on additional packages.

To start with, we need to decide on the best way to do this. We can use an event or an interface. In general, listening in on an event is simple. The PCL listens for an event generated from the platform.

This was easy. Wow! This is going to be a short chapter!

Except that it isn't. The problem is not so much the change in the network state; it's more in getting the initial state. In this case, we will use the standard interface or the injection method.

Setting up the event system and interface

The interface only needs to be something as simple as the following code:

```
namespace connectivity
{
  public interface IConnectivity
  {
    bool NetworkConnected();
  }
}
```

 The source for the connectivity part of the chapter can be found in Chapter13/Connectivity.

To track the state of the connection, a bool variable is set up in App:

```
public static App Self {get; private set;}

public bool IsConnected {get; private set;}

public App()
{
  App.Self = this;
  IsConnected = DependencyService.Get<IConnectivity>().
NetworkConnected();
```

The reason why IsConnected is set to private set; is because the listener for the event change is in App. We will keep all the connectivity parts in one place.

The handler for the event is also fairly simple, although we need to also broadcast back to the platform to send an internal notification, as shown in the following code:

```
public UIChangedEvent MessageEvent { get; set;}
MessageEvent = new UIChangedEvent();

MessageEvent.Change += (object s, UIChangedEventArgs ea) =>
{
  if (ea.ModuleName == "Connection")
  {
    IsConnected = Convert.ToBoolean(ea.Info);
    MessageEvent.BroadcastIt("Notification", "You have {0}
connection", IsConnected ? "a" : "no");
  }
};
```

This works by the registered event listening for the Change event. When the event is triggered, ModuleName is checked to ensure that it's the event we're interested in. This means that we are able to use this in other methods and filter ModuleName. From here, act on the content.

To show what is happening, we can have a small UI, as follows:

```
public ConnectionState()
{
  if (Device.OS == TargetPlatform.iOS)
    Padding = new Thickness(0, 20, 0, 0);

  var titleLabel = new Label
  {
    FontSize = Font.OfSize("System", NamedSize.Large),
    TextColor = Color.Red,
    Text = "Network state"
  };

  var currentState = new Label
  {
    TextColor = App.Self.IsConnected ? Color.Green : Color.Red,
    Text = App.Self.IsConnected ? "connected" : "disconnected"
  };

  Content = new StackLayout
  {
    HorizontalOptions = LayoutOptions.CenterAndExpand,
    VerticalOptions = LayoutOptions.FillAndExpand,
    Orientation = StackOrientation.Vertical,
    Children =
    {
      titleLabel,
      new Label{ Text = "Current state : " },
      currentState
    }
  };

  App.Self.MessageEvent.Change += (object s, UIChangedEventArgs ea) =>
  {
    if (ea.ModuleName == "Notification")
    {
      currentState.TextColor = App.Self.IsConnected ? Color.Green :
Color.Red;
```

```
        currentState.Text = App.Self.IsConnected ? "connected" :
    "disconnected";
        }
    };
}
```

Setting up your Android code

Setting up the connectivity code in Android is a two-step procedure:

1. The first is the creation of BroadcastReceiver.

2. The second is calling this receiver into being.

Broadcast whatcha-ma-call-it?

When something happens on the hardware level, Android broadcasts a message that any code can listen to. In order to listen to the message, a broadcast receiver is used. In the case of the connectivity broadcast receiver, the code is simple enough:

```
[BroadcastReceiver]
public class Connectivity : BroadcastReceiver
{
  public override void OnReceive(Context context, Intent intent)
  {
    var extras = intent.Extras;

    using (var info = extras.GetParcelable("networkInfo") as
NetworkInfo)
    {
      var state = info.GetState();

      var result = state == NetworkInfo.State.Connected || state ==
NetworkInfo.State.Connecting;

      // store the online state in the internal settings system

      ConfigUtils.SaveSetting("online", result, SettingType.Bool);

      // broadcast the event

      connectivity.Singleton.MessageEvents.BroadcastIt("Connection",
result.ToString());
      }
    }
}
```

To instantiate the broadcast receiver, the following code in the launcher code does the job:

```
protected override void OnCreate(Bundle bundle)
{
  var intentFilter = new IntentFilter();
  intentFilter.AddAction(ConnectivityManager.ConnectivityAction);
  RegisterReceiver(new Connectivity(), intentFilter);
```

The only other piece of code required to get this to work is to add the following line in the `AndroidManifest.xml` code:

```
<action android:name="android.net.conn.CONNECTIVITY_CHANGE"/>
```

As we will use facilities on the hardware, the following permissions are needed: `AccessNetworkState` and `AccessWifiState`.

Setting up the interface

The interface is a simple enough affair, as shown in the following code:

```
[assembly: Xamarin.Forms.Dependency(typeof(Connection))]
namespace connectivity.Droid
{
  public class Connection: Java.Lang.Object, IConnectivity
  {
    public Connection()
    {
    }

    public bool NetworkConnected()
    {
      var connected = false;
      return NetworkUtils.HaveConnection ||
      NetworkUtils.HaveWifiConnection;
    }
  }
}
```

In `NetworkUtils.cs`, you will find the `HaveConnection` and `HaveWifiConnection` code. The important lines in both properties are as follows:

```
var cm = (ConnectivityManager)Forms.Context.GetSystemService("connect
ivity");
var activeNetwork = cm.ActiveNetworkInfo;
```

To interrogate the network state, we need to use the `ConnectivityManager` service connectivity and then store `ActiveNetworkInfo`. The result from the property is then fed back to the interface.

Listening for connectivity on Windows Phone

Windows Phone is much simpler. In `MainPage.xaml.cs`, add the `MainPage` constructor:

```
DeviceNetworkInformation.NetworkAvailabilityChanged += new EventHandle
r<NetworkNotificationEventArgs>(ChangeDetected);
```

The event is simple as well, as shown in the following code:

```
void ChangeDetected(object s, NetworkNotificationEventArgs e)
{
  MessageEvent.BroadcastIt("Connection", e.NotificationType ==
NetworkNotificationType.InterfaceConnected ? true.ToString() : false.
ToString());
}
```

Adding a notification

There are two types of notification available to all platforms: internal and external. An external notification is similar to a push notification. As the notification to change the network state is purely to tell the user something and is generated on the device, it's an internal notification. Take a look at the following code:

```
static readonly int ButtonClickNotificationId = 1000;
connectivity.Singleton.MessageEvents.Change += (object s,
UIChangedEventArgs ea) =>
{
  if (ea.ModuleName == "Notification")
  {
    RunOnUiThread(() =>
    {
      var builder = new Notification.Builder(this)
      .SetAutoCancel(true)
      .SetContentTitle("Network state changed")
      .SetContentText(ea.Info)
      .SetDefaults(NotificationDefaults.Vibrate)
      .SetContentText(ea.Info);

      var notificationManager = (NotificationManager)GetSystemService(
NotificationService);
      notificationManager.Notify(ButtonClickNotificationId, builder.
```

```
Build());
    });
  }
};
```

Setting up iOS

iOS is very simple to set up and listens for events. The basis for the majority of code is based on the freely available `Reachability.cs` class from Xamarin (https://github.com/xamarin/monotouch-samples/blob/master/ReachabilitySample/reachability.cs).

This class contains just about everything required to check your connection. In `AppDelegate.cs`, a small amount of code is needed to get the `ConnectionChanged` event:

```
// set up notifications
var settings = UIUserNotificationSettings.GetSettingsForTypes(
UIUserNotificationType.Alert | UIUserNotificationType.Badge |
UIUserNotificationType, null);
UIApplication.SharedApplication.RegisterUserNotificationSettings(sett
ings);

// produce notification
MessageEvents.Change += (object s, UIChangedEventArgs ea) =>
{
  if (ea.ModuleName == "Notification")
  {
    var notification = new UILocalNotification
    {
      FireDate = DateTime.Now,
      AlertAction = "Connection changed",
      AlertBody = ea.Info,
    };
    UIApplication.SharedApplication.ScheduleLocalNotification(notific
ation);
  }
};
```

Setting up Windows Phone

Setting up the change of connectivity is simple on Windows Phone. In `MainPage.xaml.cs`, we need to subscribe to the `NetworkAvailablityChanged` event as follows:

```
DeviceNetworkInformation.NetworkAvailabilityChanged += new EventHandle
r<NetworkNotificationEventArgs>(ChangeDetected);
```

The `ChangeDetected` event is also simple, as shown in the following code:

```
void ChangeDetected(object sender, NetworkNotificationEventArgs e)
{
  MessageEvents.BroadcastIt("Connection",
  e.NotificationType==NetworkNotificationType.InterfaceConnected ?
  true.ToString() : false.ToString());
}
```

Finally, we need to implement the interface:

```
void ChangeDetected(object sender, NetworkNotificationEventArgs e)
{
  MessageEvents.BroadcastIt("Connection",
  e.NotificationType==NetworkNotificationType.InterfaceConnected ?
  true.ToString() : false.ToString());
}
class Connection : IConnectivity
{
  public bool NetworkConnected()
  {
    var rv = false;
    try
    {
      var InternetConnectionProfile = NetworkInformation.
GetInternetConnectionProfile();
      var profileInfo = GetConnectionProfile(InternetConnectionProfi
le);
      if (profileInfo.Contains("None"))
        rv = true;
    }
    catch (Exception ex)
    {
      Console.WriteLine("exception thrown : {0}:{1}", ex.Message,
ex.InnerException);
      rv = false;
    }
    return rv;
  }

  string GetConnectionProfile(ConnectionProfile connectionProfile)
  {
    string connectionProfileInfo = string.Empty;
    if (connectionProfile != null)
    {
```

```
        connectionProfileInfo = "Profile Name : " + connectionProfile.
ProfileName + "\n";

    switch (connectionProfile.GetNetworkConnectivityLevel())
    {
      case NetworkConnectivityLevel.None:
      connectionProfileInfo += "Connectivity Level : None\n";
      break;
      case NetworkConnectivityLevel.LocalAccess:
      connectionProfileInfo += "Connectivity Level : Local
Access\n";
      break;
      case NetworkConnectivityLevel.ConstrainedInternetAccess:
      connectionProfileInfo += "Connectivity Level : Constrained
Internet Access\n";
      break;
      case NetworkConnectivitybreak;
    }

    switch (connectionProfile.GetDomainConnectivityLevel())
    {
      case DomainConnectivityLevel.None:
      connectionProfileInfo += "Domain Connectivity Level : None\n";
      break;
      case DomainConnectivityLevel.Unauthenticated:
      connectionProfileInfo += "Domain Connectivity Level :
Unauthenticated\n";
      break;
      case DomainConnectivityLevel.Authenticated:
      connectionProfileInfo += "Domain Connectivity Level :
Authenticated\n";
      break;
    }
  }
  return connectionProfileInfo;
  }
}
```

Adding social media to your app

Social media sites (such as Facebook and Twitter) are fast becoming the **defacto** method of communication for people around the world. They both have massive advantages over sending messages with images via MMS or have the text size restrictions that are found in text messaging.

Adding social media in an app is not that difficult and works via a login system that passes the information to either the OAuth1 or OAuth2 authentication system for verification.

The difference between OAuth and OAuth2

OAuth2 gives the mobile developer a lot of advantages over the original version. One of the most important advantages is that OAuth2 doesn't require the app to launch a web page for authentication. The second advantage is that the OAuth2 token is short-lived: the app cannot stay live forever.

Implementing OAuth

We can implement OAuth in a number of ways. The simplest way is to install `Xamarin.Auth` via NuGet (at the time of writing, the component store only lists this for iOS and Android, whereas the version of NuGet is available for all platforms).

`Xamarin.Auth` is not PCL-compliant, so any communication between the PCL and the platform will require an injection service. This is not difficult at all.

The next way is to use a simple library such as the one held on Google Code. The site contains many different implementations of OAuth for different languages. However, the C# one only covers OAuth1, rather than OAuth1 and 2.

OAuthLib covers OAuth1 and 2. The end choice is yours. You can also write your own. In the Facebook example, a simple implementation (which is PCL-compliant) is included.

For my examples here, I'll use the `Xamarin.Auth` library from NuGet.

Installing Xamarin.Auth from NuGet

Installing any package from NuGet is the same and has been covered in *Chapter 2, Let's Get the Party Started* and a few other places. In this case, we will need the Xamarin.Auth package, as shown in the following screenshot:

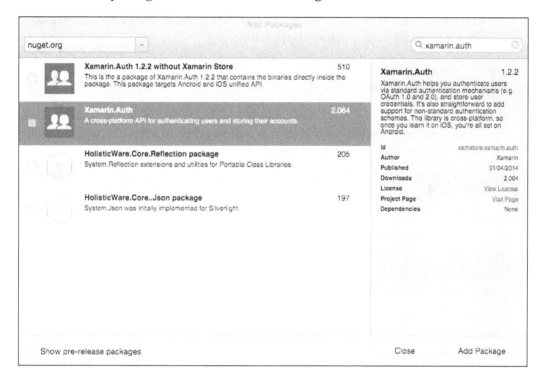

You will need to add this to each platform that is being targeted.

OAuth1 for Twitter

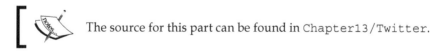

The source for this part can be found in Chapter13/Twitter.

In order to get this part to work, you will first need to register an app. This gives you a key that is required as part of the authentication system.

To register an app, perform the following steps:

1. You will need to go to `https://apps.twitter.com` and click on the **Create an application** button.

2. You will need to fill in the requested information.

3. Once filled, scroll down to the bottom of the screen, agree to the terms, and click on **Create your Twitter application**.

 The source for this part can be found in `Chapter13/Twitter`.

4. Once you have created your app, you will be taken to a details page that will look similar to the following screenshot:

5. You will need to generate an access token. You will find this by clicking on the **Keys and Access Tokens** tab. At the bottom of the screen, you will find a button to generate the token. Click on the button to generate your access token.

6. Your app will need the **API Key**, **API Secret**, and the **Callback URL**.

Once you have these, you're set to go!

Let's jump on

I will leave out the description of how to generate the UI in the PCL. However, we do need to create an interface for the platform. As always, let's keep it simple, as shown in the following code:

```
public interface IAuthenticate
{
  void AuthenticateUser(string username, string password);
}
```

Authentication in the application

The following code snippet demonstrates how to authenticate in the app (this example is from the Android version). The UserDetails class is in the PCL and is accessed through App.Self:

```
[assembly: Xamarin.Forms.Dependency(typeof(Authenticate))]
namespace Twitter.Droid
{
  public class Authenticate : Java.Lang.Object, IAuthenticate
  {
    public Authenticate()
    {
    }

    public void AuthenticateUser()
    {
      var auth = new OAuth1Authenticator(consumerKey: "YOUR_CONSUMER_
KEY",
      consumerSecret: "YOUR_CONSUMER_SECRET_KEY",
      requestTokenUrl: new Uri("https://api.twitter.com/oauth/request_
token"),
      authorizeUrl: new Uri("https://api.twitter.com/oauth/
authorize"),
      accessTokenUrl: new Uri("https://api.twitter.com/oauth/access_
token"),
```

```
            callbackUrl: new Uri("http://www.all-the-johnsons.co.uk/
    success")
            );

        auth.Completed += (object sender,
    AuthenticatorCompletedEventArgs e) =>
        {
          App.Self.User.IsAuthenticated = e.IsAuthenticated;
          if (e.IsAuthenticated)
          {
            App.Self.User.Name = e.Account.Properties["name"];
            App.Self.User.ScreenName = e.Account.Properties["screen_
    name"];
            App.Self.User.Token = e.Account.Properties["oauth_token"];
            App.Self.User.TokenSecret = e.Account.Properties["oauth_
    token_secret"];
            App.Self.User.TwitterID = e.Account.Properties["user_id"];
          }

          App.Self.MessageEvent.BroadcastIt("authenticate");
        };
      }
    }
  }
```

This is pretty much all you need to log in.

Using OAuth2

As with Twitter, we will use the Xamarin.Auth package.

The Facebook example in this chapter will need you to first register for the Facebook app and then add a new app. When presented with the option of what to target, select the **Advanced** option. This allows you to target all the platforms at once. This will give you a secret app ID that is required for OAuth2. You will also need to go to **Settings** | **Advanced**, part way down under **Client OAuth Redirect**, and enter the redirecting URL. This can be any URL that exists for testing purposes. Once the app is ready for the bigger picture, the redirect page should be a page of a website that is not publically accessible.

 The source for this part can be found in Chapter13/Facebook.

Virtually, the same code that was used for Twitter can be used for Facebook, but with OAuth2 and not OAuth1. The authenticator looks similar to the following code:

```
var auth = new OAuth2Authenticator(
clientId: "APP_ID",
scope: "", // permissions
authorizeUrl: new Uri("https://m.facebook.com/dialog/oauth/"),
redirectUrl: new Uri(""));
```

The user interface

It is worth pointing out here that the UI is not what you would expect. Most often, with a Xamarin Forms application, the UI is constructed from the PCL. Moreover, the likes of Facebook and Twitter provide their own login user interface. This is part of the remit of `OAuthAuthenticator`.

This means that the PCL UI for the content page is empty, and we rely on a custom renderer to produce the user interface with a callback to the PCL once the login has been performed.

A very simple implementation of a Facebook login (as supplied with the example code for this chapter) looks similar to the following screenshot when executed. The example is using the Windows Phone emulator under the `Windows` directory, but the same UI is produced for Android and iOS.

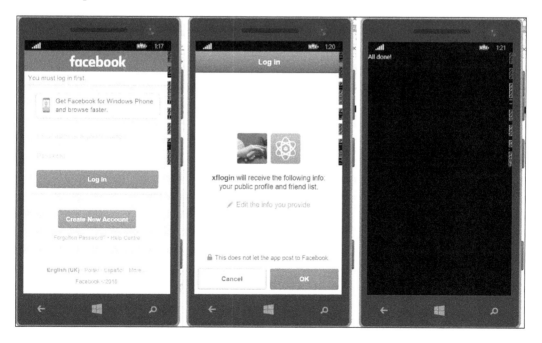

The reason why the UI is the same for the login is that it is supplied by Facebook as an embedded web page through the authenticator service.

Summary

There is nothing difficult in logging in to a social media source. It provides a very simple and effective method to log in to your app without the problems of writing your own login system; simply grab the token returned, store it on the server, and compare it on successive logins.

There are some sticking points for the flow, but nothing too terrible.

In the next and final chapter we'll tie up the loose ends and by the end of it, you will have all the tools required to create your own Xamarin Forms app. *Hang on…. it's going to be the ride of a lifetime!*

References

- https://code.google.com/p/oauth/
- https://oauthlib.codeplex.com/SourceControl/latest
- https://developers.facebook.com/docs/facebook-login/v2.3

Bringing It All Together

From developing mobile apps to using the Xamarin Forms library, we've looked at a variety of aspects until now. Everything has been done for a purpose: to show you how simple it can be to develop something effective with very little effort for three different mobile platforms. This is fine, but as with so many TV series around, there has been an overlooking arc, and this is the case here as well.

In this chapter, we will:

* Learn how to set up Azure for mobile and storage
* Take a look at the parts we've covered so far and may be missing from your application

Setting up Azure

Although I have set up Azure with the one month free version of Azure, it offers everything I need to get the code for this chapter up and running without any financial layout. Setting up Azure is a fairly painless process.

Signing up

Let's assume that you have a valid Microsoft login (this can be for Hotmail or any other Microsoft service, such as Skype). You will need to use this to sign up. The initial sign up screen currently looks similar to the following screenshot:

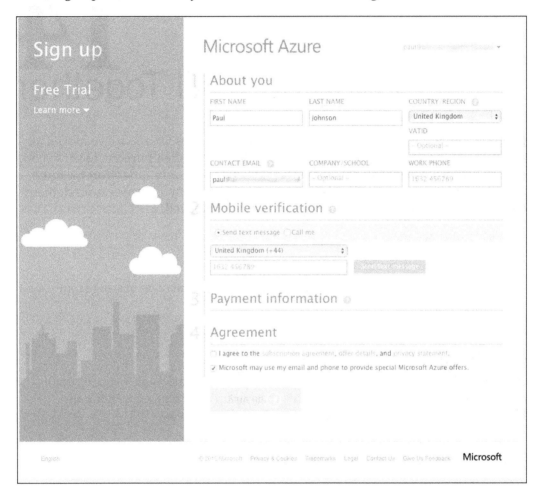

Now, perform the following steps:

1. Enter the sections as requested. You will need to expand the payment information and fill it as required. Don't worry about supplying a credit/debit card; it's never used unless you say to use it.

2. Once everything has been filled, click on the **Sign up** button. You will see the following set up screen:

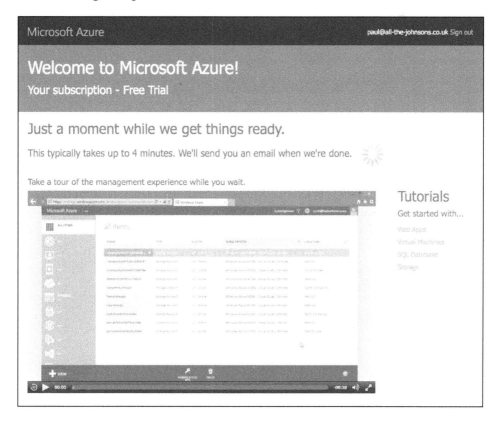

Once everything has been set up, the screen will change to this:

3. Clicking on **Start managing my service** will take you to the settings screen on the Azure web interface:

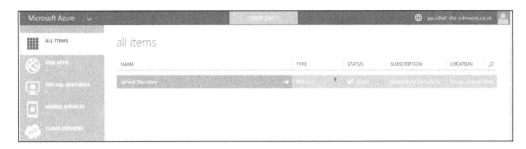

We are interested in mobile services (as we will use it for a mobile application). Mobile services allows you to set up a simplified database, add the push notification settings, and anything else you need to do. Perform the following steps:

4. When you first click on **MOBILE SERVICES**, you will be be directed to the following screenshot:

5. Click on the **CREATE A NEW MOBILE SERVICE** arrow to create the service. You will see a two bar dialog that will enable you to set up the service:

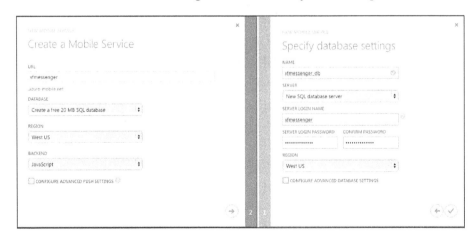

We don't need to select the advanced push settings; most of them can be set up later. Once the service has been set, you will be see the following screenshot:

6. To access the service, click on the arrow next to the service name:

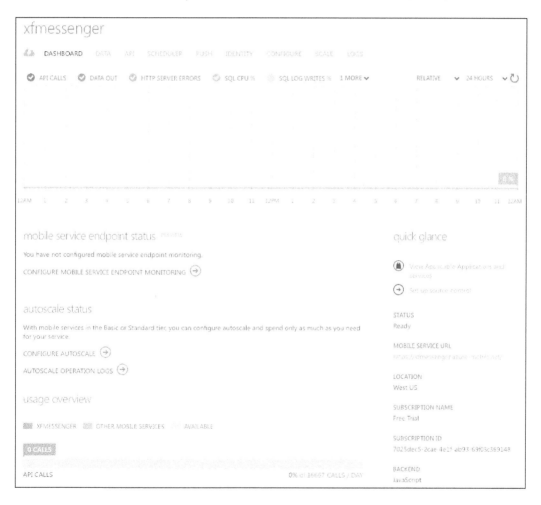

7. This may look scary, but we can ignore most of it. For example, we can quickly set up the push notification center by clicking on the **Push** option before the graph.

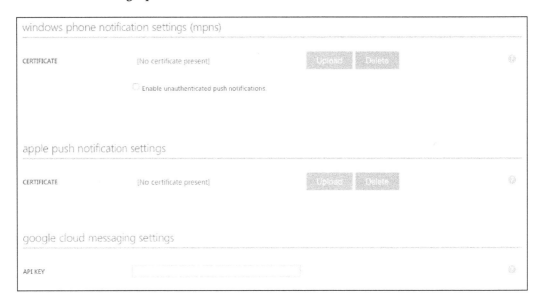

Obtaining the iOS and Android keys are covered in *Chapter 1, In the Beginning…*. Once you've added them, notifications will be ready on the server, but not in the data.

Adding data

A service without data is not of much use. Perform the following steps:

1. To add data, click on the **DATA** option. You will see a friendly message, as shown in the following screenshot:

2. Clicking on the **ADD A TABLE** arrow gives you access to a greatly simplified database view.

The data types permitted are number, string, Date, and bool. This is handy for those not used to set up a database because we don't need to worry about the type for number—it's a number. Why should the developer be worried if a value is int, double, or float? Simply put, they don't.

3. When you add the table, you will first be presented with the table name definer. This also allows the security settings on the table to be set:

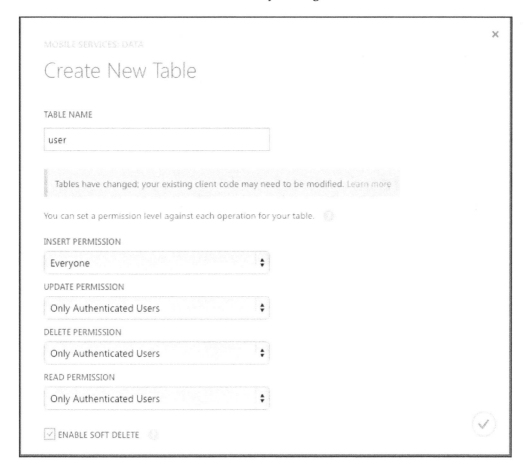

4. The permissions range from anyone using anything to admins and scripts only. Once you're happy, click on the tick.

By default, every table in Azure comes with the following table data:

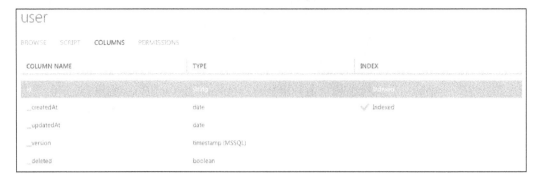

These cannot be removed. You will see that **id** is a **string**, not **int** (which is more usual for databases). This is useful as it can store a GUID, meaning that the ID is never going to be the same (the chances of two GUIDs being the same is exceptionally small). Create as many tables as you need.

Adding storage

Part of the specs for the app is that pictures and sound can be sent as part of the message. As we've seen when creating the tables, there are no blob types. Azure provides for this by using storage accounts. Essentially, the app stores the image as a blob in the storage against an ID Perform the following steps:

1. When you click on the **Storage** option, you will be presented with the familiar message that Azure gives:

2. Select **CREATE A STORAGE ACCOUNT**. A kind of wizard will appear, asking for basic details:

3. Enter the information as required and click on **CREATE STORAGE ACCOUNT**. The storage account consists of containers. Microsoft recommends that you use different containers for different types (such as images, video, and audio).

4. Once the storage account has been set up, click on **CONTAINERS** to create a new container:

5. You will be presented with a new container window. For our purposes, the access type is set to **Public Container**. Essentially, the access levels range from anyone to only those with high security levels:

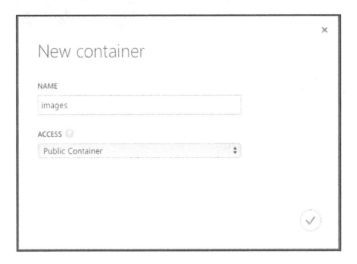

Now that we have Azure set up, we can start with the coding.

Setting up the application

This application requires you to use Azure and Azure Storage. The libraries for these can be found on either the Xamarin Component store or NuGet. You will also need the service endpoint and the application key. Perform the following steps:

1. To obtain these, log in to the mobile service. The endpoint is found on the dashboard:

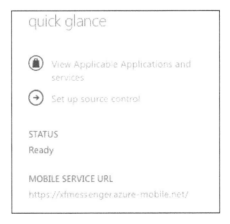

The key has to be generated. There are three buttons: **MANAGE KEYS**, **RESTART**, and **DELETE** at the bottom of the web interface:

2. Select **MANAGE KEYS**. A dialog window will appear that contains the application and the master key.
3. You will need the **APPLICATION KEY**. There is a clipboard next to the application key. This is useful because you will need it in the app:

 I have split the source into a couple of parts. The code for this section (which includes the push code) can be found in `Chapter14/xfmessenger1`.

The source code (`xfmessenger1`) sets up the database, the Azure code, and all the backend work. Rather than reworking on the previous chapters, I will concentrate on the login and on Azure.

Adding Azure

The Azure libraries can be added via NuGet or the component store. Getting Azure to work requires a two-step process: **pre** and **post** authorization.

To start with, we need to create an instance of the library, as shown in the following code:

```
public static MobileServiceClient MobileService = new
MobileServiceClient( "https://AZURE_WEBSITE_ENDPOINT", "AZURE_ID_
CODE");
new Microsoft.WindowsAzure.MobileServices.CurrentPlatform();
```

`CurrentPlatform` needs to be called in the platform code.

This sets up the basics; however, to use the service, we need to authenticate. There is no way to do this directly, so a server method (known as an API call) needs to be called. The following code snippet assumes that there is a network connection:

```
var resp = await App.Self.MobileService.InvokeApiAsync("login",
HttpMethod.Get, usrData); // usrData is a dictionary containing the
login data
if ((bool)resp["authenticated"])
{
  App.Self.MobileService.CurrentUser = new MobileServiceUser(userid)
  {
    MobileServiceAuthenticationToken = token = (string)resp["token"]
  };
```

`MobileService.CurrentUser` has to be instantiated; without it, no further calls to the server can be made. `MobileServiceAuthenticationToken` also needs to be stored.

Once this has occurred, the application can proceed.

Adding the Azure login API

Azure allows development with either Node.js or .NET. Perform the following steps:

1. To set up the custom API, go to the mobile services menu option on the Azure web interface, select the instance created, followed by **API**. By default, the service will come without any services written:

2. When you click on the **CREATE A CUSTOM API** arrow, it will display the following dialog window:

> The preceding example is typical for a new custom API. These should also be considered as the minimum levels of permission. This gives the API a layer of protection because without the key being present, the login will automatically fail. It is not as important for the signup process (in fact, this doesn't require an API call, just a direct insert into the database for the new username and password).

3. When you're happy, click on the tick icon; you'll be presented with a script editor, which is very similar to the one in Visual Studio.

> In the source directory, you will find a sample login script that will provide the minimum requirements for login. For the login to work, it requires `Dictionary` to be passed in. This contains the username, password, the device ID, the phone operating system, and the phone OS version. The password is encrypted before leaving the phone (it is never wise to send passwords *in the clear*).

The script editor is simple to use, and if you make a mistake, you will see the following error. The red wavy line indicates where the error is:

```
else
{
    thisisanerror

    failAuth(request);
}
```

4. Once the script is complete, click on the **Save** icon. The service will store the new script, and once it's complete, you'll see the following screenshot:

Putting some meat on the bones

Now that the backend is more or less how it needs to be, we need to concentrate on the frontend. To start with, we need to test the signup and login part of the app. An example of this is in the source code for xfmessenger1.

We start off with a simple option to sign in or sign up; selecting one of these leads to their respective interface.

Sign up and log in with the same code

The sign up process is a two stage process with the second being the same as the login process, the difference being that sign up inserts directly into the database, whereas login uses the API, which in turn, does the Azure database search.

The automatic login

This can be achieved by storing the user details in the platform settings system or in the custom XML method. Depending on what you will do with the data depends on whether you go the XML route or the settings route. The login test should be performed on the application setting. If the username and password exists, then the login can just go forward. However, the problem here is data security. If the phone is stolen or even just sold without the user having first signed out, then all the messages, and so on, will be available to the new owner.

We can negate this problem to an extent using the same kind of system as Apple uses with their fingerprint system; after a period of inactivity, force a login.

The required data to sign up

There are two source files called `details.cs` and `user.cs` in the `Classes` directory. These contain the required data. Some properties will be autofilled by the app, whereas others require user input.

In general, anything with ID in the name being filled by the app are always strings. We will use a string to keep inline with how Azure stores internally. To ensure that the IDs are unique, **GUID (Global Unique IDentifier**, also known as a **UUID — Universal Unique IDentifier**) is used. A typical GUID looks like this:

```
736c5547-bdb4-4890-a5d8-6ad717cb04ed
```

If you consider that each character can be any one of 36 characters (0-9, a-z) and that there are 32 characters that will give a possible 5.3×10^{36} combinations of characters, there is virtually zero chance of any two GUIDs being the same. The letter U in GUID is well deserved!

The following table states the methods to accept the user details:

user.cs	details.cs
string username { get; set; }	string firstname { get; set; }
string password { get; set; }	string lastname { get; set; }
	DateTime birthday { get; set; }

The application will enter any other values (such as the link between user and details objects).

 For a good example of an app-filled class, `phone.cs` fits the bill. All the details here are supplied from the phone directly.

The data organization

You may be wondering why the contents of `details.cs` are not just in `user.cs`. They would reasonably look to be one of the same. The reason is that details do not need to be associated with a user, but they can be associated with a contact. The person running the app should never know the username and password of the contact, and the contact should also not know the login details of anybody else.

This kind of separation is not uncommon when you use databases, and in terms of efficiency, it is better than having a large object for data. In general, keeping data models as small as possible makes for greater efficiency. This goes double for the likes of mobile devices that have limited read/write access speeds.

 A reasonable explanation of the GUID math is outside the remit of this book. A fairly good and simple to understand discourse can be found at `https://en.wikipedia.org/wiki/Globally_unique_identifier`.

Wrapping up the login and base settings

The source in `xfmessenger1` contains everything required to log in, sign up, and create the database the app uses, create the initial settings for the internal system, enable push notifications, and alert the app as to when the device is in and out of range.

Take a moment to see how it is written. If you have created your own Azure service to test the code, create the mobile service, and tables to mirror these in the `Classes` folder (however, remember that `id`, `__createdAt`, and `__updateAt` are already going to be in the database tables in the Azure service and are automatically populated by Azure Mobile Services), you should find that you are able to sign up and log in without an issue on any of the supported platforms.

The Azure Storage

Part of the application allows images and audio to be sent to the recipient. In order to do this, we need to utilize the Azure Storage.

 The source for this part can be found in `Chapter14/AzureStorage`.

In the first part of this chapter, we set up the Azure Storage service as part of setting up Azure.

We have already created the storage, but now, we need to configure the mobile service to use it. Head back to the Azure management portal and click on the Azure Storage menu option. Make a note of the storage account name and the primary key. These will be required to configure the mobile service.

Perform the following steps:

1. Once you have made a note of all the values, go to the mobile service and select the **Configure** option. Then, scroll down to the app settings section:

2. You will need to create two new name/value pairs:

    ○ STORAGE_ACCOUNT_NAME: This is the name for your storage

    ○ STORAGE_ACCOUNT_ACCESS_KEY: This is the primary key for the storage

3. Once you're happy with this, click on the **Save** icon.
4. We next have to add a script to the database table. Select **Data** on the mobile section and the storage table.
5. Once selected, click on the **Script** option and replace the **Insert** script with the contents of the `blobinsert` file in the `Chapter 14/Azure Scripts` folder.
6. Click on **Save**, and the storage is now set up on the server.

Storing data

In each project foldwer, there is an image of a dog, a cat, and a small audio file as well. We will upload each of these to the Azure service.

Setting and storing

Using storage with Xamarin Forms is not difficult, but it does all that needs to be performed on the platform level, rather than in the PCL. Let's consider the Android version (the sample already has the `Internet` permission set). Perform the following steps:

1. The first step is to set up the container and the resource name:

    ```
    storageItem.containername = "images";
    storageItem.resourcename = filename;
    ```

2. Then, send it to the server. This is an asynchronous process that returns an empty string of SAS, as shown in the following code:

    ```
    await storageTable.InsertAsync(storage);
    ```

3. Check whether the string is null or empty, and if it isn't, send the following file:

    ```
    if (!string.IsNullOrEmpty(storageItem.SasQueryString))
    {
      var cred = new StorageCredentials(storageItem.SasQueryString);
      var imageUri = new Uri(storageItem.ImageUri);

      var container = new CloudBlobContainer(new Uri(string.
    Format("https://{0}/{1}",
        imageUri.Host, storageItem.ContainerName)), cred);
    var blobFromSASCredential =
        container.GetBlockBlobReference(storageItem.ResourceName);
    ```

4. Finally, upload the image as a stream, as shown in the following code:

    ```
    await blobFromSASCredential.UploadFromStreamAsync(imageStream);
    ```

The messenger application

Now that we have the storage and backend sorted, we finally need to perform the messenger part. This is split into four parts:

*   Compose
*   Send/Receive
*   Contacts
*   Push

What about displaying the messages?

Messages are just a list of uneven table items. If we attach an ID to each message list from each contact, we can display the conversation. The conversation is still just a list of uneven table items. These are the simplest of tasks, so there is not much need to spend time on it.

The difficult part is the first message. If we have an ID on each message object that points to `parent/previous ID`, we can keep going backwards down the list. If `parent/previousID` is `"-1"`, then it is at the top of the list.

For the conversations, if we have a list of all the objects with `parentID` of `"-1"`, then we will have the initial message display.

The message composition

This can be done via a text entry on a keyboard or speech to text. To prevent excessive message sizes, we can set an arbitrary limit of 500 characters for the message.

Speech to text

This is another platform-specific feature, so it needs to be accessed through `DependencyService`. In order to trigger the speech input, we will add a button that then fires the DS. We can take the returned text and then use `Substring(0, 499);` to truncate the string to 500 characters.

 An example of this can be found in `Chapter 14/SpeechToText`. The example is for Android and Windows Phone only, as Apple currently does not give the developer's access to this extremely useful resource.

The message composition

We could always use a straight `Entry` gadget, or we could make it look good. In this case, we will use a custom renderer to place a background on the entry and then add it.

Lazy image loading

The one way that we can make the application feel more responsive is to employ a technique called lazy loading. This is very commonly used in desktop and mobile arenas, most notably on web browsers. Here, the text is rendered with placeholders of the correct size being inserted. The images are then downloaded on a different thread, and once available, it is rendered.

The example of this can be found in Chapter 14/LazyLoading and Chapter 14/LazyWebLoading.

This can be seen to greatest effect when you use the likes of Facebook, and when you view a gallery. It would be horrendously slow to wait for every photo to download and then to render the images at the end. Chances are that the end user will think that it's crashed or similar and leave. While we know that something is happening, the end user won't, and at the end of the day, it is the end user experience that determines whether your app is the chosen one or someone else's that may not work as well, but renders quickly.

We can do this lazy loading in our app too.

Essentially, we will pass the image filename (or URI) in its own thread and load it asynchronously. Once the `Completed` property is raised, the image can be rendered. Once the file is loaded, a placeholder is shown.

Contacts

A messenger app is nothing if you cannot send a message to someone. We can gather contacts in a number of ways:

- Scrap the users contact list
- Via one of the social networks — use contacts from there
- Have the end user invite someone directly

Using social media

Typically, this requires that the user logs in to the social media provider, and when the authentication process is being processed, permission to access contacts and images is requested at the same time.

 An example of getting the contacts list from Facebook is provided in Chapter 14/FacebookContacts. The example also includes an example of how to send an e-mail without using the native e-mail client.

Once the permission has been granted, it is just a case of downloading the contacts, grabbing the e-mail address, and having the app (or server) send out an e-mail that invites the end user to download the app and sign up. At the same time, a details object can be created on the server for them. A token is sent as part of the e-mail to sign up, in which it is then associated with the user and the details automatically.

The direct invitation

This can be performed via SMS or e-mail. The question is which one you should use. To answer this, you need to consider the murky world of marketing and the user product lock-in.

For all of its user friendliness, Apple has a massive amount of product lock in. The rational behind this is that Apple wants to ensure the end user experience, and the best way to do this is to have absolute control. Without the use of a web service that has an SMS gateway, the end user is locked in iMessenger.

This is not a problem until you try to produce your own messenger application that uses the default SMS gateway or OS-specific provided methods. At this point, it doesn't matter how good your product is; the user still has to use a competitor's product in place of yours.

 Android is not as restrictive (you can send a message without any user interaction), and Windows Phone allows you access to the SMS base without using their product, but the user still has to approve the sending. The only advantage of using the default SMS software is that the user will pay for them.

Using a web service is a better idea, but this requires a server with an SMS gateway installed (which will also cost the end user per message). Does it?

The likes of an SMS gateway works by the message coming in with an approved ID, data, and the recipient phone number as part of the data packet. The service then checks the ID and sends out the message. If you're lucky, the service will check whether the phone number is valid.

Now, let's consider what we can do when we send data to the server:

1. The user creates the message with a contact attached.
2. The user sends the data to the server. The data will include the user ID.
3. The data arrives at the server and is stored.

At the point of storing, if push notifications are set up, it is possible to send out a message from the server to the recipient to tell the software that they have a new message.

The format of the notification can contain a large amount of data, but it's never a good idea to send a large amount of data via push for no reason other than there is no absolute guarantee of a message getting through. A far better idea is to implement a two-way notification.

This two-way system works like this:

1. The user sends the message. It contains the message ID, the contact ID, and the message.

2. The server sends out the notification to the contact, but it includes the return ID.

3. The recipient receives the push and sends back the return ID.

4. The server receives the return ID and sends a message back to the originator to say that the message with the original ID has been received.

Are the words "I have a cunning plan" marching with ill-deserved confidence in the direction of this?

They are. If you look at this, if step 3 fails, then there is no way for the server to know that it has failed. We can build a three strike fallback in the notification system based on `DateTime`. If the receipt is not received by the third attempt, the server sends out a failed message to the sender.

However, this does lead to the question of interval for the `DateTime` event. It's too short and pointless, too long, and the convenience of the messenger is lost. For the sake of argument, the example in the Azure Scripts directory is set to 5 minutes.

Displaying and storing the attachments

Displaying attached images is not difficult and can be done in the PCL. The audio has to be performed on the platform with the facilities they provide.

 The source code in `Chapter14/PlayingAudio` demonstrates how to perform this task.

The issue with attachments is the storage. SQLite should never be used to store large objects; it is not designed for this. The storage of **BLOB (Binary Large OBject)** will cause SQLite to suffer from significant slowdowns in terms of operation and data retrieval. In order to keep the storage in the PCL, we need to store the BLOBs on the device as whatever they are and then retrieve them using the file stream objects.

Using file streams to save and load

This is achieved using the `StreamReader` and `StreamWriter` classes. Remember that in the PCL, the .NET library is only a subset of the full library with the code guaranteed to be available on all the platforms.

In its simplest form, reading a stream is conducted like this:

```
string line;
using (var reader = new StreamReader("file.txt"))
line = reader.ReadLine();
Console.WriteLine(line);
```

Writing a stream is slightly more involved (not really). Take a look at the following code:

```
using (var writer = StreamWriter("important.txt"))
{
  writer.Write("Word ");
  writer.WriteLine("word 2");
  writer.WriteLine("Line");
}
```

`StreamReader` and `StreamWriter` can also read and write asynchronously. This will help in speeding up the saving process. It also allows lazy loading on recall.

And that's it!

This chapter has covered all the aspects required to produce a half decent messenger application. You can find the final version with just about everything covered in this book (not just this chapter) used to produce the messenger application in the code for this chapter.

Summary

There is nothing difficult in producing a functional Xamarin Forms application. The difficulty comes with the styling of the application, and to some extent, overcoming the shortfalls via injection techniques. Hopefully, this book would have helped you to produce functional and good-looking Xamarin Forms applications for business, pleasure, or personal use for yourself.

I conclude by fulfilling a long time promise that I made to someone very close and dear to me for the end of my second book — *the butler did it!*

Index

Symbol

.NET generics
  about 76
  class usage, restrictions 76-78
  linked lists 82
  methods 78-82

A

abstraction layer, standard UI login
  about 47
  device, setting 49, 50
  login button 51
  uniform size, ensuring 48
address book
  address storage class, creating 170, 171
  BindingContext, using 188
  incorporating, in messenger
    application 169, 170
  internal address book, accessing 171
  viewing 182-186
  WeakReference 186-188
  Xamarin Mobile component, using 176
Aggregate method 102
All method 102
Android
  about 247, 248
  broadcast receiver, creating 256, 257
  connectivity code, setting up 256
  connectivity, listening on Windows
    Phone 258
  geolocation events, adding to 210, 211
  interface, setting up 257
  maps, setting up 41
  notification, adding 258

  setting up, for push notifications 199, 200
  WebViews 40
  Xamarin Forms, instantiating within 26
Android custom renderer 56
Android native platform storage 220, 221
Android push notifications
  additional permissions 202
  broadcast receiver 203-205
  setting up, in app 201, 202
Android service
  about 205, 206
  actions, handling in code 207
  receive 207
  register action 206
  return value, using 206
  unregister action 206
Android UI 113-117
Any method 102
Apple developer console
  URL 12
application
  backend storage 8
  certificate, exporting for Azure 16-18
  cross platform considerations 4, 5
  design templates 2
  internal data structure 6
  iOS profile, creating 10-13
  messenger application UI, list 2
  other considerations 3
  packages, adding 18
  planning 1
  push notifications, configuring 14-16
  push notifications, creating 14-16
  push notifications, setting up
    for Android 8, 10
  push notifications, setting up for iOS 10

shopping list 2
speech to text and text to speech 3
As a loop method 96
Azure
  adding 280
  application, setting up 278, 279
  automatic login 282
  base settings, wrapping up 284
  data, adding 274-276
  data organization 283
  login API, adding 280-282
  login, wrapping up 284
  required data, for sign up 283
  same code, logging up with 282
  same code, signing up with 282
  setting up 269
  signing up 270-274
  storage, adding 276-278
Azure Storage
  about 284, 285
  data, storing 285
  setting 286

B

BasicUI 46
BindingContext
  using 188
  versus WeakReference 188, 189
binding project
  background, implementing 159
  background, implementing
      for Android 160, 161
  creating 150-153
  data, adding to List 154-156
  drawable image, converting to bitmap
      image 163-166
  extension method, creating 161
  horizontal position, setting 158, 159
  IValueConverter, using 157
  list of strings, binding 153
  List<string> container, creating 154
  message addition, simulating 166-168
  message reply, checking 156, 157
  new message, adding to list 166
  text height, obtaining 161, 162
  text typeface, considering 162, 163

text width, obtaining 161, 162
trigger, using 159
BLOB (Binary Large OBject) 7

C

cells
  about 22
  EntryCell 22
  ImageCell 22
  SwitchCell 22
  TextCell 22
checkboxes, Xamarin Forms labs
  about 239, 240
  Android 241
  in PCL 243
  iOS 240
  Windows Phone 242
complex UI example, custom renderer
  about 54-56
  Android custom renderer 56
  iOS custom renderer 57
contacts, messenger application
  about 288
  direct invitation 289
  social media, using 288
cross-platform, considerations
  about 4, 5
  language considerations 5
  online translation services 5
cross-platform settings system
  about 224
  Android IUserSettings interface,
      creating 226, 227
  initial data, creating 225
  iOS IUserSettings interface,
      creating 228-230
  preferences, loading 228
  preferences, saving 226, 227
  Windows Phone IUserSettings interface,
      creating 230
custom renderer
  about 51
  complex UI example 54
  creating 51, 52
  customizing, for Android 52, 53
  implementing, on iOS 53, 54

D

data
finding, with LINQ 95
database helper class
about 85
creating 86
data classes, interfacing with 86
generic types 85, 86
database helper class, creating
about 86
code 90-92
data, adding to SQLite database 88, 90
data back out, getting 92-95
database connection 86, 87
database, setting up 88
Func delegate 92
data binding
history 147, 148
in mobile arena 149, 150
data, ordering
about 97
OrderBy 97
OrderByDescending 98
t=>t? 97
defacto method 262
Dependency Injection (DI)
about 33, 68, 72
implementing 34, 35
Inversion of Control (IoC) 34
design templates
URL 2

E

error code
ACCOUNT_MISSING 206
AUTHENTICATION_FAILED 206
INVALID_PARAMETERS 206
INVALID_SENDER 206
PHONE_REGISTRATION_ERROR 206
SERVICE_NOT_AVAILABLE 206
event system
setting up 254, 255

F

First method 96

FirstOrDefault method 96
Func delegate 92

G

Garbage Collection (GC) 186
geolocation events
adding, to Android 210, 211
adding, to code 210
adding, to iOS 211
gestures
about 36
gesture recognizer, adding 36, 37
GET
and POST 134
GetSet class 232
GPS
about 210
defining 210
map, adding 213-215
map types 216
pins 216
used, in PCL 212
using 191
Xamarin Forms map, creating 213
GUID (Global Unique Identifier)
about 283
math, URL 284
package creator, URL 251

I

Inline method 97
interface
setting up 254, 255
internal address book
accessing 171
native implementation 171
native implementation, for
Android 172-174
native implementation, for iOS 174, 175
internal data structure
about 6
contacts 7
message 7
messenger data structure 7
Inversion of Control (IoC) 68

W

WeakReference
  about 186-188
  long weak reference 187
  short weak reference 187
  versus BindingContext 188, 189
web service 136
WebViews
  about 36, 37
  generated web page, displaying 38
  web page, displaying 38
  web page, displaying for Android 40
  web page, displaying for iOS 39
  web page, displaying for Windows
    Phone 40
  web page, displaying from file 38, 39
Where method 95
Windows Communication
  Framework (WCF)
  about 133, 141, 142
  web reference, adding 143-146
  web service, using 142, 143
Windows Phone
  about 250, 251
  adding 27
  connectivity, listening 258
  importing, from Mac into
    Visual Studio 27-30
  libraries, adding 30, 31
  maps, setting up 41
  modifications 129, 130
  setting up 259
  WebViews 40
  Xamarin Forms, instantiating within 27
  XAML code, modifying 31, 32
Windows Phone native platform
  storage 223, 224

X

Xamarin.Auth
  installing, from NuGet 263
Xamarin Forms
  about 19, 20
  cells 22
  information, storing 25
  instantiating, within Android 26

  instantiating, within app 25
  instantiating, within iOS 26
  instantiating, within Windows Phone 27
  layouts 21
  pages 20
  parent property 120
  size property 117-119
  views 21
  working with 23-25
Xamarin Forms labs
  about 237
  checkboxes 239, 240
  installing, in project 238, 239
  resolver 243
Xamarin Mobile component
  about 180, 181
  components, mixing with packages 179
  errors 180
  installing, through component
    store 177, 178
  installing, through NuGet 178
  using 176
XLabs
  URL 243
XML-based solution
  about 231, 232
  GetSet class 232
  serializer class 233, 234
  UserData class 232, 233

Y

yEd Graph Editor
  URL 2

Thank you for buying
Cross-platform UI Development with Xamarin.Forms

About Packt Publishing

Packt, pronounced 'packed', published its first book, *Mastering phpMyAdmin for Effective MySQL Management*, in April 2004, and subsequently continued to specialize in publishing highly focused books on specific technologies and solutions.

Our books and publications share the experiences of your fellow IT professionals in adapting and customizing today's systems, applications, and frameworks. Our solution-based books give you the knowledge and power to customize the software and technologies you're using to get the job done. Packt books are more specific and less general than the IT books you have seen in the past. Our unique business model allows us to bring you more focused information, giving you more of what you need to know, and less of what you don't.

Packt is a modern yet unique publishing company that focuses on producing quality, cutting-edge books for communities of developers, administrators, and newbies alike. For more information, please visit our website at www.packtpub.com.

About Packt Open Source

In 2010, Packt launched two new brands, Packt Open Source and Packt Enterprise, in order to continue its focus on specialization. This book is part of the Packt Open Source brand, home to books published on software built around open source licenses, and offering information to anybody from advanced developers to budding web designers. The Open Source brand also runs Packt's Open Source Royalty Scheme, by which Packt gives a royalty to each open source project about whose software a book is sold.

Writing for Packt

We welcome all inquiries from people who are interested in authoring. Book proposals should be sent to author@packtpub.com. If your book idea is still at an early stage and you would like to discuss it first before writing a formal book proposal, then please contact us; one of our commissioning editors will get in touch with you.

We're not just looking for published authors; if you have strong technical skills but no writing experience, our experienced editors can help you develop a writing career, or simply get some additional reward for your expertise.

Xamarin Mobile Application Development for iOS

ISBN: 978-1-78355-918-3   Paperback: 222 pages

If you know C# and have an iOS device, learn to use one language for multiple devices with Xamarin

1. A clear and concise look at how to create your own apps building on what you already know of C#.

2. Create advanced and elegant apps by yourself.

3. Ensure that the majority of your code can also be used with Android and Windows Mobile 8 devices.

Xamarin Mobile Application Development for Android

ISBN: 978-1-78355-916-9   Paperback: 168 pages

Learn to develop full featured Android apps using your existing C# skills with Xamarin.Android

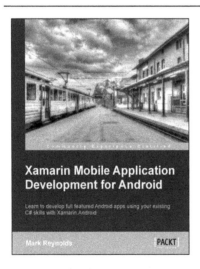

1. Gain an understanding of both the Android and Xamarin platforms.

2. Build a working multi-view Android app incrementally throughout the book.

3. Work with device capabilities such as location sensors and the camera.

Please check **www.PacktPub.com** for information on our titles

Xamarin Essentials

ISBN: 978-1-78355-083-8 Paperback: 234 pages

Learn how to efficiently develop Android and iOS apps for deployment using the Xamarin platform

1. Explore the Xamarin platform and understand the architecture behind Xamarin.iOS and Xamarin.Android.

2. Learn how to build and run iOS and Android apps using Xamarin Studio and Visual Studio.

3. This is a practical tutorial with a clear and concise approach that teaches you how to create, share, and reuse code across your iOS and Android apps.

Xamarin Cross-platform Application Development

ISBN: 978-1-84969-846-7 Paperback: 262 pages

Develop production-ready applications for iOS and Android using Xamarin

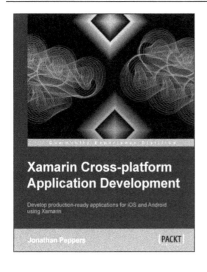

1. Write native iOS and Android applications with Xamarin.

2. Add native functionality to your apps such as push notifications, camera, and GPS location.

3. Learn various strategies for cross-platform development.

Please check **www.PacktPub.com** for information on our titles

www.ingramcontent.com/pod-product-compliance
Lightning Source LLC
Chambersburg PA
CBHW062102050326
40690CB00016B/3178